Baby Boomers,
Generation X
and
Social Cycles

Volume 1

North American Long-Waves

Baby Boomers, Generation X and Social Cycles

Volume 1

North American Long-Waves

Edward Cheung

Longwave Press

Toronto
2007

U.S. EDITION ISBN: 978-1-896330-00-6

Canada Cataloguing in Publication Data

Cheung, Edward, date-
    Baby boomers, Generation X and social cycles / Edward Cheung. -- Expanded ed.

Includes bibligraphical references and index.
Contents: v. 1. North American long-waves.
ISBN 978-1-896330-06-8 (v. 1)

1. Population--Social aspects.
2. Population--Economic aspects.
3. Social change.
4. Long waves (Economics)
5. Social movements. I. Title.

HB849.44.C54 2007   304.6   C2007-900616-7
Printed in China.

For orders or enquiries, please contact Longwave Press at:

www.longwavepress.com

To Idealism

Acknowledgments

I never expected that writing this book would be a journey of twenty years. It is the completion of one journey and now the start of another. I am grateful to the many people who have supported me along the way. Many thanks to Mary Field for listening to my ramblings and for providing me with helpful feedback throughout the book. Getting this book completed would have been so much more difficult without you. Thanks to Gillian Meecham for all your efforts in proofreading and correcting. You have provided much variety and rhythm to my writing. Any errors that remain are, of course, entirely mine. Thanks to Tom and Suzanne Hong, Leong Goh, Philip Cheung, Allen Lee, David J. Taylor, Ivan Sing, Baldev and Maninder Nijjar and Danny Emoff for your help in the various stages of this book. Thanks to the staffs of the Toronto Public Library, Ryerson University Library, York University Library, the University of Toronto Library and Boston Public Library for assistance in finding the required material. Thanks to the many people who have kept Kondratieff's work alive through all these years and the many historians whose careful research I have depended on. And of course, thanks to Nikolai Kondratieff, the person who started it all 80 years ago. I believe that it is now time that he should receive the recognition long due to him for his contribution to mainstream economics.

Contents

LISTS OF FIGURES AND TABLES

D*efinitions*

BEA - U.S. Bureau of Economic Analysis
HSTUS - Historical Statistics of the United States: Colonial Times to 1970.
SAUS - Statistical Abstracts of the United States
USCB - U.S. Census Bureau
USDA - U.S. Department of Agriculture
USPTO - U.S. Patent and Trademark Office

BOC - Bank of Canada
HSTCA - Historical Statistics of Canada
STATSCAN - Statistics Canada

Equation Definitions:
Percent Change per Decade: $F(t) = (Y(t) - Y(t-10))*100/Y(t-10)$

P*reface: Volume 1*

When I started research on the subject of long-waves and demographics in 1988 the population explosion as an impending crisis was still on the minds of most people. Population growth was seen as a threat to our immediate future. The growing concern now is the low birth rate among the industrialized economies. How consensus has changed over the last several years! The population concerns are now more in line with the conclusions that I have drawn in this book; that slowing or declining population growth would raise a new set of issues about the economy and our social well-being.

Since the publication of the first edition of this book in 1994 it is heartening to find books and articles that have used many of the original concepts introduced here, such as that social movements come in waves in relation to demographics and that the fluctuations in population growth cause shifts in aggregate demand producing long term fluctuations in economic growth.

The study of demographics is sometimes like the folk story of the blind men and the elephant. Having never seen an elephant before, upon touching the elephant's leg, one man exclaims it's a tree. Upon touching the trunk, another man exclaims it's a snake. Yet another exclaims it's a rope after touching the tail. Each man interprets the elephant depending on what he is touching without a complete concept of the whole.

Without a valid demographic model, claims of demographic relationships are often based on one-off observations or ideology. Thus it is often difficult to resolve what real impact population changes have on our social environment or our economy. The consequence is that studies of population growth and decline often give contradictory results; both population growth and decline can be cited as having either positive or negative impact on our social well-being by different schools of thought. There are few theories, if any, that can relate the many economic, social and political relationships to demographics as well as the long-wave. With over two hundred years of history and statistics, the long-wave establishes historical precedents allowing for the validation of relationships, and precedents for the understanding of future events. The ability to validate relationships is extremely important to any science and extremely rare in the social sciences. For that reason alone the long-wave should rank among the best of the social sciences.

While a few decades ago the world was troubled by the possibility of a population explosion, in the last few years Western governments have turned their attention to the issues related to a shrinking population. This is the new impending crisis. The ageing population of Europe is projected to decline by more than ten percent by 2050. A population almost equivalent to that of Canada is projected to disappear from continental Europe. With it European governments foresee a looming crisis involving shrinking work forces, inadequate pension funding and social security and economic uncertainty. The spectre of an ageing and declining population is becoming a worldwide reality. The solutions to our problems lie in understanding our past. It is time to give Nikolai Kondratieff and other long-wave pioneers their rightful place in history.

Edward Cheung,
January 2007.

*P*reface: 1994 / 1995

We live in a world that is constantly changing. Explaining change has always been difficult. Often it is attributed to the social and economic conditions that arise. But ultimately, unless change can be related to earthquakes, storms, drought and other natural occurrences, divine intervention or extraterrestrial beings, the economy, government policies and international affairs are the result of the actions taken by the population.

The cycle of events that we will be considering is approximately fifty-four years in length, and is referred to as the long-wave. Fifty-four years is about the entire length of the most active part of most people's lives. There are many theories about the long-wave, but up until now, all are lacking in the analysis of the population and its composition. This is where this book begins.

By examining the population, it is possible to observe the intimate relationships between its composition and the activities that society undertakes. The population is composed of people of different ages and in varying proportions. A generally young society would have different needs than a generally old society and the perspective and approach to obtaining these needs would be different. These in turn determine society's changing social and economic policies. As the composition of the population changes, almost all aspects of social life change with it.

1 THE LONG-WAVES OF SOCIAL CHANGE

The demographics of many nations were changed dramatically after World War II by what is known as the "Baby Boom." The Baby Boom generation or Gen-B brought us rock & roll and made Woodstock a landmark in time. In their activism they mobilized the civil rights movement, the women's movement and the urban reform movements. They brought in the liberal governments of the 1960's but with time switched to the conservative governments of the 1980's. In the 1960's Gen-B moved away from a traditional education to bring back a progressive education as a new teaching philosophy, only to revert back to a traditional education again by the 1990's. The rock & roll generation, hippies, yuppies (young urban professionals), dinks (double income no kids), the MBAs who took credit for corporate profits in the 1980's and financial advisors who took credit for mutual fund and investment returns during the stock market boom of the 1990's; these are a few of the cultural icons that represent the changing times in the lives of the Baby Boom generation. Each represents a phase of the Baby Boomers progressing from youth to maturity, emerging from being young rebels to being guardians of the establishment.

History was made and is still being made by Gen-B. As Gen-B ages, health care, social security, retirement pensions and the uncertainty about whether there are enough funds for these programs when Gen-B retires, have been growing concerns. That the world has been changed by the Baby Boom generation is without question. Society has had to change to accommodate Gen-B. Gen-B, because of the large numbers, has changed the social, political and economic systems of society.

And where is Generation X in all this, those born after the baby boom? Compared with Gen-B, there are few cultural icons that can be as strongly identified with Gen-X. Neither would the Gen-X cultural icons be representative of the spirit of the times. If the media had not caught on to the term *Generation X* from the book of the same title, the collective impact of this generation could have been overlooked altogether.[1]

Baby Boomers were born at a time when the birth rate was increasing. Generation X was born at a time when the birth rate was decreasing. Gen-X was too young to be involved in any of the activist movements of the 1960's and 1970's and when Gen-X came of age, the movements were drawing to a close. The world was becoming a different place in the 1980's. The conservative governments of Ronald Reagan and George Bush were elected in the U.S., the conservative government of Brian Mulroney was elected in Canada and the conservative government of Margaret Thatcher was elected in Britain. Societies around the world were becoming more conservative.

Economically the 1980's and 1990's were difficult decades for everyone, but in particular Gen-X bore the brunt of the burden of fiscal restraint. While the average real wage gain for the decade of the 1950's was 43 percent and for the 1960's, 37 percent, the highest wage gains in a century, the early 1980's were hit by a recession that was the worst since the Great Depression of the 1930's. The unemployment rate in the 1980's went over 10 percent. While the average wage held steady throughout the

1980's, on closer examination, for Gen-X joining the work force, that is those between 18 and 24, there was a real wage decrease of over 25 percent. This meant that those with longer employment histories continued to enjoy real wage gains.[2]

The permanent layoff rate for men aged 15 to 24 was 11.8 percent compared to 7.1 percent for men 55 to 64. Ten years later, in the recession from 1990 to 1992, those that moved into the age group of 25 to 34 again had the highest permanent layoff rate, 10.5 percent compared to 7.9 percent for those aged 45 to 54. Those aged 18 to 25 had the second highest layoff rate of 10.2 percent.[3]

The recession of 1990 to 1992 eliminated many permanent positions which were replaced with temporary positions and contract work; work for which younger workers could not qualify for lack of experience. From the mid 1980's to the mid 1990's the hiring rate for those between 25 and 34 fell 15 percent but for those between 45 and 54 the hiring rate increased by 10 percent.

While those born between 1932 and 1971 had a 70 percent chance of leaving home by the age of 24, those that left home in the 1980's faced a period of high unemployment. The probability of leaving home by the age of 24 for those born after 1977 had dropped to only 54 percent.[4] The social and economic environments through which Gen-B and Gen-X have grown up are significantly different. These have shaped the attitudes and outlooks of each generation.

Social history can be divided into periods of activity and inactivity. The cultural predominance of Baby Boomers overshadows all that which is Gen-X. When Baby Boomers were growing up, society entered a period of high activity and now that Baby Boomers are growing old, society is entering a period of low activity.

The early 1900's to the 1920's was another period of high activity known as the Progressive Era; an era that reflected a baby boom that has long been forgotten and relinquished to the archives of history. Activists were out in full force during this era, in their idealism, to stop drunkenness, to further the egalitarian rights of women, and to alleviate the conditions of the poor. The movement to prohibit the consumption of alcohol culminated in the passage of laws banning the manufacture, distribution and consumption of alcohol nationwide. The women's movement rallied and won the right to vote by 1920. The settlement-house movement began when youths moved into the poor districts of cities to provide assistance to those living in poverty, establishing a "settlement" in their midst. These activities marked the beginnings of social work. Progressive education was in full swing in all the public schools. The new music of this era was called Jazz. After the 1920's many of these movements came to an end. The conservative administrations of presidents Harding, Coolidge and Hoover in the U.S. marked the end of the Progressive Era. The conservative government of Richard Bennett was elected in Canada.

In the 1920's the stock market began to soar. There were mergers and acquisitions taking place across the country. Investment trusts came into existence and became extremely popular with investors, as popular as mutual funds were in the 1990's. In 1929 the stock market crashed marking the beginning of the Great Depression. During the depression all the issues of an ageing and retiring population came to the surface. Social security, retirement pensions and hospital insurance were made available to many people for the first time.

On the heels of Gen-B of the early 1900's was a group similar to that of Gen-X of today. This group came of age in the 1920's, paralleling Gen-X of the 1980's. But the 1920's generation was not as fortunate because many lives were put on hold during the Great Depression. History rotates around the two alternating generations of Gen-B and Gen-X, but Gen-X will never eclipse the profound effects of Gen-B on the social, political and economic structures of society.

This book is about change; change in the social, political and economic systems of society brought about by the changes in the composition of the population. Mostly, this change has been brought about by a cycle of baby booms, which has emerged every 50 to 60 years, followed by the lack of change, when Gen-X arrives.

When we map the periods of inflation with social history, we find that periods of high activity occur at periods of high inflation and periods of low activity occur at periods of low inflation or even deflation. These periods of high inflation and high activity were preceded by baby booms, and the periods of low activity and low inflation were preceded by periods of declining birth rates.

To understand the relationships between population growth, the economy and social change, we begin with the work of a Russian economist by the name of Nikolai Kondratieff. In the 1920's Kondratieff started to evaluate the nature of capitalist economies. As he analyzed the data on commodity prices, wages and other economic statistics, he discovered that developed economies fluctuated in cycles of 50 to 60 years in what he called "long-waves."

Figure 1.00 shows three and a half long-waves since 1789. Each wave has been labelled I, II, III, and IV. The straight lines indicate the major price trend of each section of each wave. The convoluted line is the U.S. wholesale price index, the statistical variable of this graph and an indicator of inflation. The waves of the statistical variable, some of which have a tendency to shift with time, are labelled usD, usE, usF and usG to help us keep track. For Canada these will be referred to as caD, caE, caF and caG. For our purposes, the long-wave is viewed as consisting of five major sections: the rising slope, the peak, the primary decline, the secondary decline and the trough. In 1814, 1864, 1920 and 1974, similar inflationary pressures peaked followed by a sharp decline in prices and a recession. A period of recovery then followed. A sense of economic security and prosperity is dominant at this time. Historically, prices have continued in a declining trend producing a deflationary environment. As Kondratieff noted, there were more years of prosperity on the rising side of the long-wave than on the declining side. The first two long-waves of our analyses reached bottom in 1843 and 1897 in the midst of a depression. Commodity prices of the third long-wave declined into 1932 in the midst of the Great Depression but began an early upswing with the advent of World War II and the rebuilding of Europe thereafter. Without the enormous spending of WWII and the rebuilding afterwards, the downswing may have lasted until the 1950's. Kondratieff's work had anticipated the Great Depression by about a decade.

There were others who wrote about economic cycles before Kondratieff, but Kondratieff did the most work on the subject up to and during his time and the Harvard economist Josef Schumpeter made the lasting association between Kondratieff and the long-wave, now also known as the Kondratieff wave. Many theories have been developed about the long-wave since the 1920's. This is the first book to relate the Kondratieff long-wave to demographics.

There is one additional time period that we must keep track of in addition to the long-waves. This is a mildly inflationary period on the downswing of the first long-wave labelled usδ (us delta), that can be found in figure 1.00, from which came the rise of Jacksonian Democracy. We give it a rough date of between 1825 and 1840. This period was preceded by an increase in birth rate that was not large enough, in relative terms, to generate a complete long-wave of its own. Although the events in this era, which led to the presidency of Andrew Jackson, may seem relatively minor with respect to the long-wave, as we do our correlations, we will find that some events are significant enough that, without giving them proper attention, this study would not be nearly as complete. Similar sentiments culminated in the Rebellion of 1837 in Canada, led by William Lyon Mackenzie. For Canada this period will be referred to as caδ (ca delta). What is important to this study is the understanding of the cyclical relations that emerge and not the cyclical periodicity.

Historians tend to place usδ at either the end of the first long-wave or at the beginning of the second long-wave depending on how one views the continuity of history. We will follow this treatment of history in our historical analysis; however in the statistical data in figure 1.00 usδ shows up as an entity of its own, being at the end of the first long-wave.

With the turning points of the long-wave and usδ, we can begin to evaluate how the composition of the population affects the interests and pursuits of society. We use these sections and turning points of history, not so that we can attempt to fit all our data into a mold, but so that we can observe and understand relationships. If the data fits these points well, then there must be strong relationships. If the data does not fit these points well, then there may be other influences to consider, or that the relationships may be weak, or there may be no relationship at all. Evidence suggests that the long-wave and the conditions of usδ all occurred when they did largely because of a dynamically changing population. As we examine the long-waves of the last two hundred years, we will find that a similar set of activities tends to repeat for each upswing and another similar set tends to repeat for each downswing.

Long-Wave	Long-wave Phase	Years
Wave I	Upswing	1789 - 1814
	Downswing	1814 - 1843
	usδ upswing	1825 - 1840
Wave II	Upswing	1843 - 1864
	Downswing	1864 - 1897
Wave III	Upswing	1897 - 1920
	Downswing	1920 - 1932
Wave IV	Upswing	1932 - 1974
	Downswing	1974 - 20??

Table 1.00 - Long-wave Phases

Each upswing of the long-wave is preceded by a baby boom. Following each baby boom is a baby bust. In the 1990's, this generation was called "Generation X." Gen-X was still in school when the great social movements were coming to an end and when most political upheavals were just about settled. When Gen-X came of age and entered the work force, there was a recession looming over the horizon. In sharp contrast, the baby boom generation was an idealist generation. Gen-B was a great constructor of change. It was in the early years of this generation that the women's movement and the civil rights movement took root. Gen-B could afford to be idealists. The large numbers were the reason for the great prosperity that developed. As Gen-B made its way into the social movements and into the corporate boardrooms, the camaraderie that developed was one that was never fully experienced by Gen-X. And as Gen-B ages, an economic decline follows many years later.

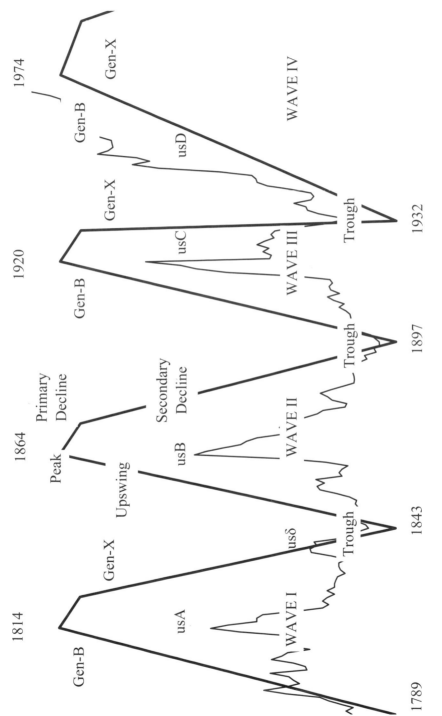

Figure 1.00 – U.S. Wholesale Price Index – 3 1/2 Long-waves

The generally accepted length for the term "generation" is between twenty and thirty years. There is no agreed upon scientific definition for the term and its usage has always been arbitrary. There may be other groupings of generations, but these two groupings of Gen-B and Gen-X are sufficient for the purposes of this study.

Unlike more populous countries such as the larger countries of Europe, or the United States where the population was originally concentrated along the eastern seaboard, Canada's population was scattered thinly along the Canada-U.S. border with an equally thin line of communications. Canadian population reached 25 million 130 years after the U.S. and about 200 years after France. Canada began as a colony and even after Confederation, remained under the governance of Britain for an extended period of time. For these and other reasons Canadian history is not as eventful as that of the U.S. or the larger countries of Europe. This study will concentrate largely on the events of the United States, the world's largest economy, and that of Canada. The demographic principles developed here, however, are relevant to other countries as well.

Since Baby Boomers are born before each bout of inflation, near the trough of the long-wave, by the time the next trough is reached 50 to 60 years later, the Baby Boomers will have aged considerably and are ready for retirement. Thus the long-wave is a reflection of this alternation between a generally young society and a generally old society.

The young and the old have different needs, different abilities and different perspectives. As the composition of society changes from proportionately young to proportionately old, the activities that society undertakes reflect this change. When society is young, it is full of energy and vitality. It looks upon the world as a place to explore and experience. It is full of idealism as to how the world should be, or could be, and it has the energy to make its demands known. When society is old, the energy greatly diminishes. The old have had their fill of experiences. Few things can excite the old as they can the young. Peace and stability are valued. The old are practical and cautious. These and many other differences between the young and the old determine the outcome of social movements, political elections and economic growth. The clustering of different activities at each phase of the long-wave reflects the changing needs and perspectives of a society growing from youth to age.

Co-incident with the youthful upswing of the long-wave and its ageing decline is the rise and decline of institutions. When the population is young, the institutions are proportionately populated by the young on the upswing of the long-wave. By the downswing, that which was once proportionately young has become proportionately old and is ready to be replaced by a younger generation. Thus the long-wave, being 50 to 60 years in length, is the lifecycle of those born during the baby boom years, which we have labelled as Gen-B, reflecting their movement through the social structures of society. The long-wave is in effect the change of leadership, followers and institutions. By examining the many aspects of social life such as the reform movements, popular music and the economy according to the divisions of the long-wave, the effects of a changing population will become apparent. These changes are reflected in almost all aspects of life.

2 SOCIAL MOVEMENTS: UNITED STATES

In this chapter, we examine several social activities that, at certain phases of the long-wave, have commanded sufficient interest from society to constitute a national movement. Within each movement, we find youthful idealism and energy on the upswing of the long-wave, followed by declining interest and participation on the downswing of the long-wave. Different historians have taken different approaches to the history of each subject matter to be investigated, but the vigor of youth, the declining interest that comes with age, and the passing of institutional leadership becomes apparent as each movement is examined.

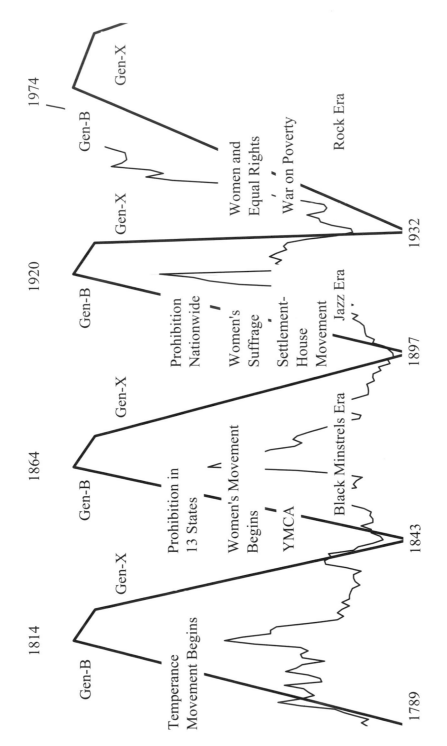

Figure 2.00 - Social Movements (U.S.)

Prohibition

There was a considerable amount of drinking and drunkenness in late eighteenth century America. Almost everyone drank liquor. The slave trade used liquor as a currency of exchange, doctors prescribed it as a preventive and a cure for all sorts of diseases, and employers provided it abundantly to their workers. There were even agreements in work contracts that stated that workers were to have a certain number of days off just for the purpose of getting drunk. Many employers found that owning a tavern or a distillery in addition to their other ventures made good business sense. The employers would dispense the wages in the tavern and since the employees were there, they were obligated to buy a few drinks before leaving.

Town meetings and court sessions were often held in taverns so that "lawmakers and judges could be close to a source of inspiration."[1] The clergy was heavily involved with liquor. Many owned distilleries and saloons. When a chaplain complained to Benjamin Franklin that people did not attend prayer meetings, he suggested that rum be served after the meetings. The chaplain took his advice and had no need to complain again. From the teething pains of a child to the ailments of the aged, the "Good Creature of God," as liquor was called in colonial legislation, was used by men and women, young and old.

In 1810 it was estimated that the average drinker consumed at least twelve gallons of hard liquor a year. This is not the watered down grog that is popularly consumed today. These spirits were mouth singeing, throat burning pure alcohol. There was so much drinking and drunkenness that a reference in the Old American Encyclopedia of 1830 stated, "Sots were common in both sexes, of various ages, and of every condition."[2] From birth to death, liquor was almost as important as bread.

Between the early eighteenth century and the early nineteenth century estimates reveal that the per capita consumption of alcohol almost tripled. The increases in the consumption of alcohol and the general level of drunkenness in Britain, Canada and the U.S. did not go unnoticed. As part of a movement to combat drunkenness in Britain, the artist William Hogarth created the now famous drawings of "Beer Street" and "Gin

Lane" in the 1751. In the drawings the artist contrasts the prosperous street scene of beer drinkers with that of the chaotic street scene caused by the stronger drink of gin. A drunken mother central in the "Gin Lane" drawing lets her child fall out of her arms and over a stair railing.

The colonies attempted to enforce legislation on drunkenness with flogging, confinement to the stocks or even expulsion from the colony, but these punishments were seldom imposed nor were they successful. There was difficulty in finding a jury sober enough to convict. When the jury was sober however, they dared not convict lest the same fate fall upon them some day. There was not a great deal of incentive for governments to prosecute because the duties collected on liquor were a large source of revenue.

In 1785 the first scientific paper was published to deal comprehensively with the effects of liquor. The most prominent doctor of his time, Dr. Benjamin Rush was the chief physician of the Continental Army and one of the members who drafted and signed the Declaration of Independence. He was an advocate of women's education, a founder of the first anti-slavery society in America and a great practitioner of heroic medicine. He was also the first to write a psychiatric paper in the U.S. in which his greatest contribution to the field was his theory that mental illness was a disease. In the area of substance abuse, his paper "An Inquiry into the Effect of Spirituous Liquors on the Human Body and Mind" concluded that liquor had no nutritional value and caused and aggravated diseases. The arguments against liquor presented in his paper would be used throughout the history of the temperance movement.

WAVE I

On the first upswing of the long-wave in 1808, Dr. Rush's paper came into the hands of a twenty-three year old doctor by the name of Billy J. Clark. In the community of Moreau, New York, a land of lumberjacks and rafters where the only leisure was to be found in the half dozen local taverns, Rush's essay spoke clearly to Clark. Clark contacted his pastor, a man barely a year older than Clark, to form the first and most influential temperance society of the time. Members were required to inform on one another. The members agreed to a penalty per offence of 25 cents if caught drinking and 50 cents for getting drunk. No member was to serve alcohol on any occasion.

As a result of the efforts of this society, other temperance societies sprang up in Connecticut, Massachusetts, New York, Rhode Island, Vermont, New Hampshire, Maine and Pennsylvania and articles on the problems of intemperance began appearing in religious periodicals.[3] On the first upswing of the long-wave, the formation of temperance societies set into motion a flurry of activities, but what seemed to be a promising start for the temperance movement had deteriorated by the downswing of the long-wave. In 1823, the Boston Recorder reports:

> We have to report that the efforts for reform are so few and feeble. The laws are poorly executed. Nothing comparatively is yet actually accomplished. Moral societies which sprung into being a few years ago as if by magic, at the alarming prevalence of vice, are merged nearly into oblivion. Their influence was gone even sooner than their name. Intemperance now walks at large aided rather than opposed by law.[4]

WAVE II

Despite the failure of the temperance movement, alcohol could not cease to be a concern for long. Politicians were able to command complete voting blocks with a few barrels of cider. Drunkenness was seen as the cause of decay, destroying both body and spirit. Contrary to the beliefs of happiness and prosperity as set forth in the Constitution, where there was drunkenness, there was seen widespread poverty. The temperance movement came back with astonishing vigor on the upswings of each of the next two long-waves. Through the efforts of the Revs. Justin Edwards and Lyman Beecher, the first of two of the greatest prohibition movements began to take form. Lamar Beman, writing in 1915, places these two prohibition movements on the upswings of the second and third long-waves in the following manner:

...there have been two great Prohibition movements that have spread over the country and commanded a large measure of public attention.... The first of these two movements was about the middle of the nineteenth century and might be said to have begun with the passage of a state-wide Prohibition law in Maine in 1846.... The second Prohibition movement... may be said to have begun with the adoption of a state-wide law in Georgia in 1907.[5]

It was in 1810 that Lyman Beecher attended an ordination where there was so much liquor that it "looked and smelled like the bar of a very active grog-shop." There, he pledged that he would "never attend another ordination of that kind...." In 1825, Beecher gave his first temperance sermon. The following year, Justin Edwards formed the American Society for the Promotion of Temperance, later shortened to American Temperance Society.

Through their united effort, over eight thousand temperance societies were formed by 1836 with a membership exceeding 1.5 million. To unite these organizations, the American Temperance Society became the American Temperance Union. At first these societies believed in moderate drinking and attempted to help their members in meeting that goal. But soon many members pledged that they wanted to abstain from liquor totally.

One notable group that formed in this era was the Washingtonians. Their history may be said to have begun on the evening of April 6, 1840, when six tradesmen met at Chase's tavern in Baltimore, as they had been doing for countless nights. Except on this night, there was a Rev. Matthew Smith of New York holding a temperance meeting at a nearby church. Two of the men decided to go to hear the Reverend. After the meeting, the two men went back to the tavern and proposed that they form a temperance club of their own. Within a week all six men had signed the pledge of abstinence. The Washington Temperance Society, or the Washingtonians as they were called, was thus formed. Central to their method of gaining converts was the public confession. A reformed drunkard would give an emotional testimony about the horrors of his drinking life and how, after throwing away the bottle, his problems were cured. Then the audience was asked to sign a pledge of abstinence.

Their greatest convert was John Henry Willis Hawkins. Hawkins, like many men of the time, spent much of his life in a drunken state. He had apprenticed as a hatter and recalls that, of the sixty names that he had found written in his master's old books, all but one went to the drunkard's grave. It was the pleading of his daughter one night, "Daddy, please don't send me for more whiskey again!" that set his resolve to stop drinking. Through his leadership, chapter societies were organized in numerous states. Pledges of abstinence came in by the thousands. Whenever they held parades, banks and businesses closed to welcome them. At its height, the Washingtonians claimed the support of over 600,000 people. However the group dissolved within a decade, the members having to join an ever-growing number of other temperance societies. Another group worth noting was the Women's State Temperance Society formed by Susan B. Anthony and Elizabeth Cady Stanton in 1852. Within two years it became dominated by men and subsequently ceased to exist.

With its growing membership, it was becoming apparent to the temperance movement that temperance was only one of many issues that it had to address. Speakeasies, the name given to illegal drinking spots, dotted the countryside. Some were no more than dilapidated shacks where violence flourished. In the cities, saloons dumped their wastes onto the streets, leaving behind the slimy slippery froth on the sidewalks. Later they became commonly associated with brothels. Women would walk blocks around these establishments to avoid them. A change in the philosophy of the temperance movement was forthcoming, and this was to include extending its arena of action to changing the law.

The first person to advocate the statutory prohibition of liquor was General James Appleton. When he was elected to the Maine legislature in 1836, he presented a bill restricting the sale of liquor to quantities of less than twenty-six gallons. The bill came close to passing but was defeated by one vote. Another nineteen years of lobbying was needed before the first effective prohibitory law could be passed, and this came through the efforts of Neal Dow.

As a young man in Portland, Maine, Neal Dow wanted to study law, but his father kept him working in the family tannery. When he had time to spare he would visit the local temperance society where he came under the influence of General Appleton. Dow developed an abhorrence for liquor that would be with him for the rest of his life. He took the Appleton bill to the Maine legislature five times and each time it was voted down.

Dow could not be deterred from his goals. Eventually, Dow inherited his father's prospering business and not long after, became a director of about a half dozen corporations. His influence grew considerably. He continued to organize temperance societies and to encourage people to vote for temperance candidates irrespective of political party.

By now the temperance forces had developed considerable literature for the dry cause. The public was inundated with scientific facts about the consequences of drinking. Fashioned after the French and English medical journals, reports by eminent doctors of spontaneous combustion due to over-consumption of alcohol or burning up while breathing too close to an open flame filled the literature of the time. Statistics were used to prove that parents who indulged in alcohol did great injury to their unborn children. All sorts of diseases were associated with the drunkard.

In 1847, Dow began his attempts to enter the political arena and finally became the mayor of Portland in 1851. Within his first month of being mayor, he presented his bill for the sixth time to the state legislature. By now, Dow had control of both the legislature and the governor, having successfully elected the dry temperance politicians into place. His bill providing for the total prohibition of liquor was passed by a vote of 18 to 10. Anyone storing, selling or manufacturing liquor was subject to search and seizure, fines and imprisonment. Dow personally led many of the raids. Prompted by this victory, prohibition forces in other states pressed for similar bills. In 1852, Minnesota, Rhode Island, Massachusetts and Vermont passed prohibition measures; in 1853 Michigan; in 1854 Connecticut; in 1855, Indiana, Delaware, Iowa, Nebraska Territory, New York and New Hampshire. In all, thirteen states enacted prohibition laws. But after the New Hampshire victory, the abolition of slavery became a greater national concern. Many prohibition leaders were also abolitionists and directed their attention in that direction. This left the prohibition movement to go its own way. All states except Maine either repealed or altered their prohibition laws. The United States Brewers Association, organized in 1862, became a powerful "wet" force in the repeal of regulatory statutes. The Revenue Act of 1862 taxed liquor outlets and gave the brewers even more say in government. As Herbert Asbury observes:

> Throughout the long, depressing period from the middle of the 1850's to the early 1870's, the liquor traffic, particularly the brewing industry, waxed prosperous, powerful, and arrogant — the brewers even demanded that the government remove all restrictions from their operations and no longer require them to keep books. The temperance reformers, on the other hand, floundered helplessly, stripped of virtually everything save the shining armor of righteousness. Every move they attempted was met by the screaming protest, "Don't destroy the liquor traffic now! The government needs the money!"[6]

Following an influx of a large number of German immigrants, German beer was becoming well established in America by the 1870's. Its lower alcohol content was preferred over hard liquor amongst an older population. The per capita consumption of absolute alcohol declined throughout the downswing of the long-wave. From 1850 to 1910 the per capita consumption of beer increased by more than 1000 percent while wine doubled and distilled spirits decreased from 2.24 gallons to 1.43 gallons. Beer would eventually surpass distilled spirits as the preferred alcoholic beverage. In 1917 at least 90 percent of all alcohol consumed was from beer.[7]

Two relatively minor movements on the downswing of the second long-wave broke the decline in prohibition activity. The first was the woman's crusade that began in 1873 and lasted about a year. The second was led by the Woman's Christian Temperance Union after the woman's crusade came to an end.

The woman's crusade came from "divine inspiration" to take up where the men had failed. Women from across the country gathered in saloons praying and singing praises, driving saloonkeepers out of town. In their attempts to shut down the sources of liquor, the women faced mobs, clubs, hatchets and an arsenal of free-flying food. This era produced some of the most legendary tales in the history of prohibition.

In Ohio, a saloonkeeper by the name of John Van Pelt, known as the "wickedest man in the entire state," encountered a visit from a group of these crusaders. Twice a day a group of about forty women would enter the saloon to pray for him. When his axe-swinging episodes failed to dissuade them, he dumped a bucket of dirty water on them followed by a bucket of beer. Public outrage, especially from the women's husbands, put him behind bars for a week. When he was released, the battle carried on for another three weeks. Finally, Van Pelt announced a complete surrender "not because of law or force, but to the women who have labored in love." With tears streaming down his cheeks, he axed his entire stock of whiskey and beer.

In another episode, the bar keeper loaded a cannon in front of his saloon and threatened to blow up the first crusader to approach. Scores of crusaders lined up in front of the cannon while their fearless leader lifted herself onto the barrel and led the women in singing. The bar keeper gave in, explaining he could not stand their singing.

In 1874 the Woman's Christian Temperance Union was organized. Led largely by Frances Willard until her death in 1898, the WCTU focused on temperance education for the young and obtained legislation requiring such programs in all schools in virtually every state. The WCTU did not limit its interests to alcohol. It had forty-five departments, each attending to a different social concern including women's suffrage. In 1881 the WCTU, along with the National Temperance Society and the Prohibition Party, managed to get eight states to enact statewide prohibition into their constitutions. Many were overturned almost immediately because of legal technicalities or they were ruled unconstitutional by the courts. In less than a decade, only three states retained prohibition. The two movements came and went, and although many had anticipated them to be another great wave of prohibition activity, it was not until the upswing of the third long-wave that the nation focused on this issue once more. On the whole, the downswing was relatively calm in terms of social activism.

WAVE III

The upswing of the third long-wave began with the unforgettable personality of Carry Nation. For about a decade, beginning around 1900, this hatchet-wielding lone crusader was demolishing speakeasies wherever she went. More often than not, the authorities were afraid to prosecute for fear of having to admit openly the types of establishments in their district. If Carry Nation gave the liquor establishment headaches, there was one organization that wanted to remove a few heads. This was the dry force's most potent weapon, the Anti-Saloon League of America. In the late 1800's the saloons had become such vile establishments that no one, not even members of their own industry, had a good thing to say about them. The Anti-Saloon League's purpose was to bring the saloons and all liquor interests to an end. It promised to usher in an era of clean living and clear thinking.

Howard Hyde Russell, a successful lawyer and a graduate of Oberlin College, had turned against alcohol because of its effect on his alcoholic brother. In 1893, he organized the Ohio Anti-Saloon League with the concept that it would support any candidate who would support prohibition, regardless of their political party or religious denomination. Within two years, the national Anti-Saloon League of America was organized to unite all prohibition societies. Russell was named its superintendent. With him, Russell took on a recent Oberlin graduate, Wayne Bidwell Wheeler. Through the Anti-Saloon League and the WCTU, the dry forces gathered to do battle against liquor once more. This time it would be to put prohibition into the Federal Constitution.

In the years to follow, Wheeler proved himself to be the prime mover of prohibition. He studied law and became an attorney for the Ohio League in 1898 and eventually the general counsel of the national League. John D. Rockefeller, Andrew Carnegie, Henry Ford and Pierre Du Pont were among his supporters. One donation that proved its value was a tract of land in Westerville, Ohio. On it the League built it's own printing plant and within three years was grinding out 250 million pages of dry propaganda. That constituted only about half of all the literature published by the dry camp. Independents such as Yale's economist Irving Fisher made their own contributions by publishing all sorts of wonderful statistics about the benefits of prohibition. By 1916 the League had obtained 3,500,000 pledges of total abstinence. At its climax, there were over 50,000 trained prohibition speakers, speaking at every opportunity across the country.

The brewers, distillers, wineries and other liquor interests did not stand idly by. In 1915 an estimated 450 million pieces of literature were distributed for the wet cause. Newspapers were bought out to write wet editorials and politicians were bought out to vote for wet legislation. This is not to say that the dry cause limited itself to totally legitimate means. Only that the wet cause was continually exposed.

Between 1907, when Georgia first passed its statewide prohibition bill, and 1912, five states were already dry. By 1913 the League felt that it had elected enough dry members to Congress to pass a nationwide prohibition bill. Over five thousand men and women marched to Washington in December of that year to present the proposed amendment to the Constitution. When the bill came up for debate the following year, over six million petitions were sent to Congress. And when the bill failed to get the necessary two-thirds majority, the League concentrated on the elections of 1916 to elect more dry Congressmen. The League had done such an effective job that before all the votes could be counted the League knew that prohibition would be the way of the future.

The Eighteenth Amendment was adopted by the Senate on August 1, 1917 with a vote of 65-20 and by the House on December 18. In 1919, the National Prohibition Act, also known as the Volstead Act, was passed over the President's veto and went into effect January 16, 1920. By the time the Act was ratified, 33 states were already dry. The dry forces now awaited the beginning of an era of clean living and clear thinking.

But the era was neither as clean nor as clear as the dry forces had anticipated. Prohibition faced improper enforcement. The courts were swamped with offenders and there were never enough prohibition agents to enforce the law. In some areas, there was no enforcement at all. Worst, prohibition put liquor under the domination of bootleggers and gangsters. By the time gangsters like Johnny Torrio and Al Capone rose to notoriety, they were netting over forty million dollars a year in liquor activity alone. Police, politicians and prohibition agents came under their payroll. Speakeasies arose by the thousands. Boys who were not allowed even to mention liquor before were now bragging about how drunk they could get while girls listened admiringly. The morality of the day gave the wet forces a mighty arsenal, and of course, they blamed it on prohibition. When the Great Depression came, prohibition took its share of the blame.

Long-Wave	Long-wave Phase	Long-wave Period	Blocker's Prohibition Phases
Wave I	Upswing & Downswing	1789 - 1843	1748 - 1840
Wave II	Upswing	1843 - 1864	1840 - 1860
Wave II	Downswing	1864 - 1897	1860 - 1892
Wave III	Upswing & Downswing	1897 - 1932	1892 - 1933
Wave IV	Upswing	1932 - 1974	1933 - 1980

Table 2.00 - The Prohibition Movement and Long-wave Phases

By the late 1920's, on the downswing of the long-wave, the prohibition movement deteriorated once more. There were defections into the wet camp from within and without the League such as John D. Rockefeller and Pierre Du Pont. And the women, who had been fighting for the dry cause for almost a century, were replaced by the "New Women," who were not inclined toward prohibition. When Franklin D. Roosevelt was elected President in 1933, he took the wet platform and the

Eighteenth Amendment was repealed. There was not much more than a whimper of protest from the drys.

The prohibition movement never regained any of the lost ground. On the fourth upswing of the long-wave, breath analysis tests have been implemented for drivers and drunk driving has become a part of the criminal code, but these efforts to control alcohol consumption and its effects are relatively minor compared to all that went on in the past.

Temperance historian Jack Blocker makes no mention of long-waves in his book, but his division of temperance history, except for the clustering of early years, has turning points that align closely with that of the long-wave turning points as shown in Figure 2.00. Blocker says of his division of history:

> Different periodizations could easily produce other cycles and a different progression within some cycles. Alternative periodizations, however, will not do justice to both the changes and the continuities in the experience of temperance reformers.[8]

After the lifting of prohibition, the consumption of alcohol increased on the upswing of the fourth long-wave until 1981 when, throughout the 1980's, the consumption of alcohol began to decline.[9] In the 1990's, coffee houses replaced bars as the fashionable place to gather and socialize. Low-alcohol light beer became popular on the downswing of the fourth long-wave just as lower alcohol German beer had become popular in the 1870's over hard liquor, on the downswing of the second long-wave. Even alcohol-free beer and wine have found a market. And restaurants no longer frown on patrons who order water instead of liquor.

The Women's Movement

From the beginnings of colonial America, women had no legal rights to property, to education or to employment. Women had limited say in the issues concerning the community in which they lived, and were not allowed to address groups of men who formed the societies that dealt with these issues. Throughout history, there were many instances of women attempting to exert their actions beyond their sphere of "proper conduct," but most were isolated and did not become matters of national concern.

In the 1830's, the movement for the abolition of slavery was gathering momentum and fostered the involvement of thousands of individuals, many of them women. Although men were the ones who sat in the abolitionist societies, formed the membership and set the agendas, much of the grass roots agitation came from women. They helped with petitions, set up meetings and informed and encouraged people to attend. They were also engaged in the dangerous Underground Railroad, at times risking their lives in encounters with ruthless mobs in order to help slaves escape to freedom. Despite their effective participation, they were left without a say and without a role in many of these societies. Very few societies allowed women to be members and even fewer allowed them to address their meetings. Through their involvement with the anti-slavery movement, women were brought to think about rights of their own.

The first prominent figures to arise from this era were the sisters Angelina and Sarah Grimke. Born to a wealthy slave-holding family, the Grimke sisters turned to Quakerism because of their abhorrence for slavery. They joined the American Anti-Slavery Society in 1835 and were appointed as agents to speak to women's groups. Under the guidance of Theodore Weld, who later married Angelina, the two sisters developed well-honed skills in speechmaking. Soon, men wanted to attend their meetings too. Their speaking to mixed groups of men and women, "promiscuous gatherings" as they were referred to at the time, and in particular, to groups of men, aroused much opposition from the clergy and even among some abolitionists themselves. Addressing the public was criticized as unwomanly and unchristian. Thus the Grimke sisters found that they were forced to defend their actions and the rights of women.

WAVE II

After the Grimke sisters, many more women took to the lecture circuit. Lucy Stone joined the forces of the Anti-Slavery Society in 1848 and began lecturing for the abolition of slavery and the rights of women. In July of the same year, on the upswing of the second long-wave, approximately 300 women gathered to draw up the "Declaration of Sentiments" at the Wesleyan Church of Seneca Falls, New York. Organized by Lucretia Mott, Elizabeth Cady Stanton, and several other women, this was the first Women's Rights Convention and officially marked the birth of the women's movement. Taken after the "Declaration of Independence," the "Declaration of Sentiments" stated:

> The history of mankind is a history of repeated injuries and usurpations on the part of man toward woman, having in direct object the establishment of an absolute tyranny over her. To prove this, let facts be submitted to a candid world.[10]

The "Declaration" went on to state that a woman had no right to vote, was forced to submit to laws in the formation of which she had no voice, was considered civilly dead once married, had no rights to property or wages and, among many other items, had no opportunities for quality education and earned a penance for her work. Since Seneca Falls, a women's convention was held almost every year up until the Civil War.

Though the convention was a bold venture for many of these women, it did not appear to be unusual for the spirit of women at that time.[11] Women were making progress in many fields on their own. A number of female writers successfully published books. Harriet Beecher Stowe published *Uncle Tom's Cabin* which sold over 300,000 copies in one year. Catherine Beecher, active in many reforms, founded the National Board of Popular Education and the American Women's Educational Association. Dorothea Dix attempted prison reform. Antoinette Brown was ordained as a minister. Harriot Hunt pioneered in medicine. Maria Mitchell was elected as a member of the American Academy of Arts and Science for her work in astronomy as the discoverer of the Mitchell comet. Clarina Nichols was a newspaper editor. Dr. Elizabeth Blackwell founded a forty-bed hospital. There were many female anti-slavery societies also. With much hardship, women made their way into professional careers and prominence, and at times were given opportunities to address legislatures and committees. During the Civil War, Dorothy Dix organized and headed the Sanitary Commission and women provided nursing services to the army for the first time.

Prior to the Civil War, women had not formed a national organization to coordinate their efforts. The movement depended on individuals and small groups that sprang up in numerous states. Without a coordinated effort, many had to find their own means of funding to promote the cause. They travelled from town to town, gathering signatures and sending petitions. They gave speeches and organized meetings, often not knowing if the crowd would be generous enough to help support their expenses or would run them out of town. Without the vote, they did all that was in their power to bring about reform. Some, such as Susan B. Anthony, went as far as breaking Federal election laws by illegally registering and voting in the presidential election of 1872.

At the end of the Civil War, the American Equal Rights Association was formed to support the enfranchising of Negroes and women. When the legislation, the Fourteenth Amendment, was proposed, some women felt that the opportunity had come for them to receive the vote, but to their dismay, they discovered that it would apply to males only. Even among the women themselves there was no widespread desire to be enfranchised.[12] Control over their own wages, being able to have the same education and career opportunities as men and getting the custody of children in a divorce were of greater concern. Stanton, one of the founders of the Association, had strong feelings about the vote and felt betrayed. She believed that the vote would bring about equal working conditions and wages, open more opportunities in education and professions and give women the moral power to halt crime and misery. With a growing rift between herself and the women of the movement, Stanton broke away to set up her own organization.

Stanton and Anthony had met in 1851 and their relationship lasted throughout the history of the women's movement. In 1869 they formed the National Woman Suffrage Association with their periodical "Revolution." Lucy Stone, Henry Blackwell, Julia Ward Howe and a few others formed the American Suffrage Association in November of the same year with the "Woman's Journal" as their periodical. Both organizations believed in getting the vote for women but differences lay in how this was to be done.

The actions of the NWSA did much to alienate their organization. Anthony encouraged working women to form unions, yet their journal, "Revolution" was printed in a non-union shop that paid low wages. She went as far as urging women to better themselves by being strike-breakers. Then there was the Victoria Woodhull sex scandal, a woman to whom they gave their full support to be the next president of the United States. Their association with free love only served to confirm public suspicions about the women's movement.

By the downswing of the long-wave, it was no longer seen as improper for a woman to address public audiences. Jeering and heckling gave way to acceptance. But the women's movement was on the decline. Individuals and ever-smaller groups fought for and sometimes won victories, but they no longer had the same level of support, even from women themselves. As Eleanor Flexner noted, there was a "steady trend of the suffrage movement toward the conservative and the conventional during the last twenty years of the nineteenth century..." and that even "Susan Anthony herself would have thought twice about flouting Federal election laws and going to jail...."[13] The women's movement floundered for almost three decades on the downswing of the long-wave.

WAVE III

While the women's movement itself was floundering, women did continue to make progress in many areas. In 1890 over 200,000 women were listed as farm owners. There were many female blacksmiths, bookkeepers, nurses and accountants. Numerous educational institutions that at one time were open exclusively to men began opening their doors to women. Female colleges such as Vassar, Wellesley and Smith were graduating increasing numbers. More women made their way into professions than ever before. By 1890, over 2,500 women had a Bachelor of Arts degree and there were over 250,000 women teachers compared to 90,000 in 1870. In the medical profession, there were about 4,500 women working as doctors or surgeons and in related areas compared to 544 in 1870.[14] By 1900 seven out of ten colleges were co-educational. With their growing professional status and a need to associate with people of similar interests, women's clubs were organized. In 1890 the General Federation of Women's Clubs was formed to give the clubs a national unity. As the long-wave began its ascent, the right to vote began to receive increasing attention. Through women's clubs and the Woman's Christian Temperance Union, the women's movement began to develop strategies once more toward securing the vote.

In 1890, Alice Stone Blackwell, daughter of Lucy Stone and Henry Blackwell, negotiated a merger between the two main suffrage organizations and formed the National American Woman Suffrage Association (NAWSA). In 1893 Lucy Stone passed away. Between the years 1896 and 1910, called the "doldrums" of woman suffrage because of its inactivity, Elizabeth Cady Stanton and Susan Anthony passed away and left the united organization under new leadership.[15] In 1904 the International Woman Suffrage Alliance organized under the leadership of Carrie Chapman Catt, a teacher, school administrator and journalist who had served for four years as NAWSA's president. In 1907, Harriot Stanton Blatch, daughter of Elizabeth Cady Stanton, organized the Equality League of Self-Supporting Women, later called the Women's Political Union. As an increasing number of new faces and names became associated with the suffrage movement, an increasing number of suffrage organizations came into being. A new generation of women began to bring new urgency to a cause that the previous generation had left unfulfilled. Women began travelling from town to town once again, speaking on the suffrage issue, breathing a new life and a new vitality into the women's movement. Billboards, pageants and plays were used to promote suffrage for women. Petitions and telegrams flooded legislators, trying to persuade them to support the suffrage cause. Since women had been a part of the temperance movement long before the brewers and distillers organized, the liquor interests became the biggest opponents of women's suffrage. These interests feared that with the women's vote, their industry would be doomed for certain.

Blatch devised the widely popular suffrage parade. Women, from the factory worker to the housewife to the doctor, gathered to march by the thousands. The public reacted with hostility at first but as they grew accustomed to the marches, there came much respect. Women paraded in all the cities where they could organize and as often as they felt necessary. Other more militant, though smaller groups, physically attacked members of the government, seeking violent confrontations in hopes of changing public sentiment.

One violent confrontation occurred when Alice Paul, a social worker who was involved with a militant suffrage group in Britain, came back to America to do her doctoral studies. She was appointed to the Congressional Committee of NAWSA. In 1913, she organized a parade of 5000 women to march to Washington on the day of Woodrow Wilson's inauguration. Unlike the pleasant marches before, near riots broke out and the Pennsylvania National Guard was called in.

With ensuing differences between NAWSA and Alice Paul, an earlier-formed Congressional Union led by Alice Paul broke from NAWSA and became an independent organization. The Congressional Union later became the Woman's Party. One of their strategies was to campaign against Democratic candidates whether or not they believed in woman suffrage. Since the Democrats formed the government, it was Alice Paul's belief that the party in power must be held responsible and punished for not giving women the vote.

With 2,000,000 members in New York City alone, NAWSA should have been a formidable organization. But throughout this period NAWSA was wrestling with inadequate leadership and unworkable policies. In 1917, in a state of virtual collapse, it summoned Carrie Chapman Catt back to lead the organization. By this time, women were able to vote in presidential elections in twelve states and Jeanette Rankin of Montana had become the first elected congresswoman.

When America entered the First World War, women were needed for the war effort. Thousands came into the job market, taking jobs that were regarded as men's work. The militant Woman's Party began picketing the White House and holding bonfires, something never done before by any other group. At first the pickets were peaceful. But when the pickets included protests against the war, riots broke out. The women were arrested and jailed. When they refused to eat in protest they were force-fed.

Women's suffrage was passed by Congress in 1919, seventy-two years after its conception. Ratification by the necessary number of states was completed on August 26, 1920.

Along with the third long-wave came the young flapper, a sensual and worldly creature who gave birth to the cosmetics industry and the beauty salon. Before 1920 only a handful of people were recorded as paying taxes in the cosmetics industry. By 1927 over 18,000 businesses and individuals were paying taxes under this category. Once, putting on rouge was done only by disreputable women, now the new woman made it acceptable. Once speakeasies and bars were patronized only by men, now women, who had fought for prohibition for over a century, were there too. No other explanation can be made for this radical change in behavior except the long-wave. With the upswing of the long-wave came the sexual revolution. Victorian prudishness was cast aside and Freudian psychology was elevated to a new science. It would not be until the downswing of the fourth long-wave that the validity of Freud's methods would be openly called into question. Contraceptives were promoted and drew considerable controversy. On the downswing of the third long-wave, William O'Neill observes:

> For social feminists as a whole, the 1920's was a period of defeat and decay.... [and thereafter] Regardless of the fate of its parts, the women's movement as a whole was dead. After the depression the phrase itself passed out of the language, testifying to the fact that public women no longer felt themselves part of some kind of corporate body, however loosely defined. The sisterly feeling between women's organizations, and the vague unifying ethic accompanying that feeling, did not survive the 1920's.[16]

WAVE IV

The upswing of the fourth long-wave brought in another sexual revolution. Love-ins, free-love communes and public nudity expressed the freedom of the 1960's. Abortion rights and universal access to contraceptives were promoted and drew considerable controversy. The women's movement saw its second revival under the banner of Women's Liberation, with women taking to the streets and protesting once more. In 1963 Betty Friedan wrote *The Feminine Mystique* and with a group of several other people, formed the National Organization for Women (NOW). They pressed Congress to open hearings on the Equal Rights Amendment, a document that had been compiled by Alice Paul shortly after women had won the vote. The ERA was never ratified. By the long-wave decline in the 1980's, the media began asking, "Where did the women's movement go?" Yet women continue to make great strides in the work place and in their careers, becoming corporate presidents and chief executive officers, sitting on committees, boards and legislative bodies, not unlike the women who made progress for themselves on the downswing of the previous long-waves. In schools, young girls outperform boys academically and in university courses, women outnumber men as women have begun to outnumber men in entering university. An older society has shown itself to be supportive of the roles and aspirations of women on the primary decline of the long-wave.

At the same time that the long-wave shifted from the upswing to the downswing, the shift in concerns changed from the issues of womanhood to the issues of motherhood, morality and domestic affairs. With the downswing of the first long-wave came the formation of mothers' associations, on the second long-wave, the social purity movements culminated in the formation of the American Purity Alliance. The current long-wave decline is seeing a renewed focus on the home and family with the rise of family values, parental leave, daycare and childcare.

In a footnote, William O'Neill makes the following observation about the participants of the women's movement. It should be noted that the dates fall neatly on the long-wave turning points, clearly marking the long-wave of institutional change:

> Generation is not a very exact term, but when speaking of the suffrage movement it seems fair to say that there were three distinct waves of women involved over time. The founders surfaced in the 1830's and 1840's and dominated the movement until the seventies and eighties. These included Mrs. Stanton, Miss Anthony, Lucy Stone, Amelia Bloomer, and many others, some of whom retained authority to the century's end. The second generation developed in the 1880's and 1890's. It included women like Carrie Chapman Catt, Anna Howard Shaw, and Harriot Stanton Blatch, who led the movement to final victory. A third generation consists of the younger women who emerged in the twentieth century, were active in the last years of the struggle, but... never enjoyed the cohesion or the prestige of earlier generations.[17]

Urban Reform Movements

Like the other movements already examined, improving the city environment to better accommodate its residents, addressing the issues of slums and ghettos and helping the poor receive greatest attention on the upswing of the long-wave. Long-wave characteristics of urban reform movements may be found in the building of the YMCA, founded by George Williams in Britain in 1844, in the settlement-house movement, which began in 1884 in Britain with Samuel Barnett and moved to America several years later with Jane Addams as a central figure, and in the War on Poverty in the 1960's.

The YMCA

The YMCA began in London with George Williams who, in 1843, formed a group called the Young Men's Missionary Society at his employer's cloth business. The success of the Society led Williams to think about including workers from other businesses. Williams discovered that many shops already had informal groups of their own. In organizing many of these groups together, the Young Men's Christian Association was founded in 1844. From the activities of bible-reading and spiritual discussions, the "Y" eventually expanded to sending out missionaries and inviting some of the world's foremost authorities to speak on different subjects. It acquired its own library and athletic facilities. By 1855, the YMCA had become a world-wide movement. Williams was knighted in 1894 for his service to humanity.

The Young Men's Christian Association was first organized in America in 1851 by Captain Thomas V. Sullivan. By 1860 there were 203 associations with 25,000 members in Canada and the United States.[18] The "Y" provided a home for young men coming into the cities looking for work. It had four departments, physical, educational, social and religious. Through the "Y" came the invention of basketball and volleyball. Swimming and water safety were taught and pioneering inroads were made in night school and adult education.

We can summarize the many changes in the YMCA with Owen Earle Pence's history of the American YMCA published in 1939. His division of the YMCA's history is very close to that of the long-wave turning points. The introduction and expansion of the "Y" occurs on the upswing of the long-wave while the downswing is a time of establishment and adjustment. Pence introduces his study with the following:

> The approach to the study requires examination of the entire eighty-eight-year history of the Y.M.C.A. in North America. This undertaking appears feasible only when certain general periods are recognized as follows:
>
> An Introductory period from 1851 through the Civil War;
> A period of Establishment from 1866 down to about 1900;
> A period of Expansion from 1900 through the World War;
> A period of Readjustment from the World War to the present;
>
> These periods do not embrace identical time-spans, but within each of them a broad unity of organizational behavior will later be shown. There may be a certain danger in assuming that the apparent unity in the complex events of such periods of organizational development is really significant. The writer must

assume responsibility for defending whatever significance he attaches to them.[19]

WAVE III

A graduate of Oxford in 1865, Samuel Barnett was ordained a clergyman of the Church of England in 1867. After working at St. Mary's Church at Bryanston Square for a few years, Barnett was offered a charge in a poor section of London. On the first Sunday, only six people showed up, and they were there not to listen to Barnett, but to ask for assistance. By the end of the first year, Barnett had organized a school for 142 children, adult classes, choir and a host of other programs. Eventually, Barnett purchased a building to house fifty families because of the poor housing conditions in the area. With the help of a few philanthropic individuals, his social services program expanded.

In 1883 a group of Oxford students were contemplating how they could help the poor when they heard Barnett give a talk about plans to start a University Settlement. The following year Toynbee Hall was established. The settlement was named after a young man by the name of Arnold Toynbee, uncle of the historian of the same name, who was interested in the movement but had died before it started. The settlement began with thirteen volunteers.

The settlement provided classes and a library so that people could improve themselves. Settlement volunteers were involved in attacking social problems, providing legal aid to individuals and support for unions. Numerous societies were organized to cater to varying interests such as the Nursing Society, the Scientific Reading Club, Adam Smith Club, Leonardo Sketching Club, Football Club and many, many others. Barnett believed that universities should provide adult education classes to those in need and he pursued that course until the universities agreed. Barnett also wanted the government to provide unemployment benefits and health care; he would not see these implemented during his lifetime.

Not long after the founding of Toynbee Hall, Edward Denison paid it a visit and on his return to New York City, he and a few others opened the University Settlement. It became the first settlement-house in America.

W. J. Ashley, a graduate of Oxford, was influenced by the ideals of Toynbee Hall. When he established the Department of Political Economy at the University of Toronto, his efforts led to the founding of the University of Toronto University Settlement in 1910.

When Jane Addams and her friend Ellen Starr were touring Europe, they too visited Toynbee Hall. Addams was inspired by the care it provided to the poor and in 1889, she and Ellen Starr rented a house in a downtrodden neighborhood of Chicago, built earlier by Charles J. Hull, to be a settlement in that area. Hull-House provided an array of social services to those in need, from kindergartens for young children and group activities for older children to special interest and discussion groups for adults. As different needs appeared, Hull-House responded with the resources at hand. When a group of women went on strike and worried that they may not have enough money to pay their rent, a boarding club was set up to provide facilities. Many who needed emergency shelter went to Hull-House.

About 50,000 people visited Hull-House the first year. By its tenth year, the settlement had a staff of 25 volunteers. As the settlement expanded, Hull-House came to occupy almost the entire city block, consisting of thirteen buildings.

Owing to their concerns for the social conditions in the neighborhood, Hull-House workers came to sit on numerous committees and headed many government agencies; among them, the Civic Federation Committee on Industrial Arbitration, the committee overseeing the Juvenile Court in Chicago, the Children's Bureau of the United States, and the National Consumers' League. Jane Addams was even appointed as garbage inspector when Hull-House Women's Club reported the lack of adequate garbage collection in the neighborhood. Some of its volunteers went on to pursue other occupations successfully, such as Alice Hamilton who became the first female professor at Harvard Medical School, Gerard Swop who became the president of General Electric and William Lyon Mackenzie King who became the Prime Minister of Canada.[20]

As the number of settlements grew, the National Federation of Settlements and Neighborhood Centers was founded in 1911 to unite the settlements. By 1913 there were approximately 400 settlement-houses across the United States. For a time before World War I, the most popular single women in America were settlement-house workers, with Jane Addams well ahead of the list. But like all reform movements, it came to an end. Allen Davis observes:

> Social work in the 1920's was rapidly becoming professionalized, and more concerned with psychiatric case work than in social reform. Most settlements... were in financial trouble, and they found it much more difficult to recruit able and energetic young residents.[21]

After 1920 the settlement-house movement declined and Jane Addams became a forgotten heroine of history until the 1960's brought in the "War on Poverty."

Another movement worth noting is the Boy Scouts. The Boy Scouts saw incredible growth on the upswing of the third long-wave. Beginning in 1907, Robert Baden-Powell, a semi-retired inspector-general of the British Army, began encouraging boys in the London area to organize groups of Scouts. By 1909 there were over ten thousand members. Boys roamed around the countryside practising their scouting skills, building campfires and seeking to do good deeds. In 1910 Baden-Powell resigned from the army to work full-time with the Scouts. His weekly publication, "Scouting for Boys" and its promotion by other organizations, such as the YMCA, greatly increased interest in scouting. By 1912 the Boy Scouts had become a worldwide movement. Baden-Powell's sister Agnes led the Girl Guides, which was formed soon after the Boy Scouts began. After 1920 the rapid expansion of the Boy Scouts slowed.

WAVE IV

Just as urban reform received much attention on the third long-wave upswing, the fourth long-wave brought many to fight for the cause of the poor. These attacks on poverty received official government involvement when the Johnson administration announced the "War on Poverty" in 1964 with the passing of the Economic Opportunity Act. It was hoped, according to the Office of Economic Development, that by 1976 the number of poor in the nation would be reduced to zero. In 1967 the President announced that $25 billion would be spent on programs to eliminate poverty, more money than would be spent in the Vietnam War. But by the downswing of the long-wave, social work, which had made the War on Poverty so vital, had lost its vitality and food-banks have become a supplement for government shortfalls.

Popular Music

Around the 1840's, the first definitive form of a widely popular style of music was beginning to sweep through America. Like each of its successive forms, it found its greatest popularity on the upswing of the long-wave, and then diminished on the downswing of the long-wave. Since none of these forms of music contained any of the idealism or aesthetic values usually associated with the European orchestral or operatic traditions of music, to which all music was compared at that time, each form also met with controversy and opposition. These three forms of music are known as the Black Minstrels, Jazz and Rock. No other type of music gained as great a following as these three, nor has any faced as much opposition. Each musical form dominated one long-wave.

WAVE II

Black Minstrels was the first music to gain wide popularity in America and would remain America's most popular entertainment form for about half a century.[22] As far back as the late eighteenth century, white actors in English plays would darken their faces with burnt cork to imitate Negroes. By the time the form was fitted for American entertainment, the Negro was portrayed in comic relief. In the late 1820's black-faced white American performers toured the nation as part of larger entertainment formats. Adapting British melodies to Americanized lyrics, they alleged that what they were doing were Negro songs and dances. One of the most famous performers was Thomas D. Rice who introduced and popularized the plantation slave character "Jim Crow." Dressed in patched rags, he would jump, hop and move his body in the most awkward manner while singing his ditty:

> Come listen all you galls and boys
> I'm just from Tucky - hoe;
> I'm goin to sing a leetle song,
> My name's Jim Crow.
> Weel about, and turn about, And do jis so;
> Eb'ry time I weel about, I jump Jim Crow.[23]

In plays or short skits, the "Jim Crow" character could boast of superhuman feats. Whether it was outsmarting his master, fending off his captor, or taming the wild frontiers, his exploits never cease to amaze. He boasted that he could "wip my weight in wildcats" and "eat an Alligater" or "tear up more ground dan kifer 50 load of tuter."[24] Another popular character was "Dandy Jim." Dressed in the most pompous fashions, Dandy Jim had a more sophisticated personality. He was both "larnd" and "skolarly" and could give a discourse on any subject at a moments notice. He spoke with such absurdity that it produced episodic outbursts of delirium from members of the audience.

The popularity of the minstrels began gathering momentum on the upswing of the second long-wave with the performance of the 'Virginia Minstrels', a part of a circus act at the New York Amphitheatre on the Bowery in 1843. Introduced by the New York Herald as an Ethiopian band "entirely exempt from the vulgarities and other objectionable features which have hitherto characterized Negro extravaganzas," four white actors, with their faces darkened, played Negro music with fiddles, tambourines, bones and banjos and exaggerated their movements and accents as to imitate the Negro working in the plantation.[25] Robert Toll gives a vivid description of their performance:

> The Virginia Minstrels combined the raucous qualities with what audiences believed were Negro song, dance, dialect, and humor and presented them with a vitality, exuberance, and rapid-fire pace previously unknown on the American stage. They were something new, unusual, and compelling. They burst on stage in makeup which gave the impression of huge eyes and gaping mouths. They dressed in ill-fitting, patchwork clothes.... Once on stage, they could not stay still for an instant.
>
> Even while sitting, they contorted their bodies, cocked their heads, rolled their eyes, and twisted their outstretched legs. When the music began, they exploded in a frenzy of grotesque and eccentric movements. Whether singing, dancing, or joking, whether in a featured role, accompanying a comrade, or just listening, their wild hollering and their bobbing, seemingly compulsive movements charged their entire performance with excitement. They sang and danced rousing numbers and cracked earthy jokes. From beginning to end, their shows provided an emotional outlet.[26]

Each act, although well prepared, was adaptable to the different situations that may arise, leaving room for considerable improvisation. The music was played by ear and the instruments were tuned to keep any would-be Beethovens at a safe distance. The spontaneity of the acts and the ability to accommodate the mood of the audience gave the Virginia Minstrels a strong appeal. People went to see the show over and over again.

The astounding popularity of the Virginia Minstrels gave birth to a complete stage show of its own. It established the format that many minstrels followed for decades. It also set little boys' ambitions to become minstrel actors and a good number eventually did. Later, when it became acceptable, Negroes publicly performed the same acts.

At the time of the minstrels, a divergence was forming in the concept of the theatre. Early American theatre entertained both the rich and the poor. Since theatre offerings were limited, class differences did not dictate which form of entertainment one was to attend. With the onset of the minstrels, more variety was available. The upper societies looked down upon the minstrels, and so remained with the traditional theatre. There was opposition to the new music because it lacked the idealism usually associated with traditional music. One musician likened the minstrels' popularity to a "morbid irritation of the skin" which "breaks out now and then." Those who enjoyed foot stomping, tobacco chewing, whistling, yelling and spitting went to the minstrels show. They often tried to participate or influence the stage acts. When they liked the performance, they would applaud for an encore and even throw money. If they did not, the performers were pelted with whatever was at hand and some were even driven out of town. The cakewalk, an exaggerated parody of slave owners walking, became the latest craze.

After the Civil War, on the downswing of the long-wave, variety shows began to gain popularity as "wholesome family entertainment." The minstrels had to alter their shows in many ways to adapt to changing tastes. Some even dropped the Negro subject altogether. Many minstrels left the four-man format and featured lavish productions with fancy costumes and staging. Except for their names, these productions were virtually indistinguishable from variety shows. A refinement in the minstrel acts had begun. Robert Toll explains:

> In the 1870's and 1880's... the large minstrel companies... successfully appealed to families by offering them "clean, bright, amusement", where they could enjoy good wholesome fun together. Only a few years earlier proper society would have looked with "holy horror" at a lady attending a minstrel performance, the editor of the "Clipper" observed in 1879, "but now, and very properly too, our fair ones turn out in numbers second to none."[27]

One minstrel performer lamented:

> They have refined all the fun out of it... Minstrelsy in silk stockings, set in square cuts and bag wigs... is about as palatable as an amusement as a salad of pine shavings and sawdust with a little

salmon, lobster, or chicken... What is really good is killed by the surroundings.[28]

At its height of popularity in the 1860's there were at least sixty recognized companies and many more borderline troupes, totaling about 150 altogether, performing the shows across America. By 1877, the downswing of the long-wave, the number of recognized companies in the country fell to about twelve.[29] The popularity of minstrel shows went into a tailspin decline.

Two of the most distinguished minstrel composers were Daniel Decatur Emmett and Stephen Collins Foster. Emmett, a member of the Virginia minstrels, composed over 300 songs, among them "Dixie" and "Road to Georgia." Emmett gained much of his musical experience as an army musician. He joined in 1834 and was discharged a year later for being underage. He then joined a circus as a musician where he wrote his first minstrel song. From there the minstrels became Emmett's lifetime occupation. Foster, also a composer of traditional music, assigned his earlier authorship to minstrel actor E.P. Christy because of the fear of what his association with "Ethiopian music" might do to his reputation. Foster's minstrel music actually sold much better than his other works and when he discovered that it was becoming accepted even among "re-fined people," he wanted his authorship reinstated and proposed to become, "without shame or fear," the best Ethiopian songwriter there was. Among Foster's compositions were "Oh, Susanna," "Camptown Races," "Old Folks at Home," "My Old Kentucky Home," and "Jeanie." Foster's songs made a fortune for his publisher but he himself died a pauper's death at the age of thirty-seven.

Between the minstrels era and the jazz era, Tin Pan Alley, march bands, vaudeville, burlesque and variety shows kept America entertained. Symphonies and operas were becoming established. But by the 1890's a new music was beginning to get public attention once more. This was "Ragtime."

WAVE III

Ragtime received its first public introduction at the Chicago World's Fair in 1893. Exactly how it was introduced is unknown for lack of records, but it is believed that a large group of pianists, such as Scott Joplin, converged upon the Fair to display their musical talents. The new music, syncopated minstrel songs, became the delight of many fans on the third long-wave upswing. At its height, one musician stated ragtime was in the "affections of some 10,000,000 or more Americans."[30]

But despite its popularity, ragtime became embroiled in controversy. Opposition came from many quarters because of its departure from traditional values and familiar musical sounds. The American Federation of Musicians pledged that they would not play ragtime because they believed that it would ruin "legitimate music." Ragtime did not contain any of the aesthetic forms usually associated with traditional music. As one song of a jealous lover states, "And I done him, cause I loved her. I carved him long, I carved him deep..."[31]

People caught dancing the "Turkey Trot" were taken to court or fired from their jobs. In New York, the Commissioner of Ports issued the order that ragtime was not to be played in the free summer concerts at the city docks. The Superintendent of Vocation Schools banned ragtime from its music program.[32]

Ragtime reached its height of popularity in the early 1910's, but it was soon replaced by jazz. And when jazz came, the music controversy opened even wider, because jazz was "ragtime raised to the Nth power."[33]

Like ragtime, the early history of jazz is unclear, but by 1900 New Orleans had become the center of jazz. Commonly believed to be from the brothels and saloons, the new music, heavily syncopated, full of squeaks and squeals and moans and groans came forth. The very first jazz was played mostly by musicians with no formal musical training. They played from their hearts and emotions and what sounded good was right. One story followed that the first person to play jazz was a blind paperboy known by his peerage as "Stale Bread." Having acquired a violin from a passing minstrel show, he and his "moaning and soothing melodies... [were]... threatening to corner the trade, playing as he sold his papers." Soon enough, others joined with him until there were five all together, none of whom could read music. This group became known as "Stale Bread's Spasm Band."[34] Early jazz was highly improvised and very little was written down. No piece was ever played exactly alike.

In 1917 the "Original Dixieland Jass Band," a group of five white New Orleans musicians, played to the first public audience in New York at Reisenweber's Restaurant. Within a few weeks, they were playing to a full house. They produced the first jazz phonograph record that sold into the millions.[35]

The association between jazz and moral and social problems continued to develop from the ragtime era, but by now, it appeared to be more evident than ever. With the increasing popularity of the music came a growing opposition from the establishment. The traditional musicians dismissed jazz as nothing but noise. It was considered earthy and sensual. The jazzmen lived unconventional lifestyles. They played all night and slept all day. Jazz as it existed at the time was rough. Notes seem to emanate out of nowhere. The patrons could hardly sit still while the music was playing. New dances had to be introduced to dance to the accelerated rhythm. H. O. Brunn explains the opposition:

> It was not the music itself, of course, so much as the manners and customs associated with it that alarmed civic leaders. Shimmy dancing, bootleg hooch, female smoking, and premarital sex appeared as a shattering distortion of contemporary ethics. No tradition seemed too sacred. Even the heretofore stable English language seemed doomed, as the word "neck" rapidly changed from a noun to a verb. The elders saw it as the end of the world. This revolt of the younger generation was induced by deep-seated psychological ills, and while jazz may have been only the outward manifestation, it was everywhere recognized as the cause.[36]

In a speech before a thousand public school teachers in Kansas City, the Superintendent of Schools stated:

The nation has been fighting booze a long time...I am wondering whether the jazz isn't going to have to be legislated against as well. It seems to me that when it gets into the blood of some of our young folks, and I might add older folks too, it serves them just about as good as a stiff drink of booze would do. I think the time has come when teachers should assume a militant attitude toward all forms of this debasing and degrading music.[37]

High schools such as Fall River banned jazz from their dances because it was a "travesty on music."[38] Even Mr. and Mrs. Henry Ford announced a war against jazz by kicking off a costume party.[39] In April 1922, New York's Governor signed the Cotillo Bill which gave the Commissioner of Licenses in New York City authority to prohibit dancing wherever and whenever he saw fit. He promptly banned dancing after twelve midnight.[40]

As the sides clashed on the jazz issue, acceptance of the new music was growing even among the most outspoken of critics. On the decline of the long-wave, just like the black minstrels earlier, jazz went through a refinement process as traditionally educated musicians began borrowing from its theme. Some began to recognize jazz as "the most important musical expression that America has achieved."[41] Led notably by Paul Whiteman, symphonic jazz and the jazz orchestra began to develop.

On February 12, 1924, Whiteman gave the first jazz concert ever at the classical music stronghold of Aeolian Hall. He wanted to demonstrate to the world, and in particular, to the elite of the music world, that jazz had progressed considerably and was deserving of recognition. Yet fearful of rejection, he carefully entitled his debut "An Experiment in Modern Music." The tickets could have sold ten times over that night. All permissible seating and standing room was filled. An impressive roster of musical dignitaries was invited. The first piece that Whiteman played was "Livery Stable Blues," as it was played ten years earlier. The audience applauded, not realizing that Whiteman was attempting to show the progressive improvements made on jazz. Just as much as jazz had changed, it was evident that the audience had changed also. Even after they had played all their scores the audience continued to yell for an encore. The resounding success of the concert was heralded by the most prestigious of periodicals. Later that year, even Carnegie Hall opened its doors to Whiteman's orchestra.

The success of refined jazz sounded the death knell to improvised jazz. Jazzmen that could only improvise and could not play from a score found it increasingly difficult to get jobs. For the jazzmen, refined jazz demanded a radically different lifestyle. The long hours of rehearsals and study meant that it was necessary to keep a disciplined life. The days when the jazzman could pick up a saxophone and play with nothing more than raw emotions and gut feelings were coming to an end. The wildness of jazz was ending with it.

In just over a decade a conservative shift was moving over America. A word analysis of jazz lyrics from the early 1920's to the late 1930's by Neil Leonard reveals this transition taking place. Before 1928, jazz lyrics were usually:

> ...frank statements of fundamental human problems and feelings, uninhibited utterances of joy, humor, love, sensuality, anger, sorrow, pain. They found expression in simple, salty language, concrete figures of speech, and strong rhythms. Such lyrics allowed jazz singers to improvise easily and to evoke deep feelings in some listeners.
>
> ...singers laughed in the middle of them and added their own amusing words or intonations which slanted the joke in the direction desired. Singers viewed sex humorously referring to sexual relationship ironically or metaphorically. Thus, on "I'm Not Rough" Louis Armstrong speaks of sexual gratification in terms of mental satisfaction, "It takes a brown skin woman to satisfy my mind"; and on "Dropping Shucks" he responds to his lover's infidelity with the lines: "I told you sweet mama way last fall, You come and find another mule in your stall."
>
> ...But after 1928 jazz lyrics exemplified the traditional inclination of Americans to divorce music from practical affairs.[42]

By 1928 Louis Armstrong was singing:

> When you smiling, When you smiling,
> The whole world smiles with you ba-ba-ba-bo

Ah when you laughing babe, when you laughing,
The sun comes shining through... [43]

Benny Goodman was among many who benefited from the re-finement of jazz. By buying the rights to early recordings and making refinements, Goodman was able to produce records that would outsell their original. But the popularity of jazz was on the decline.

By the 1930's, virtually all opposition to jazz had stopped. By the 1940's jazz was accepted as if it had always been a part of the culture. From the 1990's looking back into the 1940's, jazz represents an era of moral stability and romanticism.

WAVE IV

Bill Haley is usually credited for introducing the music that became rock and roll. He had been experimenting with the fusion of country music and rhythm and blues, and in 1952, on the upswing of the fourth long-wave, produced his recording "Rock the Joint." When it sold 75,000 copies, Haley knew that he had a formula for success. His next hit, "Rock Around the Clock," was featured in the movie "Blackboard Jungle." The movie pushed sales of the record to the 3 million mark.

As with jazz and black minstrels earlier, as the popularity of rock and roll spread, so did the opposition grow, and as modern technology enabled the music to spread to many parts of the world, opposition quickly followed. The first cities to ban rock and roll were Bridgeport and New Haven Connecticut in 1955. Later in Britain, numerous cities banned the first rock and roll movie named after the song "Rock Around the Clock" starring Bill Haley and the Comets. Theatres in Germany could not obtain insurance when they decided to show the film. In Indonesia, the head of the film censor board was kidnapped and ordered not to release the film. France attempted to legislate a ban on all rock shows but failed to get the resolution passed.[44] In the communist bloc, rock and roll music was banned on the basis that it was decadent capitalist propaganda attempting to subvert their governments. Jail sentences were given to anyone playing the music. When fifteen youths chanted, "Long live Elvis Presley" through the streets of East Germany they were given jail sentences of between six months and over four years. Delegates from eight communist countries including the Soviet Union held a meeting in Prague, Czechoslovakia, calling for "better jazz from Eastern Europe to control rock 'n' roll."[45]

Bill Haley began rock and roll, but it was Elvis Presley who became its most popular singer. A Memphis truck driver who had a flair for wearing flashy pink and black outfits with large wing collars, Presley began his musical career in the tiny recording studio of Sam Phillips. Phillips was looking for someone who could imitate the voice of an anonymous recording that he thought could be a hit. Having heard some personal recordings that Presley had made for himself in the studio, Phillips invited Presley in to try out. But despite Presley's ability to imitate various artists, nothing suitable for recording was produced. This was after numerous sessions spanning a period of several months. Nevertheless Phillips sensed that Presley had some hidden talent, and in the evenings after work, they would get together to continue their experiments. Then one summer evening, while taking a break from rehearsals, Presley picked up his guitar and began banging on it, partly improvising and partly singing, "That's all Right." Phillips quickly recorded the song and it was from this jam session and another that followed that Elvis made his first commercial record. By the fall, the songs were rated numbers two and three on the Billboard charts. It was not the knowledge of music that made rock popular, but the spirit in which the music was played. Traditionally trained musicians found it very difficult to duplicate rock, but as the success of later groups such as Duran Duran and the Sex Pistols showed, musical training was not necessary. The members of these groups had never touched a musical instrument before they thought about forming a rock band. And they managed to gain much recognition.

Rock stars became idols to many youths. Some would follow them on their tours across the country, never missing a single show. The incessant beat accompanied by the loud volume with which youths played the music on their modern technological innovation, called the stereo, became a constant source of irritation for many parents. The term "generation gap" came into vogue in an era when parent-child conflicts became as prevalent as they were difficult to explain. People dancing by themselves, without a partner and "doing their own thing," was totally foreign to Western culture. Sociologists could only speculate on what it all meant. In the summer of 1969 a concert organized for 200,000 people became a free-for-all with 500,000 in attendance. The concert that became known as Woodstock lasted four days and is remembered as a celebration of peace, free love and the hippie movement. Some also remember it as the greatest rock concert ever.

Leonard Bernstein made early attempts to refine rock, but it did not gain much following until the decline of the long-wave. Once again, this new music, which by now has aged over 50 years, could be heard re-written in the orchestral format, often known as the warm and soothing sounds of "elevator music." In the 1980's even some of the hardest rock bands could be seen with orchestras. Like the refinement of black minstrels and jazz, rock audiences now look for a similar, yet gentler sound. Some find it in the "golden oldies" of the 1950's. Whereas some radio stations once lured their youthful audiences with promises of playing only the top ten hits all day long, before the 1980's was over they were promising never to play the same song twice the same day. And like black minstrels and jazz, rock has found acceptance among its critics also. The authors of the Rolling Stone Magazine note that even "conservative newspaper columnist George Will told of attending a Bruce Springsteen performance and coming away a classical-music snob born again into rock-and-roll fandom."[46] While the Nixon administration attempted to censor rock lyrics, both Ronald Reagan and Walter Mondale used Springsteen's "Born in the U.S.A." in the 1984 presidential election. Rock has made its way into the establishment. But even so, the new music has been on the decline.

In the December 13, 1990 issue of Rolling Stone Magazine, several musicians were asked the inevitable question, "Is Rock and Roll Dead?" David Byrn of the Talking Heads says, "As I define it, rock and roll is dead.... the music is no longer vital."[47] Although not all agreed that it is dead, most sense a decline. One musician replied, "No, but it's been comatose awhile." Rock and roll has gone the way of black minstrels and jazz. Even the expression "generation gap" has virtually passed from usage.

Music is a form of expression for people all over the world. On the upswing of the long-wave, with a growing population of youth, attention given to popular music is particularly intense; for the young like the spontaneous, but the old like the sentimental, the nostalgic and the refined. Even on the first long-wave of our study, we find evidence of what may be the first music craze. In 1810, the Mirror of Taste and Dramatic Censor of Philadelphia reports:

> In no country of the world is the practice of music more universally extended and at the same time the science so little understood as in America. Almost every house included between the Delaware and the Schuykill has its piano or harpsichord, its violin, its flute or its clarinet. Almost every young lady and gentleman, from the children of the Judge, the banker, and the general, down to those of the constable, the huckster and the drummer, can make a noise upon some instrument or other, and charm their neighbors with something which courtesy calls music. Europeans, as they walk our streets, are often surprised with the flute rudely warbling "Hail! Columbia" from an oyster cellar, or the piano forte thumped to a female voice screaming "O Lady Fair!" from behind a heap of cheese, a basket of apple whiskey;[48]

Revivals Of Religion

Churches are the western world's oldest social institutions where not only the clergy but also the laity have a participatory role. Regardless of how we view religion today, religion has been an integral part of most cultures and religious sentiment has a tendency to change with the long-wave. The understanding of history would be incomplete without the understanding of the role of religion. With the long-wave paradigm we can observe how changes in demographics have affected church history and transformed institutions.

The first signs of the Great Awakening to mark the beginnings of the Evangelical Era appeared in the 1720's under Theodore Frelinghuysen in the Raritan Valley area of New Jersey. In the churches that were once marked by formalism and lack of vitality, great revivals appeared accompanied by intense emotional outpouring. Signs of this Great Awakening, of which we have the best accounts, came to New England in 1734. Where there was wide irreverence for religion a year earlier, there were now quaint religious stirrings. When the Reverend Jonathan Edwards, later to be the president of Princeton University, rose to his pulpit and read his sermons, faintings and weepings followed. Interest in religion had so encompassed the town, "that it seemed to be full of the presence of God... never so full of love, nor of joy..." and that there was "scarcely a single person in the town, either old or young that was left unconcerned about the great things of the eternal world."

From the coastal areas to the frontiers and from the cities to the rural communities, the religious excitement spread. Even in isolated regions of the country, there were outbreaks of revivals.[49] Out of a population of 1 million people in New England, thirty to forty thousand faced conversions between the years 1740 and 1743.[50]

Edwards had never witnessed such interest in religion before. He carefully analyzed the revivals, doing case studies and waiting months to see if the many conversions were permanent. In the end, Edwards came to the only conclusion possible at that time, that it was "a marvelous work of God, a shower of divine blessing." Since the puritans arrived in America, there has always been the sense that God had chosen them to play a special role in the world. And everywhere could be seen the wonders of God's blessing. Many felt surely that God's kingdom was at hand. From this Awakening arose the concept of "disinterested benevolence." Men who were regenerated by the Spirit of God no longer acted from self-interest, but in the interest of one's fellow human being. This development set many on the road towards social reform. Samuel Hopkins, a pupil of Edwards, began a campaign against slavery in his community. For the last thirty years of his life he was preoccupied with bringing an end to the institution.

Edwards wrote a book about the Great Awakening entitled, *A Faithful Narrative of the Surprising Work of God, in the Conversion of Many*

Hundred Souls, in Northampton.... Drs Watts and Guyse of London wrote in the preface to this book:

> ... never did we hear or read, since the first ages of Christianity, any event of this kind so surprising as the present narrative hath set before us.... It is worthy of our observation that this great and surprising work does not seem to have taken its rise from any sudden and distressing calamity of public terror that might universally impress the minds of a people: here was no storm, no earthquake, no inundation of water, no desolation by fire, no pestilence or any other sweeping distemper, nor cruel invasion by their Indian neighbors, that might force inhabitants into a serious thoughtfulness, and a religious temper by the fears of approaching death and judgment.... But in the present case the immediate hand of God in the work of his Spirit appears much more evident, because there is no such awful and threatening Providence attending it.[51]

Yet by 1760 the Great Awakening came to an end. The revivals disappeared almost as quickly as they came. For many, the reasons for their disappearance were as puzzling as the reasons for their appearance. As one observer wrote, "the years since the great ingathering of the First Awakening had been hard to understand. God seemed almost to have withdrawn his blessing from New England, and above all from those who most cherished 'true doctrine'."[52]

Since the Great Awakening, revivals have been sought continually by churches on both the upswing and the downswing of the long-wave, but strong interest in religion has consistently accompanied the upswing of the long-wave. The intense energies that accompany revivals on the upswing are absent during the downswing. The result is that the upswing of the long-wave is noted by historians for its "great awakenings" or periods of great revivals. By the downswing of the long-wave, religion becomes more conservative.

WAVE I

As the first long-wave began its ascent, the full tide of revivals came back by 1800 in the Second Evangelical Awakening. One contemporary wrote, "God, in a remarkable manner, was pouring out his Spirit on the churches of New England.... Within the period of five or six years... not less than one hundred and fifty churches in New England were visited with times of refreshing from the presence of the Lord."[53] At Yale University, under its President Timothy Dwight, one third of the student body professed conversion. Among the students was Lyman Beecher, father of Catherine, Harriet and Henry Ward Beecher.

The revivals in the more settled regions remained relatively calm, without many emotional spillovers as church leaders were determined not to have the emotional excesses of the first Awakening. In the frontier states however, no such restraint was implemented. In Kentucky in 1801 for example, under the Reverend James McGready, a camp meeting revival was organized at Cane Ridge. With its largest city barely exceeding two thousand, Cane Ridge drew a crowd estimated at between ten and twenty thousand. The meeting continued for seven days until provisions ran out. There the "multitudes thronged and writhed" in such a manner that it "has challenged the descriptive powers of many historians."[54]

The Second Awakening furthered the benevolent principles of the First Awakening. Numerous mission societies, volunteer organizations, benevolent foundations and moral reform societies were organized. The American Board of Commissioners for Foreign Missions, American Tract Society, American Education Society, Hartford Asylum for the Education and Instruction of the Deaf and Dumb, Hartford Retreat for the Insane and the Colonization Society were among the many that came to being. By the downswing of the long-wave, revivals were beginning to be incorporated as a regular part of many churches and sporadic regional instances of enthusiasm continued, but the urgency of the revivals ceased. On the whole, they were known as "times of indifference." The peak of the revivals came to an end before the 1820's.

Almost a hundred years after the first stirring of Edwards' revivals, the nature of revivalism went through a dramatic change. Through Nathanial Taylor, Lyman Beecher and Charles Finney came the development of modern revivalism and the New Haven Theology.

Charles Finney was born on August 19, 1792 in Warren, Connecticut. Finney respected and sometimes involved himself with the church, but he had never considered himself a religious man. Once asked about the Christian faith he replied that it was hardly consistent with the profession that he was to follow. In the third year of his law career, Finney had an intense conversion experience. He gave up his career as a lawyer to study for the Presbyterian ministry. The demand for his preaching after he was ordained reached its highest pitch in the second half of the 1820's. The fires of revivalism burned wherever Finney went. In his revivals he included addresses on the pressing issues of the time. With regard to temperance he says, "Resistance to the Temperance Reformation will put a stop to the revivals in a church...."[55] With regards to slavery he states that, "Revivals are hindered when ministers and churches take wrong ground in regard to any question involving human rights."[56] Not only must the church not condone slavery; it is just as wrong to be neutral with the issue.

Many of Finney's associates were leaders in social reform. After serving some time as Finney's assistant, Theodore Weld became a founder of the American Anti-Slavery Society. Arthur Tappan, another one of Finney's followers, became its first president. The brothers Arthur and Lewis Tappan were wealthy and influential merchants who founded the first national credit rating agency in America that subsequently became Dun and Bradstreet. Abraham Lincoln worked as one of the agency's lawyers. Dedicated to the cause of philanthropy, the brothers gave generously to humanitarian organizations. When William Lloyd Garrison was imprisoned for libel, the Tappans bailed him out even though they had never met him. They supported Garrison's fledgling newspaper the "Liberator" also. When it came to supporting benevolent societies, the Tappans were at the top of the list.

When the founders of the Oberlin community approached Weld to be an instructor at Oberlin College, Weld referred them to Finney.

With the agreement that the community would allow blacks to register at the college and that the abolition movement be allowed to operate, Finney and other reformers established their faculty there.

Oberlin was the hotbed of activism. John Brown, who attempted to lead the slave revolt in the South, surveyed the land for the college. Owen Brown, his father, was on the board of trustees. Howard Russell and Wayne Wheeler of the Anti-Saloon League were among its graduates.

Oberlin was the first coeducational institution granting full degrees to women even before the women's movement had taken form. Lucy Stone, Antoinette Brown and Betsy Cowles were among the many feminist graduates of the college. It was a period in history that had notions that women possessed superior virtues and that they were a better reflection of Christian values. The community believed that men could learn much from them. Frequently men participated in what were usually regarded as women's work, such as baking, cleaning and setting tables. Although Lucy Stone and Antoinette Brown complained that the curriculum was not advanced enough for women, many complained that it was too progressive. When a group of female students were asked to form a mixed class with men so that they could exert their good influence, the women protested that modesty would prevent them from reading in front of men. Oberlin was also the first college to teach music in America.

From Oberlin operated one of the most important depots of the Underground Railroad. Hundreds of slaves stopped there for refuge on their way to freedom. Both students and professors faced the dangers of the mob and the wrath of the law in their efforts to help slaves. Sometimes they even rescued fugitive slaves from the hands of the authorities.

Despite Finney's wide appeal, his theology kept him in controversy with the established Calvinism of the Church. Finney had great difficulty reconciling his ideas with Calvinism. Calvinism insisted that personal salvation was determined by the arbitrary will of God and that it was God, not man, who brought about revivals. Finney believed that salvation was available to anyone and that man had the freedom to choose or reject it. Man was able to choose his eternal destiny. Revivals were the "right use of constituted means", which God has given the evangelist as a method of bringing about conversion.[57] This was a complete turnaround from Jonathan Edwards' revival experience in 1734, which he attributed directly to divine intervention. Revivalism changed from "a shower of divine blessing" to a profession.

For over a decade, the theology of Calvinism had been on the decline. The optimism at usδ and the belief in the common man made Calvinism a doctrine that few could identify with. Calvinism believed that some were made to be instruments of silver and others instruments of gold, that some were made to be vessels for wine, others to be common receptacles, that the King was king because of the election of God. But in America the President was not a person of royal blood but a commoner. He was not anointed by bishops and cardinals but elected by the votes of the people. Calvinism believed that many are called and few are chosen, that heaven was the entitlement of God's chosen few and privileged elect and not for all believers. But in America, all men are created equal and the theology of the elect no longer made any sense. By the 1830's a generation was born under the political system of democracy that made the theology of Calvinism outside the experience of most people. Whereas Calvinism may have been acceptable to the hierarchical social systems of Britain and Europe, it became increasingly out of place in America. America was not governed by class and privilege, but by social rights, egalitarianism and the democratic process. Even in England the land-owning nobility were rapidly losing status to those who started life working with their hands, the industrialists. The theology of predestination and determinism was given up for the theology of free will. Had Finney's theology not reflected the popular sentiment of usδ, he would have been expelled for heresy. Instead, within two years of Finney's publication of *Lectures on Revivals*, the once united Presbyterian and Congregational churches split over the definition of Calvinism. Through Beecher, Finney and Taylor's New Haven Theology, the protestant churches of America changed from predominantly Calvinist to predominantly Arminian.

Then there was the rediscovery of perfectionism. A copy of John Wesley's *Plain Account of Christian Perfection* fell into Finney's hands while he was studying the doctrine of sanctification. He believed that all Christians could attain a higher state of life. Revivals had always meant the conversion of sinners, but to Finney and his colleagues, revivals were the taking of the first steps towards perfectionism, which meant: "perfect trust and consecration, the experience of the fullness of the love of Christ."[58] A Christian must live more than a nominal life. A Christian should be trying to attain higher forms of holiness, and what better way to show it than in acts of benevolence and a commitment to the welfare of others. This perfectionism empowered a wave of activists on the second upswing of the long-wave.

Finney, like the faithful believers of Edwards' time, felt that they could help usher in the one thousand years of peace before the return of Christ. With the optimism of usδ, came the movement to free the slave, to build public schools, to bring equality to women and justice to the world. The post-millennial optimism of mankind perfecting the world to help usher in the return of Christ marked the spirit of activism on the upswing of the second long-wave.

WAVE II

With the upswing of the second long-wave came another upsurge of interest in revivals that culminated in the years 1857 and 1858. Timothy Smith says of this era:

> The awakening of 1858… was both the climax of these long trends and the result of united efforts by urban churchmen of many denominations. In the two years immediately preceding it, hundreds of them had labored to precipitate a national Pentecost which they hoped would baptize America in the Holy Spirit and in some mystic manner destroy the evils of slavery, poverty and greed. Thereafter, and during the Civil War especially, "union" city-wide campaigns of every description, metropolitan and rural, became the order of the day.[59]

In October of 1857, Churches began holding noontime prayer meetings in New York's financial district of Fulton Street. Newspapers that normally did not report religious events began carrying schedules of the daily prayer meetings. Businessmen sent telegraphic messages during lunch hours to other cities on their spiritual affairs. Soon the "downtown areas of Baltimore, Boston, Chicago, Philadelphia and other cities were attracting variegated audiences that included leading capitalists, prominent lawyers and judges, eminent physicians, merchants, bankers, mechanics and tradesmen." In Bridgeton where 2500 were converted, many were "highly respected... for established moral character and great social worth."[60] Even President James Buchanan took part in these meetings at Bedford Springs, Pennsylvania.[61]

The revivals quickly spread to Britain. In Wales, where the population was little more than 1 million, approximately 80,000 professed conversion by 1860.[62] A large number of revivalists were on the scene by this time. Of the "Holiness" strand William Booth founded the Salvation Army in Britain to work among the poor. Phoebe Palmer was conducting her revivals in Hamilton, Ontario and found that there was a simultaneous interest in revivals. She reported that, at some camp meetings in Ontario and Quebec, attendance went as high as five to six thousand.[63] Palmer began her ministry by conducting the Tuesday meetings in New York City in 1835 where laymen and minister could meet together to seek the ways of Holiness. She soon left for Britain to carry on her ministry.

In the South, revivals were given preference over recreation in the Confederate army. Thousands of soldiers served as part-time preachers. The regiments regularly prayed before going into battle.

The revival of 1857 to 1858 has been generally credited to the financial panic of the time. Oddly enough, it is also generally noted that this is the first time in the one hundred and two year history of the evangelical era that the nation looked toward God instead of their banker in a financial crisis. And not since then has the nation looked to God under similar circumstances.

After the Civil War, on the downswing of the long-wave, the energy of revivals subsided once more. Few had the foresight to anticipate such terrible destruction. Some blamed it on misguided zeal. With the Civil War, and the two world wars that followed, the theology of many churches changed. Overwhelmingly, the churches could no longer rise to the optimism of men perfecting the world to usher in the kingdom of God. The theology of post-millennial optimism gave way to pre-millennial pessimism. In the theology post-millennialism, Christ was to return to an earth perfected by men. Men were responsible for creating a world that would enjoy a thousand years of peace before Christ would return to usher in eternity. But now seen in pre-millennial eyes, Christ would return when the world is on the brink of destruction. If history is an indication, it is extremely dangerous that groups that hold the pre-millennial view would think that they are helping God to fulfill their interpretation of prophecy.

Shortly after the top of the long-wave, the women's rights advocate, anti-slavery advocate and America's most prominent minister, Henry Ward Beecher, was caught in the Victoria Woodhull sex scandal. He was sued by the woman's husband and acquitted due to a hung jury.

Between the years 1875 and 1885, the downswing of the second long-wave, the prominent figure of revivals was Dwight L. Moody. Whereas the evangelists of Finney's time worked in cities with populations of tens of thousands, many cities were now reaching over a million. Special accommodations had to be made for the large crowds. The massiveness of the revivals required that they be operated like a business with executive committees, finance committees and subcommittees. There were budgets, promotions and strategies.

The revivals of Moody, however, did not reach the diversity of audiences like those before him. The strong emotionalism that characterized the revivals of the upswing was not present on the downswing. He once told his well-dressed audience to leave because he had seen them before and that it was not them that he wanted to reach. Yet the intellectual, the laborer, the poor and those on the fringes of society could find no place in his message. In the depths of the depression of 1875 he told his audience in New York City, "We live in a land flowing with milk and honey… yet men complain of hard times.[64] Inner perfectionism through conversion was the solution to the world's problems. This became the tone for many revivals thereafter. In this extremely romantic era, "a prophetic faith was transformed into a sentimental moralism."[65]

WAVE III

With the upswing of the third long-wave the outlook of many churches began to change from that of an individualistic pietism to that of a social orientation. The ideas of these churches were formulated in what is known as the Social Gospel by men such as Walter Rauschenbusch and Washington Gladden. Poverty, illiteracy and the growing slums were not seen as the result of individual morality, stupidity or laziness but were seen as the result of societal problems that must be rectified. From the 1890's to the 1920's this new theology gave men and women reason to champion the poor, to elevate women and to articulate a vision of reform to improve society in the Progressive Era.

In parallel with the Progressive Era on the upswing of the long-wave was a return to interest in revivals. In January of 1901 at Bethel Bible College, a student by the name of Agnes Ozman received the gift of the Spirit and began speaking in an unknown "language." There were scattered instances of "speaking in tongues" in the past but this time it became quite contagious. Very soon many students began having the same experience. News of these happenings began to spread hither and thither and the Holiness movement began its revival. By 1906, William J. Seymour, a black, half-blind, semi-literate preacher sermonizing from a podium of fruit crates in a warehouse on Azusa Street in Los Angeles became the radiating center of the Pentecostal movement. People from across the country came to see and hear him. Through Seymour, the Pentecostal denomination laid its foundation.

Between the peak years of 1912 and 1918 approximately 35,000 revivals took place with expenditures estimated at $20 million per year.[66] One of the most prominent revivalists was Billy Sunday, a baseball player for the Chicago White Stockings who had his conversion in 1886. Convinced that he had a calling for Christian work, he gave up his seasonal baseball job at $500 a month and worked as an assistant in the Chicago YMCA for $83 a month. In 1893 he became an assistant to revivalist J. Wilbur Chapman who helped launch his career in the revival business.

In the midst of the theological and philosophical conflicts taking place in the Progressive Era, Sunday provided his audience with the "old fashioned gospel." He did handsprings, chair swings, jumping, wailing and sometimes partially undressing and re-dressing on stage. His audience laughed, jeered, cried and cheered in an evening's performance. Those who faced conversion were to shake his hand to make it final. He estimated that close to a million people shook his hands in his twenty-year career. Through Sunday, Christian salvation, patriotism, decency and manliness became synonymous.[67]

Sunday came under heavy criticism for his compensation. The free-will offerings made to pay Sunday's salary amounted to tens of thousands of dollars for each of his campaigns. It is estimated that by 1918 he had made over one million dollars in the revival business. But Sunday believed that he was well worth it. Compared to the revivalists before him, his conversions cost only $2.00 a soul.[68]

Another prominent revivalist was an Ontario woman by the name of Aimee Semple McPherson who founded the Four Square Gospel Church and built the Angelus Temple. At the height of her popularity McPherson's name appeared on the front pages of Los Angeles newspapers several times a week. Her disappearance in 1926, on the primary decline of the long-wave, left the country speculating on whether she had drowned or was kidnapped. In the course of events that followed a faithful believer and a rescue worker were killed. When McPherson reappeared a month later, she claimed that she was kidnapped but others saw the makings of a sex scandal. She was investigated, charged, and later acquitted for lack of evidence.

In 1911 there were approximately 650 full-time and 1300 part-time evangelists. But by the downswing of the long-wave they were hard pressed to find work. William McLoughlin observes that:

> half of the 650 members of the profession were still finding employment is some churches in 1931. ...there was no doubt that the one hundred year tradition of modern revivalism subsided into a relatively unimportant and unsung role in the evangelical churches for thirty years after 1920.[69]

In *Revivals, Awakenings and Reform,* McLoughlin's dates for his Awakenings align closely with that of the long-wave. Awakenings, by his definition, include revivals and theological or philosophical change. He gives thirty years for each Awakening. The long-wave itself is mostly concerned with the intense religious interest as expressed in the experience of revivals. McLoughlin's dates must therefore be given latitude. His date for the Second Awakening, 1800 – 1830, is the top of the first long-wave. McLoughlin, like many historians, formed this timeline to encompass the theological change brought about by Taylor, Beecher and Finney in the New Haven Theology at us8. The revival of 1857 – 1858 was briefly mentioned but was not included in his analysis because this period did not contain theological change. However there are historians that do classify this period as an Awakening. What he classifies as the Third Awakening, 1890 – 1920 is the upswing of the third long-wave. By the decline of the third long-wave, society was moving back to a conservative Christianity. His Fourth Awakening beginning in 1960 is the upswing of the fourth long-wave.

WAVE IV

On the upswing of the fourth long-wave, Pentecostalism continued to gain many adherents. The Charismatic Movement began in the Anglican Church in 1960, was adopted by the Catholic Bishops in 1967 and soon moved to other Protestant denominations as well. There were the crusades of Billy Graham, a graduate of Wheaton College, a college with roots as radical as that of Oberlin College. Television evangelists appeared on the scene. The ideas of the Social Gospel were revived and Liberation Theology became active in South America. But many churches became increasingly irrelevant; irrelevant to idealistic youth because they were no longer progressive and irrelevant in education and charitable works because education and social programs became the responsibility of the state. With the debates of the early twentieth century, Christianity became irrelevant to the sciences. Many churches could claim relevancy only in the realm of morality and matters not of this world. The Protestant churches stood at the crossroads where the Catholic Church had stood 500 years earlier. They could offer little to appeal to a new generation of young, active, idealistic youth. Throughout the downswing of the third long-wave, Church membership grew from forty percent of the population in 1930 to sixty-nine percent of the population in 1960.[70] But as the upswing of the fourth long-wave progressed, the membership numbers quickly disappeared. Church buildings became no more than empty edifices presided over by a few lonely, and often grumpy, old men. Many became condominiums and parking lots. All things religious became increasingly marginalized. There was a great deal of optimism that science would provide the answers to the world's problems.

As the Christian churches faced growing disaffection, new religions, cults and occults were there to replace them. There was the Church of Scientology, the Unification Church of the Moonies and the Hare-Krishnas. The eastern religions of Transcendental Meditation, I Ching, Zen Buddhism and Taoism saw growing adherents. In the Age of Aquarius, New Age, astrology, witchcraft, Satanism and astral projections came into the open. In some cases parents had to kidnap their own children back from cults for "deprogramming." For those with a more academic leaning, first year psychology classes in universities were filled to standing room only. The search for extra-terrestrial life received broadening interest as did UFO sightings. Youth was searching for answers to age old questions of life and went looking every which way.

The fourth long-wave upswing ushered in the era of the Cold War generating fears of a Nuclear Holocaust. The war in Vietnam created growing tensions. The population explosion led to a dim view of the future with food and energy shortages. Younger and younger children were subjected to grave moral decisions in the class rooms in case one day nuclear war, food shortages or nationwide emergencies would make survival ethics necessary. Presuppositions that were taken for granted for hundreds of years came into question. The world had entered the Modern Age. It had entered the Scientific Age. And that age begat the Age of Uncertainty. Calvinist determinism which had collapsed in the optimism of usδ came back through the works of those such as B.F. Skinner and behavioral determinism in the 1940's and 1950's, which continued to receive attention on the upswing of the long-wave. Before, man was a creature of God subject to the arbitration of divine will. Now he could be viewed as cog in a materialistic machine. There was no free will, there was no real choice. All acts past, present and future are determined. The optimism that science could solve the world's problems collapsed before the top of the fourth long-wave. In the midst of the Civil Rights Movement many churches were no longer seen as pillars of moral America but as obstacles to progress.

There was once a saying that parents should cover their daughters' eyes because hip tossing Elvis Presley was coming to town. Hip tossing was a signature style of one televangelist until he was brought down by a sex scandal. Another televangelist was convicted of mail fraud while building a Disneyland style park for Christians. His wife would appear years later in a television reality show with a porn star. The primary decline of the long-wave became an era when many ministers were brought down by sex scandals. Sex scandals involving children would plague the Anglican, Catholic and Eastern Orthodox churches when they were disclosed many years later. But as the long-wave declined, the energies of revivals and concerns about the effects of cults have subsided.

After a period of disillusionment, a survey in the early 2000's found that forty percent of Americans consider themselves to be Evangelicals. Each candidate of the presidential debates of 2004 affirmed their faith in God. Whereas the "God" word was avoided like a virus by the media on the upswing of the long-wave, it has become acceptable to talk about God in public again. There is a return to a conservative form of Christian faith on the long-wave downswing.

With the downswing of the long-wave, determinism has become a growing feature in social thought. Some geneticists say that our genes not only determine our physical features, but also our weight, preferences and habits as well.

When the young search for answers about their role in the world, their discoveries often come into conflict with the knowledge of the old. The First Awakening brought a conflict between the old side and the new side, the old lights and the new lights. The Second Awakening brought a split between the old school and the new school, the old divinity and the new divinity. These were similar to the lines drawn in other religious conflicts of the past. In the end, it is not the prodigal sons that go back to the old side, for there are too few of the old generation left to champion the old beliefs. If the sides reunite, it is usually under the banner of the new ideology.

Politics

With a broad array of changes taking place in society throughout the long-wave, the political spectrum, by necessity, must reflect these changes. Each upswing of the long-wave has brought suffrage to a different group of people. All white males won the right to vote at usδ, known as the era of Jacksonian Democracy. All black males won the right to vote at the peak of the second long-wave, but had to wait until the peak of the fourth long-wave, with the Civil Rights Movement, to restate that right. At the peak of the third long-wave, women won the right to vote.

Wars tend to be greater and more atrocious on the upswing of the long-wave. The increase in the destructive power of weapons aside; with population growth, armies become larger. With a more youthful population there is more recklessness than experience, more mindfulness of adventure and pride than consequences and more adrenaline than a fear of mortality. All these factors contribute to the escalation of war beyond the anticipation of all those involved. Often these wars go beyond the control of all those who thought that they were in control. The results are great wars at the top of the long-wave. Often there are no clear winners in a great war, but with the great loss of lives, the destruction of property, the turbulent upheaval, all sides suffer from heavy losses.

With the great social movements, war and other turbulent changes near the top of the long-wave, there are dramatic changes in voting patterns. Figure 2.01 charts the difference in percentage popular vote for president between two consecutive elections. These changes in voting patterns can be seen in the large swings at usδ and at regular intervals at the long-wave tops.

During the long-wave decline, a conservative spirit takes hold of the nation. As a reflection of the conservative mood, within several years of the long-wave top, a conservative administration is elected to power. The conservative administration elected to power immediately after the top of Wave I was James Monroe. During us8 the administrations were liberal. The conservative administrations elected to power immediately after the top of Wave II were Grant, Hayes, Garfield and Arthur; after the top of Wave III were Harding, Coolidge and Hoover; and after the top of Wave IV were Reagan and Bush. Figure 2.02 lists the presidents of these conservative administrations immediately after the long-wave tops. The conservative shift of the 1980's brought conservative administrations to many countries, including Britain, Germany and Canada.

As the long-wave decline progresses, society becomes increasingly conservative. With an ageing population, an isolationist spirit takes hold of the country. There is a diminishing desire to be involved in world affairs. The most recent period of isolationist sentiment was in the 1920's and 1930's with the failure of the League of Nations.

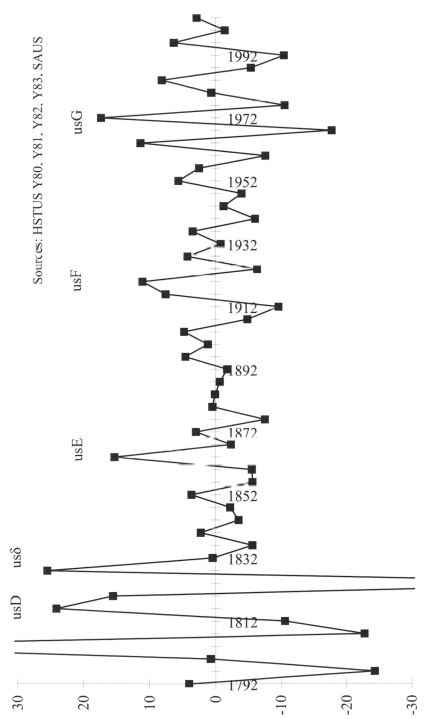

Sources: HSTUS Y80, Y81, Y82, Y83, SAUS

Figure 2.01 - Difference In Percentage Popular Vote Between Consecutive Elections For President (U.S.)

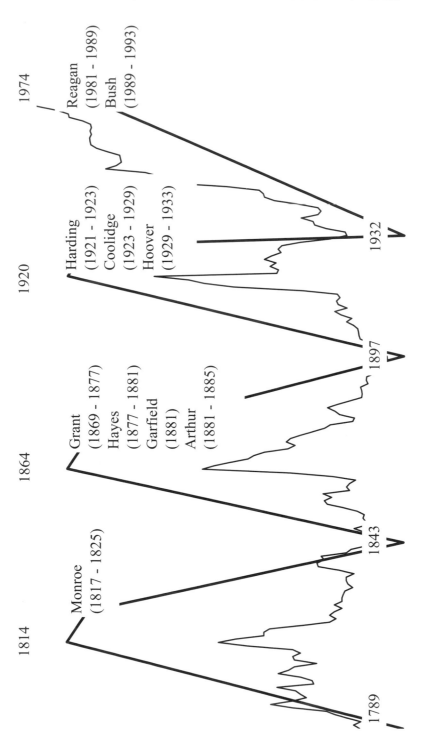

Figure 2.02 - Conservative Political Administrations (U.S.)

3 SOCIAL MOVEMENTS: CANADA

The demographics of Canada and the United States have similarities but they are not exactly the same. Because we are geographic neighbors, there is a close flow of social, economic and political exchanges. We are an influence on each other, but we also have regional differences even within the regions of each country. The social movements in Canada follow the long-wave in their own distinctive manner yet they are along similar lines as the U.S. and Britain. Again, we find that activity is most vigorous at caδ and on the upswing of the long-wave than on the downswing of the long-wave.

Prohibition

The first widely sweeping organization of temperance movements in Canada began in the 1830's at caδ with influences from both the U.S. and Britain. In Nova Scotia Rev. Lyman Beecher's speeches were found aboard a ship tossed ashore during a storm. The sermons became widely distributed and used in the temperance crusades. American influences were further strengthened with the visit of the Rev. Justin Edwards into the area. When an English temperance speaker, James Buckingham, toured the U.S. and Canada from 1838 to 1841, he found that there was more drunkenness in Toronto than in any of the bordering states and he saw more drunkenness in lower Quebec City in one hour than in all of his three years in the United States. The story only got worse when he arrived in the Maritimes.[1] In Saint John the ratio of people to liquor licenses was 50 to 1.[2]

The Canadian temperance movements began in conjunction with the revivals of Protestant Churches and the concerns of temperate Catholic priests in the Maritimes and then continued with later formed independent societies such the Sons of Temperance, the Daughters of Temperance and the Total Abstinence Society. The temperance movement slowly changed from advocating moderate drinking to advocating total abstinence. By 1844 over 10,000 people took temperance pledges in Newfoundland under Father Theobald Mathew. Subsequently his birthday would be celebrated there for over a century. There were an estimated 600 temperance societies in the Province of Canada with 150,000 Catholic and Protestant members. Tales of child and wife abuse by drunken men came to the surface where they had been kept quiet before. To replace the tavern, temperance halls sprang up across the country to provide families with a place to gather for recreation. Many of these halls became the first community halls. Instead of drinking bouts with groups of men, soirees — dinner parties for men, women and families — became the new trend.

In Montreal, a Reverend Joseph Christmas lit the fires of revivalism in the American Presbyterian Church with the perfectionist teachings of the New Haven theology and fanned the flames of temperance crusades with Benjamin Rush's essays on liquor.

For French Canadians, Father Charles Chiniquy became the center of the temperance movement. Chiniquy was an ultramontane who believed that everyone must bow before the authority of the Catholic Church. Under his leadership over 400,000 people took the temperance pledge by 1850, this being about half the population of Canada East. Before long allegations surfaced that Chiniquy was seducing the women that he attended to. Chiniquy was eventually excommunicated. He got married, became a Presbyterian minister and started a new career denouncing Catholicism. The temperance movement in Canada East was left without a charismatic speaker.

Before Toronto became known as "Toronto the Good" it was famously known as a drunken town. With a population of 20,000 in 1846, it had close to nine hundred completely unregulated liquor establishments.[3] Although there was a great deal of indifference to drunkenness, within a decade all that changed as the city's political and business leaders began adopting the temperance platform. Some of the well known forebears such as George Brown, the founder of the *Globe* newspaper in 1844 and who would be one of the Fathers of Confederation, Egerton Ryerson and William Lyon Mackenzie were staunch defenders of the temperance movement. Timothy Eaton refused to sell liquor in his stores.

As the temperance movement progressed, personal pledges changed into political action. Pressure on politicians induced Newfoundland to enact its first liquor license law in 1839. Nova Scotia limited the number of taverns that could open in various areas. New Brunswick and Prince Edward Island began regulating liquor establishments.

WAVE II

Parallel to the movement towards state prohibition on the upswing of the second long-wave in Maine in the 1840's, Nova Scotia, New Brunswick, Prince Edward Island and the Province of Canada attempted to introduce similar legislation. By 1851 seventeen counties in

Nova Scotia had stopped granting liquor licenses and close to a dozen counties were officially dry. In New Brunswick, a private members temperance bill introduced by Samuel Leonard Tilley, another future Father of Confederation, passed the legislature with a three-fifths majority to become law. But there were so many violators that it became impossible to enforce. The temperance legislation quickly lost popularity and after the election that followed, Tilley lost his seat and the law was repealed with a 38 to 2 vote. New Brunswick would be the only province to outlaw liquor in 1856 on the upswing of the second long-wave.

The Dunkin Act of 1865 opened a local option to municipalities in the Province of Canada, giving them the ability to vote on allowing liquor outlets to operate within their boundaries. Whether or not the temperance movement can be declared successful, before the century's end the consumption of liquor on the job changed from being an inducement to work that was expected of an employer to being an unacceptable conduct.

On the downswing of the long-wave a number of temperance societies consolidated into the Dominion Alliance for the Total Suppression of the Liquor Traffic. The WCTU became established across Canada by 1883. The Canada Temperance Act or Scott Act of 1878 opened the local option across the country allowing municipalities to control the sale of liquor within their boundaries; but it was found to be inadequate and like the U.S., another great wave of prohibition activity would emerge again on the upswing of the third long-wave. Attention would return to changing Federal and Provincial legislation.

WAVE III

The first attempt to put prohibition into Federal legislation was based on the election promise of Wilfrid Laurier and the Liberal party. In the plebiscite of 1898, 51.3 percent voted for the complete prohibition of liquor. But since only 44 percent of eligible voters voted, Laurier felt that the majority was too slim to pass any prohibition legislation. With the failure of the federal legislation, the temperance movement focused on Provincial changes. Prince Edward Island went dry by 1901. Saskatchewan went dry in 1915, Nova Scotia, Manitoba and Alberta in 1916, British Columbia, Newfoundland and New Brunswick in 1917. Quebec enacted wartime prohibition in 1918.

With a population of 2.5 million in Ontario, the WCTU got 825 thousand signatures for its petitions. It took three trucks to bring them to the Ontario legislature. Ten thousand marchers attended the presentation. Liberal newspapers such as *The Globe* and the *Toronto Star* were strong supporters of prohibition. The Ontario Temperance Act was passed unanimously in 1916 prohibiting the sale of liquor. All retail outlets were closed down. But to prevent damage to the agricultural industry, the production and export of liquor remained legal. For the years between 1916 and 1921 the import of liquor remained legal and personal consumption of liquor at home was unregulated.

During the election of 1919, an uproar erupted over the scandal of the Conservative government selling liquor against prohibition laws. The leaderless United Farmers of Ontario (UFO), the only party that strongly advocated prohibition, won the election with 45 seats. They formed the government in coalition with the Independent Labour Party which had 11 seats. The Conservative Party, which had had a majority government in Ontario for 14 years, won only 25 seats. The Liberal Party took 29 seats. Four hundred thousand votes against the repeal of the Ontario Temperance Act were cast in the plebiscite that accompanied the election. That was a majority of 250,000 votes.[4] Members of the UFO would eventually form the Co-operative Commonwealth Federation (CCF) and then the New Democratic Party (NDP). They would not win another election in Ontario until 1990. Prohibition took effect nationwide when the Federal Government passed prohibition legislation on March 11, 1918.

"Blind Pigs" became the name of illegal drinking spots that sprang up across the country. Unlike American speakeasies, blind pigs operated from behind locked doors and were very selective about whom they served. Many were operated by wives and single mothers from within the home. One would find out about them by referrals from a friend of a friend of a friend. When one household was taken to court for importing

1000 bottles of liquor a month, their plea was that all 1000 bottles were for personal consumption and yes, they did consume them all. Since the manufacture and export of liquor remained legal, exporters made millions by shipping the liquor to exotic destinations like Cuba and Mexico. Most of it ended up across the border in the U.S., shipped by exporters with exotic names like "rum runner." Doctors found that there was an epidemic of liquor related illnesses, for which medical alcohol was the only cure. They charged $2.00 per prescription, and some became quite wealthy from this thinly disguised sale of liquor prescription. The patient then had to line up at the pharmacist to be dispensed the dosage, along with scores of others who were caught up in the same epidemic. In one 2.5 year period, the Ontario government had purchased 750 thousand gallons of liquor for medicinal purposes.[5]

Quebec was the first province to revoke prohibition in 1919 followed by most of the provinces before the mid 1920's. Liquor sale and distribution has since come under the control of provincial governments under the entities of liquor control boards. The movement for nation-wide prohibition did not continue past the 1920's. In the 1990's and thereafter, on the downswing of the fourth long-wave, the control of liquor in some provinces has been deregulated, allowing private commercial interests to sell and distribute the product.

The Women's Movement

The women's suffrage movement had a much later start in Canada than it did in the U.S. and Britain and unlike with the British or American movements, there was no violence, suffrage parades or even public protests. Canadian women took the route of organized speeches, debates, petitions and meetings with legislators. Neither was there as much opposition. In some provinces women only had to show that there was sufficient interest to attain the vote. There were various attempts in the 1800's by women and men to give women a political voice, but the largest agitations and victories came on the upswing of the long-wave.

In the province of Manitoba, women were given the municipal franchise in 1887. There were some brief agitations by the WCTU in the early 1890's in almost all the provinces for the federal franchise, but not much of significance came from their efforts. In Alberta women were able to vote for school trustees and sit on boards. The municipal franchise came in 1894. Mrs. Gordon Grant, one of the founders of the first Children's Aid Homes in Victoria and the first woman to be elected to the Victoria School Board, led the women of British Columbia for provincial suffrage beginning in 1885, and even continuing in the years when interest was waning. Several Maritime Provinces had measures granting women the municipal franchise in the 1880's. Since 1809 the women of Quebec had participated at the ballot box until the Elections Act of 1834, which strictly prohibited females from voting.

Ontario women were granted the right to vote for school trustees in the 1850's. In the 1870's, attempts were made to enable women to vote in municipal elections and by the 1880's women with property were granted the right to vote, first on municipal by-laws, and then in municipal elections. Throughout the 1880's various municipal councils and individuals were petitioning the Ontario government to enfranchise women but without much success.

Emily Howard Stowe had to care for her children and an invalid husband while working as a teacher. Over the years she managed to save enough money to return to school to pursue her dream of becoming a doctor. When Canadian medical schools would not accept her, she and her family moved to New York where she entered the Women's New York Medical School and graduated in 1868. Returning to Toronto, she established her medical practice and began directing her efforts towards the advancement of women. In 1876, Stowe and a small group of women formed the Toronto Women's Literary Club, in large measure to discuss the issues of suffrage for women.

In 1883 the Literary Club was disbanded and a meeting was held in the Toronto City Council chambers. In attendance were approximately 130 men and women who unanimously passed resolutions endorsing women's suffrage and the formation of a society for the purpose of achieving that goal. The Toronto Women's Suffrage Association was one of the outcomes of that meeting. Through the efforts of this organization the University of Toronto opened its doors to women and the Ontario

Medical College for Women was established with Dr. Augusta Stowe-Gullen, daughter of Dr. Emily Stowe, as the first female member of the faculty. Through the efforts of other women, the legal profession began to admit women as well. By the end of the 1890's however, the legislative and professional efforts for the advancement of women were in a lull. Like the American movement, writer Carol Lee Bacchi observes that, "in 1895 the suffrage movement stood in a no-man's land," that "the few feminist founders were old and tired" and that "the vast majority of the women were unconcerned or unconverted."[6] Dr. Emily Stowe died in 1903.

WAVE III

The process of rebirth and rejuvenation of the women's movement came a decade later on the upswing of the long-wave in 1906 through the efforts of Dr. Augusta Stowe-Gullen, now in charge of the Canadian Suffrage Association, along with two other younger women, Flora Macdonald Denison and Dr. Margaret Blair Gordon. With the institutional changes came a new advocacy for women's suffrage. From St. John, Newfoundland on the east coast to Victoria, B.C. on the west coast, suffrage organizations began to form across the country. Even the prestigious National Council of Women, that had disassociated itself from women's suffrage earlier, adopted a resolution in favour of women's suffrage in 1910. The WCTU and the temperance movement were among the first to support women's suffrage because they thought it would give women a say in controlling liquor interests and other moral issues.

The churches generally supported women's suffrage in the belief that it would extend the ideals of feminine virtue across the country. At the same time the churches believed that a woman should be well educated because an educated mother would do a better job in raising children and in bringing about a higher level of education in society. Between 1880 and 1910 the Canadian Methodist and Presbyterian Churches were key proponents of the Social Gospel. Churches that supported the ideals of the Social Gospel believed in women's suffrage because it would enable women to bring about reforms to social problems. Attesting to their faith in God was their good works. Those that used theological arguments against women's suffrage soon found that their arguments held no substance. These same arguments could be heard again when the women's movement revived on the upswing of the fourth long-wave.

The Prairie Provinces were the first to enfranchise women in Canada. There was considerable support for women's suffrage from men, farmers' organizations and women's auxiliaries. In Manitoba, agitation for the right to vote in the provincial election began in 1910. Women such as Dr. Mary E. Crawford, president of the Winnipeg Political Equality League, and Nellie McClung, who would eventually serve in the Alberta Legislature, began organizing, sending petitions and getting audiences with legislators. At least ten of the League's members were journalists, ensuring that women's suffrage had wide press coverage. Manitoba became the first province to enable women both to vote and to hold provincial office. With unanimous agreement, the Suffrage Bill passed the legislature and became law on January 28, 1916. In 1917 the Political Equality League disbanded and was heard from no more.

In Alberta, the public and the press were generally supportive of enfranchising women. Two of the leaders of the movement, Emily Murphy and Alice Jamieson, would be the first women to receive appointments as magistrates. A year before the first suffrage organization, the Edmonton Equal Franchise League, was formed in 1913, the United Farmers of Alberta passed a resolution in support of women's suffrage and eventually extended its membership to women. The WCTU led the suffrage movement in agitating for changes at the municipal level in 1910. By 1916 women would be given full rights to the provincial franchise. Mrs. L.M. McKinney and Miss Roberta Macadams were the first women members of provincial parliament in 1917.

As in Alberta, the people of Saskatchewan were generally supportive of enfranchising women. The Saskatchewan Grain Growers' Association endorsed women's suffrage in 1912 with the Women Grain Growers' Association being formed at the same time. The Homemakers' Clubs in Saskatchewan provided a fostering environment for women's suffrage. The women of Saskatchewan won the right to vote in 1916.

Interest in provincial suffrage was revived in British Columbia in 1908 when the Local Council of Victoria headed by Mrs. Cecilia Spofford voted to make an endorsement. By November the Political Equality League of Victoria was established with Mrs. Gordon Grant as its president. Another league was established in Vancouver under Mrs. Lashley Hall. With these two organizations playing a central role, the provincial vote was given to women in 1917. Mary Ellen Smith became the first female member of the provincial legislature in 1918.

Ontario women had a more difficult time in securing the vote; but after the Western provinces had legalized women's suffrage, along with numerous states in the U.S. and the apparent imminent endorsement of women's suffrage in Britain, the Ontario government had a sudden change of heart and passed a suffrage bill in 1917.

Prime Minister Sir John A. Macdonald believed that women's suffrage had a role in a strong central government and introduced bills in 1883, 1884 and 1885 to entitle women to the Dominion vote, but none of these items passed Parliament. It would be 1918 before there would be sufficient political pressure to give women the Dominion franchise. The Dominion Elections Act of 1920 gave women the right to hold office. Running as an independent, Agnes Macphail became the first woman Member of Parliament in the 1921 election. She would be reelected four more times in her career.

The Maritime Provinces did not show the same amount of enthusiasm for women's suffrage as the more westerly provinces. Women won the right to vote after the Dominion of Canada Franchise Act was passed. Nova Scotia enfranchised women provincially in 1918, New Brunswick in 1919, Prince Edward Island in 1922 and Newfoundland in 1925. The last province to endorse women's suffrage was Quebec in 1940.

Yet the movement for full legal equality of women did not end there. The question of whether women were legally "persons" in the Dominion of Canada and entitled to the same privileges as men remained unanswered. The question was first put forward in Alberta in 1916 when council for the defendant questioned Judge Emily Murphy's right to hold court as his interpretation was that a woman was not legally a "person" as defined in the British North America Act. While the provincial court made the ruling in 1917 that the word "persons" made no distinction of sex, it was not clear whether the Dominion was of the same opinion. If women were not persons, then they would not be able to sit in the Senate. Judge Murphy with her four appellants Nellie McClung, Irene Parlby, Louise McKinney and Henrietta Muir Edwards took the case to the Supreme Court of Canada for an interpretation in 1927, which ruled against the inclusion of women. The matter was appealed to the Privy Council in London, which made the final ruling in 1929 that the word "persons" includes members of the male and female sex. After the 1920's, women as a collective movement, except in Quebec, were no more.

WAVE IV

The women's movement in Canada revived at the same time that the U.S. movement was reviving on the upswing of the fourth long-wave. Starting in the 1960's, women rallied on issues such as pay equity, abortion rights, employment equity and equality under the law. They made great strides in changing Canadian society by furthering egalitarian ideals. But as the long-wave declined, the frequency of collective engagements rallying for social change declined in turn.

Politics

Since Confederation in 1867 two political parties have dominated the landscape of Canadian politics. They are the Liberal Party and the Conservative Party. As the names convey, they are the mood, the politics and the ideas that have come to dominate each side of the long-wave.

In the twenty-nine years of the downswing of the second long-wave from Confederation to the election of 1896, the business-oriented Conservatives were the governing party for eighty-three percent of those years. John A. Macdonald, Canada's first Prime Minister, lost the election in 1873 to Liberal Alexander Mackenzie during the growing depression. The Conservatives won back the government in the following election but lost it again to Liberal Wilfrid Laurier during the next depression in the election of 1896.

In the twenty-five years of the upswing of the third long-wave, from the election of 1896 to the election of 1921, the Liberals were the governing party for sixty percent of those years. The Conservatives were in power for twenty-four percent of those years and the Unionists, a coalition of Conservatives and Liberals, for sixteen percent of those years.

Liberal William Lyon Mackenzie King won the election of 1926 and during the growing depression that began in 1929, several Conservative provincial governments requested federal funds. King replied that he would not give five cents to any Tory (Conservative) government. That spelled the end of the Liberals in the election of 1930. The country's first millionaire and business-oriented Prime Minister, Conservative Richard Bennett, was elected by a landslide. King had always believed that it was divine destiny that he himself became the prime minister. Now he felt that it was just as divine, that at a most difficult period, he was sitting in the opposition to chide the government on its shortcomings. And there were shortcomings aplenty to chide about. Neither Bennett nor King had any remedies to the Great Depression. It was economic heresy for anyone to suggest that the government should spend money to get the economy back on its feet or toward the alleviation of poverty, hunger or unemployment. There was a depression in the cities and drought, dust storms and depression on the farms. Employment fell by thirty percent. Thousands became hobos and drifters looking for work. Mortgages foreclosed across the country. Those that couldn't afford repairs or gas for their automobiles pulled them by horse and called them Bennett Buggies and abandoned farms that could not provide food even for their owners were called Bennett Barnyards. If Bennett had compassion for the widespread suffering, the people did not see it. During the election of 1935, King and the Liberals returned to governance with a landslide victory.

From 1935 to 1979, the Liberals governed for thirty-nine years. Only in 1957 did the Conservatives win an election, but by then they had become the Progressive-Conservative Party. John Diefenbaker, the leader, was not the traditional Conservative of decades past that sided with money and big business. As a result he did not receive the support of business. During his tenure he implemented the Canadian Bill of Rights and the Baby Bonus.

Following Diefenbaker were the Liberal years of Lester B. Pearson and Pierre Elliot Trudeau. During Pearson's term Medicare and the Canada Pension Plan were put into place. During his early years as a Member of Parliament Trudeau liberalized abortion and divorce. Trudeau declared that "the state has no business in the bedrooms of the nation." During his late years as Prime Minister he brought in the Canadian Charter of Rights and Freedoms. The popularity of his charismatic personality became known as Trudeaumania in the 1960's. In the Western provinces, the Baptist minister Tommy Douglas was the first to bring socialized medicine to Canada. He was a leader of the CCF that was formed on the basis of the Social Gospel.

During the 1980's the tide of liberalism subsided as a wave of conservatism moved in on the downswing of the fourth long-wave. Conservative leader Joe Clark held one of the shortest elected terms as Prime Minister, being in office for only eight months and twenty-seven days at the transitioning top of the fourth long-wave. The only other person that held a shorter elected term as prime minister was Conservative Arthur Meighen in 1926, of two months and twenty-seven days near the transitioning top of the third long-wave.

Trudeau was re-elected after Joe Clark, but could not rekindle the liberal climate and his personal charisma that once mesmerized the country. Brian Mulroney's business-oriented Conservatives won the election of 1984 with the largest majority in Canadian history. A number of conservative governments were elected provincially also, pursuing ultra-conservative agendas. In the 1990's the NDP was elected on a socialist agenda in British Columbia, Saskatchewan and Ontario but implemented a conservative program that could only be the envy of conservative governments. During the recession of the 1990's, social spending, health care and education funding were cut back. Individual taxes were raised and corporate taxes were kept low. The "Social Contract" in Ontario reopened civil service collective agreements and reduced the payroll by $2 billion, alienating the labor unions, one of the NDP's major supporters. The federal NDP leader Audrey McLaughlin fired her Finance Critic for challenging Ontario NDP's conservative policies. The Baby Boomers had abandoned their positions of being strident radical activists and some had entered the corporate board rooms to take up their new roles of being strident business conservatives and lobbyists.

After the fall of the Progressive-Conservative government in the recession leading up to the election of 1993, the right-wing Reform Party from the Western provinces expanded to a national scale, split the conservative vote, and left the Progressive-Conservatives out of Parliament for twelve years. Only after the Reform Party and the Progress-Conservative Party united under the Conservative banner did they finally win an election in 2006.

4 DEMOGRAPHICS AND THE LONG-WAVE

The Baby Boom that began in the 1930's was a phenomenal interruption of 130 years of declining fertility. As far as most of us can remember, there was never a baby boom before and statistics seem to corroborate this fact. Beginning with U.S. statistics, figure 4.00 shows an almost uneventful decline in birth rate per 1000 population from 1800 until 1933. To narrow the ratios, figure 4.01 plots the number of live births per 1000 women between the ages of 15 and 44 for the years 1800 to 1970. A similar pattern emerges. The birth rate per 1000 women since 1800 has declined from a high of 278 births to a low of 73 in 1933 and 1936. But on closer examination, we find that the decline in fertility has not always been uniform. There have been times when the decline slows. These are marked with the letters, usD, usE and usF for U.S statistics. In Canadian statistics these will be labelled as caD, caE and caF. Fluctuations in population growth that are too small to generate a long-wave are labelled usδ (us delta) and usγ (us gamma). At usG, as we already know, is the baby boom, when the birth rate actually stopped declining and turned up. Another observation that can be made is that sections usD, usE, usF and the peak of usG are almost regular intervals apart, approximately 40 years from the end of one section to the beginning of the next.

Year	Number of Children Under 5 Per 1000 Women 20 to 44	Increase/ Decrease Per Decade	Long- Wave	Baby Boom Intervals
1800	1342			
1810	**1358**	**16**	usD	
1820	1295	-63		
1830	1145	**-150**		
1840	1085	-60		1810 to 1860
1850	892	**-193**		50 Years
1860	**905**	**13**	usE	
1870	814	-91		
1880	780	-34		1860 to 1900
1890	685	-95		40 Years
1900	**666**	**-19**	usF	
1910	631	-35		
1920	604	-27		
1930	506	-98		1900 to 1950
1940	419	-87		50 Years
1950	**580**	**161**	usG	
1960	**717**	**137**	usG	
1970	507	-210		

Table 4.00 - Children Under 5 Per 1000 Women 20 To 44 (U.S.)

Figure 4.02 shows the number of children less than 5 years of age per 1000 women 20 to 44. As we narrow the ratios of children to population even further, we note that usD and usE now turn up along with usG while usF continues the decline, but at a slower rate. The number of children per woman in the 1800's, 1850's and 1940's was increasing while in the other decades the ratios were decreasing. When we overlay the long-wave with this graph, the most basic observation that can be made from figure 4.02 is that the periods of increase and decrease alternate with the long-wave; that is the slope, or the ratio of children to women, tends towards positive towards the upswing of the long-wave, marked by sections usD, usE, usF and usG. Table 4.00 shows the same data in table format. The periods of increase occur at regular intervals of 40 to 50 years. The decade from 1890 to 1900, usF, registers the smallest decline in the table.

The population of the United States has increased from approximately 3 million in 1790 to over 200 million by 1970. Since change is the point of our examination, we will graph the percent change per decade for the population. A decennial rate of change, the rate of change decade over decade, will help reduce small annual fluctuations to give a general trend over a longer period of time. Finding the percentage change per decade is often performed on census data that is available only once every ten years. In our case we will be performing the operation on data that is available as frequently as once a year. This process will be applied to many of the statistical series and will make them all directly comparable, whether these statistics are political, economic or social. These graphs will give the reader a good visualization of long-term trends. From figure 4.03 we can see that the population increase towards the upswing of the long-wave is greater than any increase towards the downswing. The two largest increases in population occurred at usE and usG, approximately 100 years apart, while usF has turned up. The rising slopes of this graph are not just increases but are in actual fact accelerations in the rate of growth.

Figure 4.04 graphs the percent change per decade in immigration. From an almost incomprehensible and erratic set of fluctuations when the raw data is plotted, the percent change per decade shows that

immigration accelerates during times of peace and prosperity, and de-
celerates during times of war and depression. As a percentage of resident
population, figure 4.05 shows that immigration varies from almost 0
percent to close to 1.6 percent. Figures 4.06 and 4.07 show similar characteristics for immigration to Canada. More details on the relationships
between U.S. population and immigration are given in Appendix A.

From these charts, we can observe that baby booms have accompanied each long-wave in the past, a major baby boom 100 years
apart with a minor baby boom in between. The popular belief that the
previous baby boom came after World War II or that baby booms come
after wars is not supported by these population statistics. There were no
baby booms after the Civil War; neither was there one after World War
I. And the baby boom that is usually credited to World War II began
before the war. The decline in fertility, surprisingly, stopped declining
and began turning up in the middle of the depression. The baby boom
continued for more than 20 years. If it were that the war caused the baby
boom to happen, as has been the accepted explanation for many decades,
then these men must have really missed their wives. They were having
more babies at the end of 20 years then they were at the beginning. Even
the men that didn't go to war missed their wives. They were having more
babies too.

By the late 1950's, in a prospering economy, with the absence of
any sexual revolution, or women's movement, or new discoveries in birth
control, or concerns about a population explosion, the birth rate began
to drop. There are few explanations as to why this was. The perpetuation
of the population lies in the changing psychology of the population itself.
This is the dynamic of the long-wave.

Yet figure 4.03 may not show the full extent of these baby booms.
If in 1 year, in a population of 1000, there is a death rate of 20 percent
and a birth rate of 20 percent then the net effect is a population increase
of 0. However, a new cohort group has been introduced. This group
will have similar experiences and values that those born at other times
will not have. When these cohort groups are sufficiently large, such as
Gen-B, then their presence will introduce enormous changes to society, such as the building of schools and playgrounds instead of old age

homes. Other factors such as territorial expansion and the inclusion or exclusion of other populations contribute to overall population, but there are difficulties in accounting for these factors and the various stages of acculturation.

A more revealing graph is the percent change per decade in Canadian population. Figure 4.08 shows two very distinct long-waves. Where wave usF was distorted in the American population statistics, caF is a full wave in the Canadian statistics. Similar fluctuations in population growth may be found in other countries.

Other U.S. statistics provide similar pictures of American population growth also. Figures 4.09 and 4.10 plot the percent change per decade in church membership. Many factors affect church membership. Factors such as population growth, immigration, popularity of a denomination, qualifications for membership, age restrictions, age appeal, its value as a community function, geographical location and the general religiousness of society. All these factors have varied over time. Church membership is different from church attendance in that a person could be a member and not attend church for many years. From figure 4.09, it can be seen that the growth rate in church membership reflects the long-wave. There was a sharp decline in membership during the Civil War, but it picked up again afterwards. Notice that usδ is of a significant presence. The two major troughs occurred in 1853 and 1940, with a minor trough in 1905. Figure 4.09 has remarkable similarities to figure 5.01, the percent change per decade in post office revenue, and figure 5.04, the percent change per decade in work force. Further discussion is provided in the chapter on economics.

Figure 4.10, the percent change per decade in Roman Catholic Church membership gives a slightly different picture than figure 4.09. Catholics count as members all baptized persons, which includes baptized infants. The rite of infant baptism is well practised by Catholics but not usually by Protestants. Protestant membership usually begins after reaching the age of 13. The rise of membership growth into 1959 is 15 years from the long-wave peak of 1974. The rise into 1909 is 11 years from the long-wave peak of 1920. The rise from 1940 to 1959 coincides directly with the baby boom. Without a longer statistical series, one can only suspect that the rise into 1909 is similar to the rise in Methodist membership. This series may be a better reflection of turning points in population growth than the series for Methodist membership since there are fewer variables in the intervening 13 and more years for missing registrations.

From figures 4.11 through to 4.14, we can trace what happens to a baby boom over time. Immigration continues to be a part of this series and could not be factored out. With the passage of time, as Gen-B ages, the growth of the age group to which Gen-B belongs accelerates proportionally. As this baby boom bulge moves through time, the interests of society are heavily weighted by the interests of this age group. But this statistical bulge may not retain its characteristic shape through time because not everyone lives to be the same ripe old age. Owing to accidents, war, disease and other factors causing early death, this baby boom bulge gets smaller as time moves on. Along with the impact of immigration, changing life expectancy and gender differences in life expectancy this age bulge is altered further. Evaluating the impact of the baby boom in history at the beginning when they are active is easier than at the end when they are not. The absence of reliable statistical data makes the evaluation further back into history even more difficult.

Comparing figure 4.11 with figure 4.14, we see that those over 65 years of age reached a decennial peak at about the same time as the baby boom reached a decennial peak. Extrapolating figure 4.01 by adding 60 years to the baby boom peak, we know that the most accelerative phase of Gen-B entering 60 years of age will be reached by 2017.

Canadian population graphs, figures 4.15 to 4.18, show similar changes. Baby boom caG can be traced through graphs 4.15 to 4.17. Baby boom caF can be traced through graphs 4.16 to 4.18 but appears distorted and does not trace as well as caG. In the U.S. statistics baby boom usF is barely traceable or noticeable until figure 4.14. If we compare figure 4.14, U.S. data for those over 65, with figure 4.18, Canadian data for those over 70, we find that both graphs are remarkably similar. They both start rising in 1920. The magnitude of the rise is about forty percent. They both decline into the 1970's. There is another rise and topping out in the 1980's, but the Canadian growth rate this time is greater than the U.S.

Since graph 4.14 and 4.18 are similar, we would expect usF to be as trace-able in the U.S. statistics as caF is traceable in the Canadian statistics. Unfortunately the age data does not allow us to track caF and usF as well as we were able to track caG and usG. Further discussion on population data is found in appendix A.

Even though the term "generation" is frequently used in social and statistical studies, there is no scientifically agreed upon definition for the term and its usage has always been arbitrary. The generally accepted length for the term is between twenty and thirty years, but even these boundaries are often not strictly applied in usage. Depending on which statistical series one looks at, the last baby boom peaked in the U.S. in 1957, started a slow decline into 1961 and then a rapid decline into 1975. Some identify Gen-X as those born in 1961 and after while others identify Gen X as those born after 1965. Still others identify a generation not by birth year but by the events that they encounter in life.

The label "Baby Boomers", for those born between 1946 and 1965, is statistically inaccurate also. The birth rate bottomed out between 1933 and 1936 in the U.S. The Canadian birth rate bottomed out in 1937 at about 20 births per thousand population, reached almost 25 births per thousand population by 1943, declined for a year, and then peaked at about 30 births per population by 1947. The Canadian birth rate then declined and reached a smaller peak in 1957 before declining again, as can be seen in figure 4.19. The term "post war baby boom" may be de scriptive of an era of social and historic significance, but bears no sta-tistical demarcations. It would be inaccurate to use a descriptive label in statistical and economic calculations.

Since this study uses a long-wave timeline, an exact demarcation of generations is not necessary for our study. Often circumstance and fortune determine how people will identify themselves. In our analysis Gen-B re-fers to those born at a time when the birth rate is increasing, and Gen-X refers to those born at a time when the birth rate is declining and how they affect and are affected by the social and economic situations that arise later. There may be other groupings of generations, and a more nar-row definition may be needed for other studies, but these two groupings of generations are sufficient for the purposes of this study.

Although dealing with statistics seems to be an exact science, it should be kept in mind that most historical statistics are estimates and there may be variances between one estimate and another. From the statistics that we have available, we can conclude that:

1)   There are periodic accelerations in indigenous population growth.
2)   The younger, more active population is proportionately larger on the upswing of the long-wave than on the downswing.
3)   Since a new Gen-B comes of age at about the same time as the previous Gen-B enters retirement large institutional changes take place as the long-wave moves up.
4)   Before the long-wave peak is reached, the rate of population growth declines.

As the population changes from proportionately young to proportionately old, the needs, activities and perspectives of society change with it. With these changes the long-wave cycle is generated. The patterns of population growth as manifested in population statistics are well reflected in social and economic statistics.

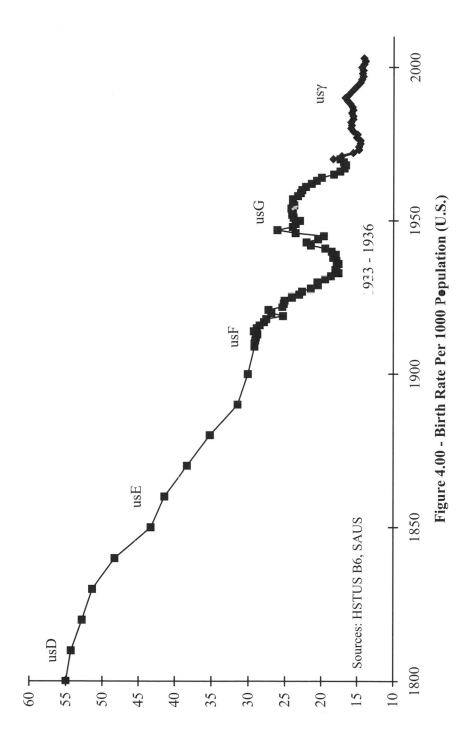

Figure 4.00 - Birth Rate Per 1000 Population (U.S.)

Sources: HSTUS B6, SAUS

1933 - 1936

usD

usE

usF

usG

usγ

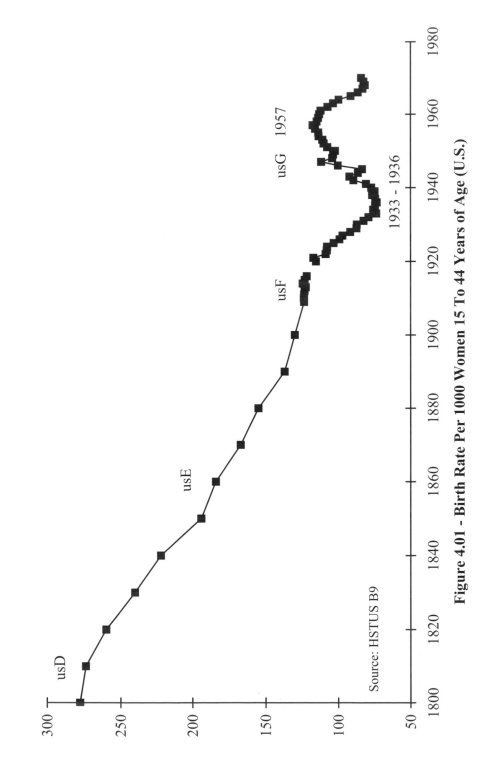

Figure 4.01 – Birth Rate Per 1000 Women 15 To 44 Years of Age (U.S.)

Source: HSTUS B9

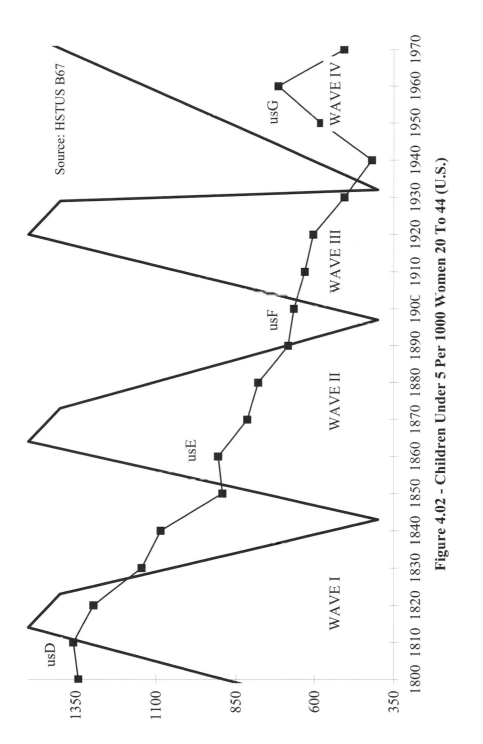

Figure 4.02 – Children Under 5 Per 1000 Women 20 To 44 (U.S.)

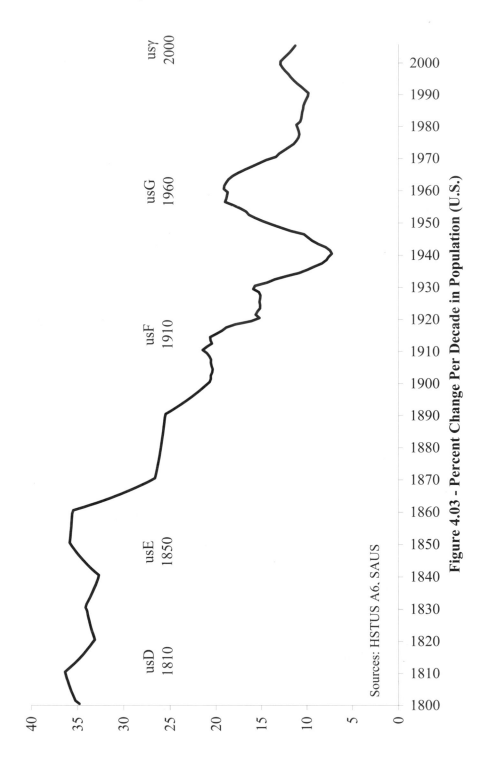

Figure 4.03 - Percent Change Per Decade in Population (U.S.)

Sources: HSTUS A6, SAUS

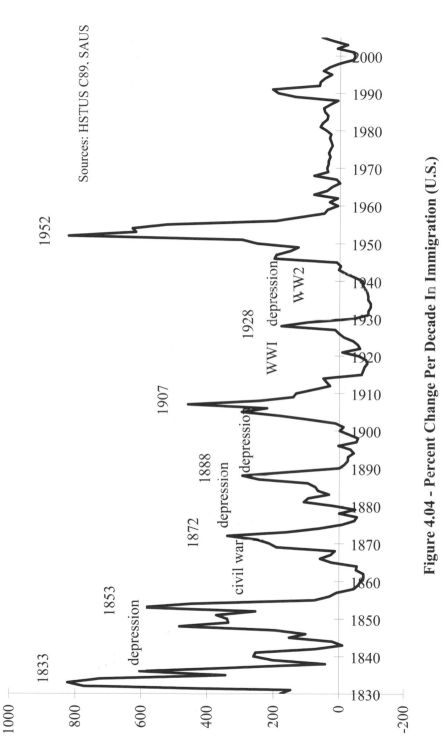

Figure 4.04 – Percent Change Per Decade In Immigration (U.S.)

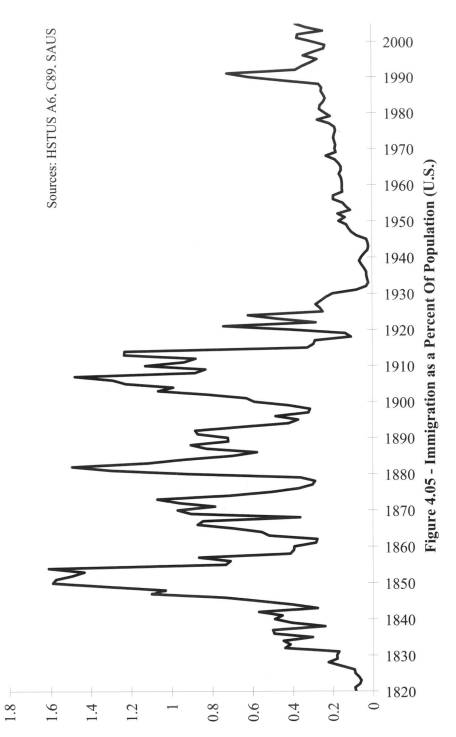

Sources: HSTUS A6. C89. SAUS

Figure 4.05 - Immigration as a Percent Of Population (U.S.)

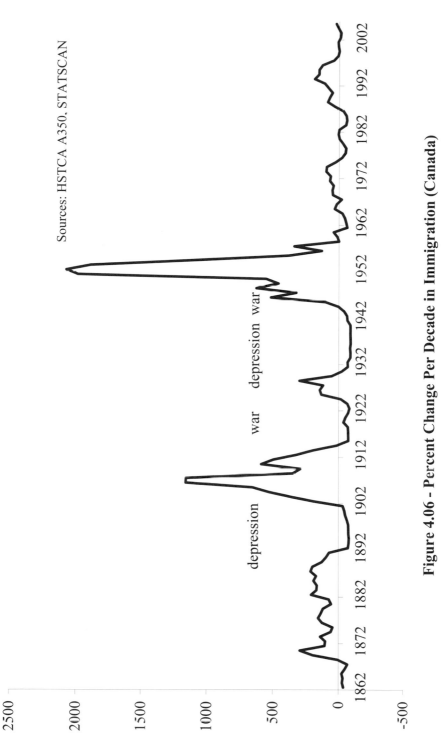

Sources: HSTCA A350, STATSCAN

Figure 4.06 – Percent Change Per Decade in Immigration (Canada)

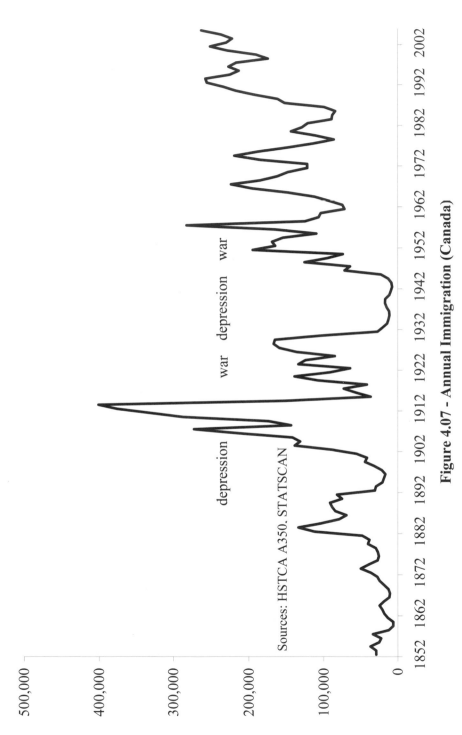

Figure 4.07 – Annual Immigration (Canada)

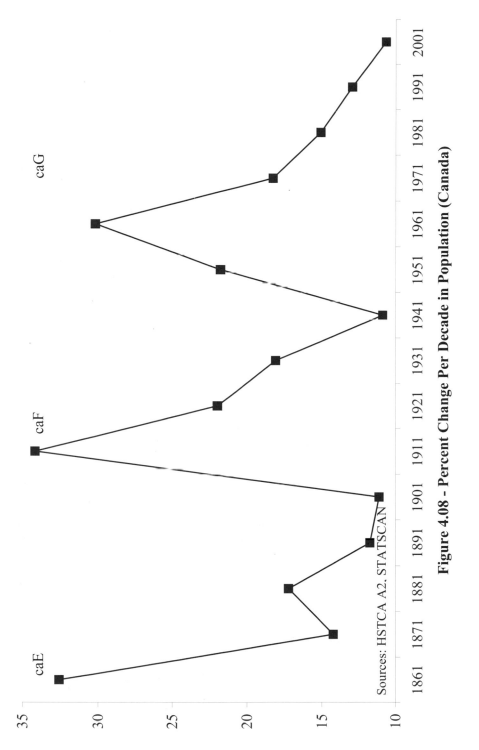

Figure 4.08 – Percent Change Per Decade in Population (Canada)

Sources: HSTCA A2. STATSCAN

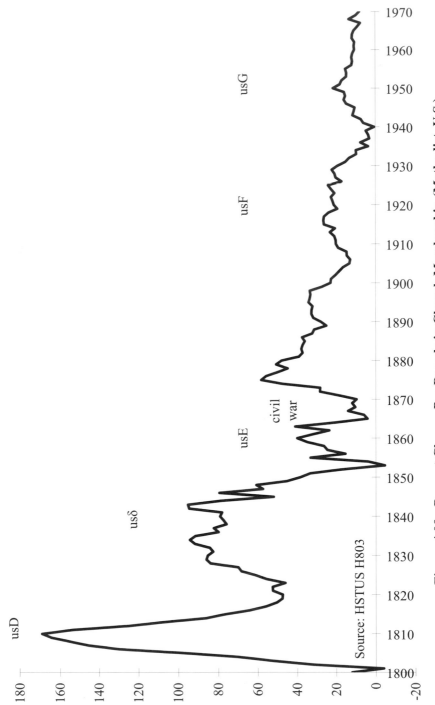

Figure 4.09 - Percent Change Per Decade in Church Membership (Methodist, U.S.)

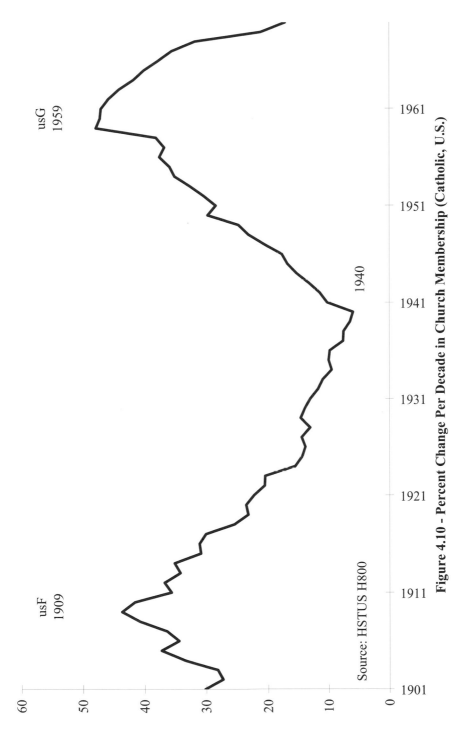

Figure 4.10 – Percent Change Per Decade in Church Membership (Catholic, U.S.)

Source: HSTUS H800

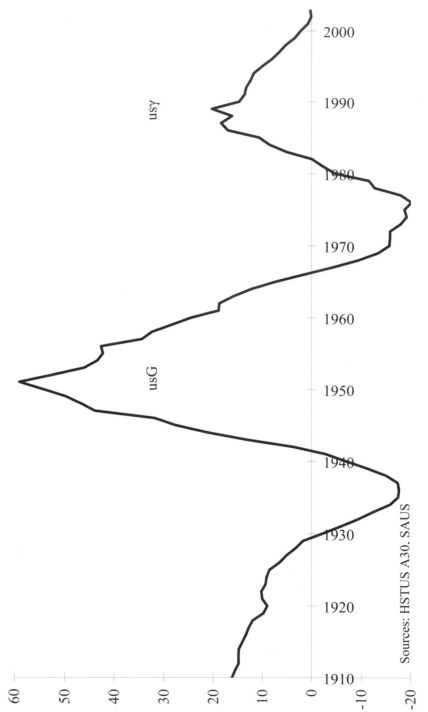

Figure 4.11 -Percent Change Per Decade in Population Ages 5 Years And Under (U.S.)

Sources: HSTUS A30. SAUS

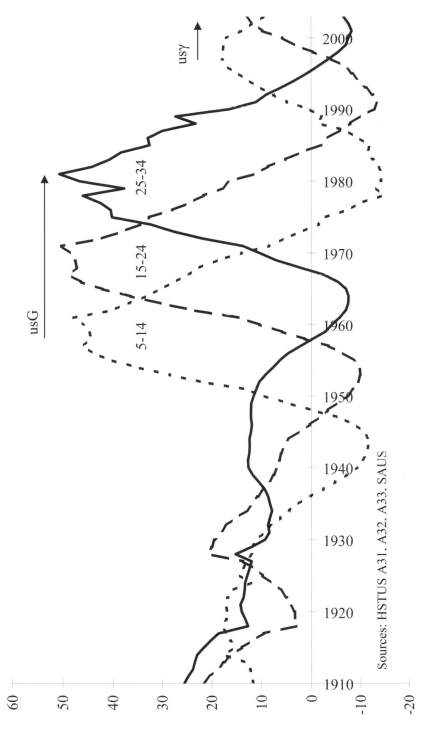

Figure 4.12 - Percent Change Per Decade in Population Ages 5-14, 15-24, 25-34 (U.S.)

Sources: HSTUS A31. A32. A33. SAUS

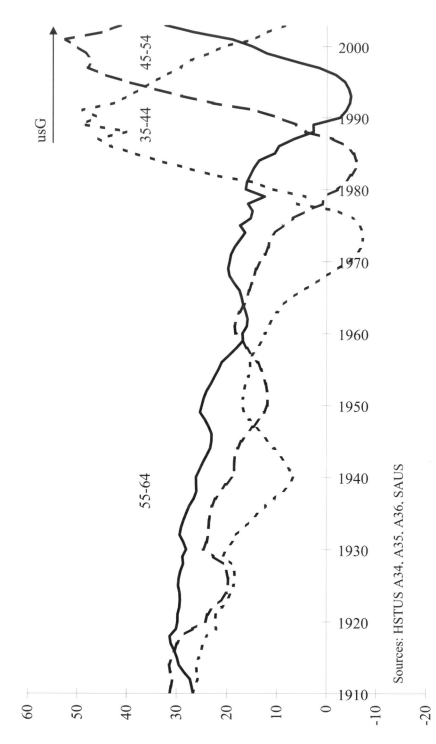

Figure 4.13 - Percent Change Per Decade in Population Ages 35-44, 45-54, 55-64 (U.S.)

Sources: HSTUS A34. A35. A36. SAUS

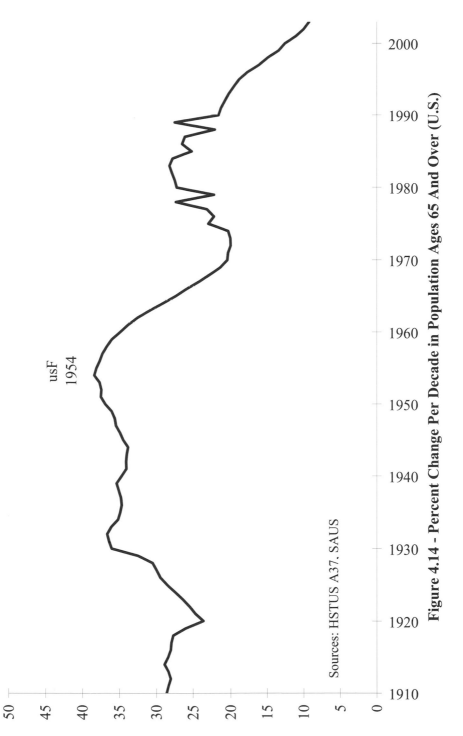

usF
1954

Sources: HSTUS A37. SAUS

Figure 4.14 - Percent Change Per Decade in Population Ages 65 And Over (U.S.)

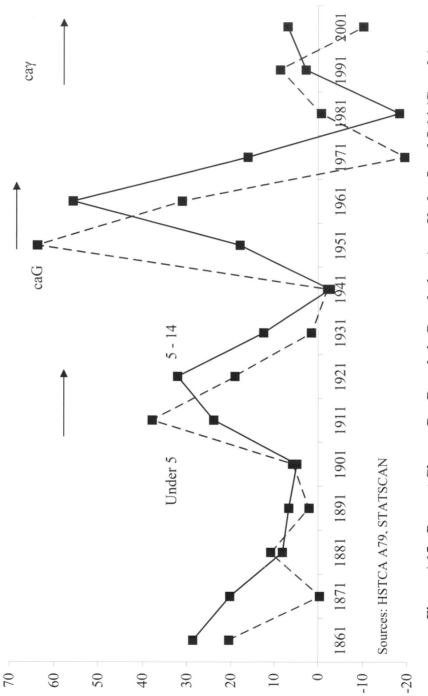

Sources: HSTCA A79, STATSCAN

Figure 4.15 – Percent Change Per Decade in Population Ages Under 5 and 5-14 (Canada)

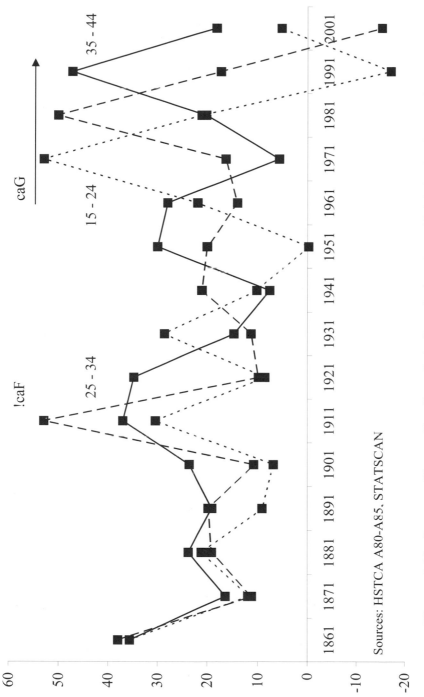

Figure 4.16 - Percent Change Per Decade in Population Ages 15-24, 25-34, 35-44 (Canada)

Sources: HSTCA A80-A85, STATSCAN

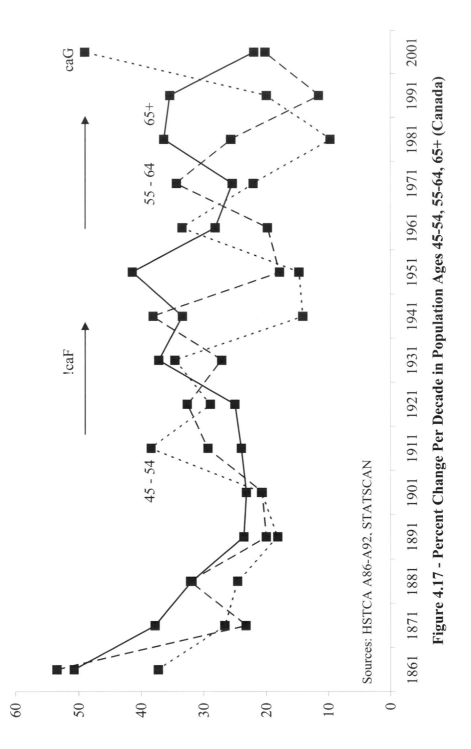

Sources: HSTCA A86-A92, STATSCAN

Figure 4.17 - Percent Change Per Decade in Population Ages 45-54, 55-64, 65+ (Canada)

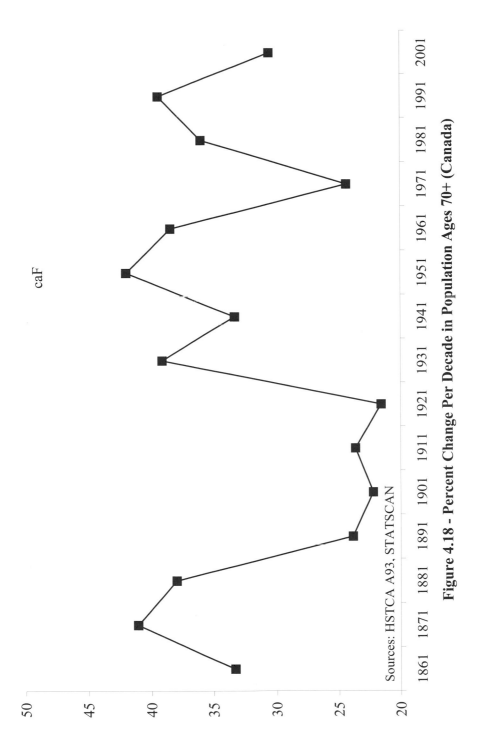

caF

Sources: HSTCA A93, STATSCAN

Figure 4.18 - Percent Change Per Decade in Population Ages 70+ (Canada)

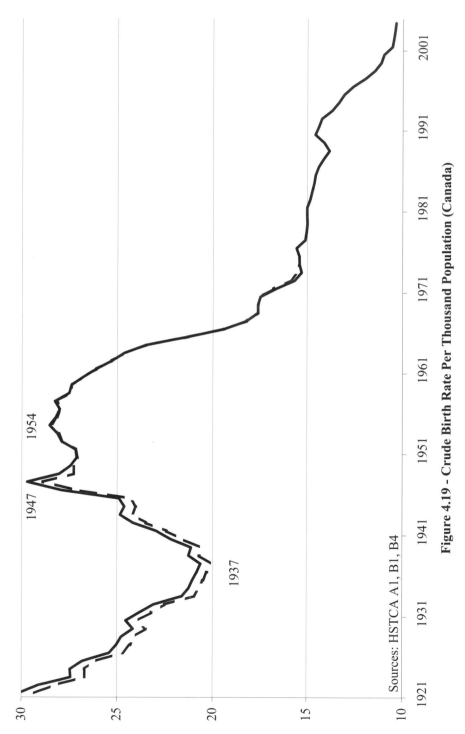

Figure 4.19 - Crude Birth Rate Per Thousand Population (Canada)

Sources: HSTCA A1, B1, B4

5 ECONOMICS

When we examine national income figures for the economy, as displayed in table 5.00, we find that over a half to two-thirds of the expenditures come from consumers. The other one-third is divided between business and government. With the large impact that consumers have on the economy, we would expect that there would be a strong relationship between the population and the economy.

Population, Labor Force and the Economy

Figure 5.00 graphs the percent change per decade in post office revenue. The post office is the nation's oldest and largest monopoly. Almost all the letters of the nation have had to use the services of the post office to get to their destinations. Its revenues are probably a better reflection of economic conditions than many economic estimates. How closely are economic conditions related to the population and the long-wave? Compare figure 5.00 to figure 4.09, the percent change per decade in church membership. Growth in church membership was below 0 in 1853. Growth in postal revenue went below 0 in 1847. Growth in church membership fell to almost 0 in 1940. Growth in postal revenue fell to almost 0 in 1936. In between these two large declines there was a mild decline in the rate of growth of church membership and a mild decline in the rate of growth of postal revenue. Since Methodist church membership starts at age 13 and after, the church membership graph must be shifted back in time to reflect population growth. Thus population growth and declines precede post office revenue growth and declines. From these two graphs, we can see that the patterns of economic growth track population growth very closely. Section usδ stands out distinctly on both graphs. What does not appear in the post office data is the effect of the small increase in birth rate usγ. Because of its small size relative to baby boom usG, the economic impact of the birth increase usγ will be mild compared to the previous baby booms. Along with the impact of the internet as a vehicle of written communications, there is good reason why usγ is not reflected in the data on post office revenue. More details on the relationships between U.S. population and other economic statistics are given in Appendix B.

	United States		Canada	
Sector	GDP (billions)	% of Total	GDP (billions)	% of Total
Government	$1721	18 %	$225	21 %
Private (Business)	$1735	18 %	$193	18 %
Consumer	$6739	69 %	$596	55 %
Other	-	5%	+	6%
Total	$9817		$1076	

Table 5.00 Contributions to Gross Domestic Product (Year 2000)

Economists such as Paul Samuelson note that population and labor are non-economic variables that grow in response to social conditions and do not change according to the state of the economy.[1] The last baby boom began in the midst of the depression and lasted more than twenty years. Population growth may be independent of the economy, but the economy is not independent of the population. Figure 5.02 displays the work force as a percent of the population and figure 5.03 displays the percent change per decade. It can be seen that labor has cyclical characteristics too. The growth of labor reaches a peak on the downswing of the long-wave. Compare the percent change per decade in work force with that of Methodist church membership. Both reflect the growth of population except that the growth in church membership and work force lags population growth because of the age requirements of church membership and the age determinants of labor. Our economic models have been mostly business focused. Through historical tradition, economic theory has come to analyze and emphasize less than one-third of the economy in business investment. Figure 5.04, the percent change per decade in work force, clearly reflects the long-wave in Canadian population. Comparing the percent change per decade in work force with figure 5.01 the percent change per decade in post office revenue and figure 4.08 the percent change per decade in population we find similar peaks and valleys.

Innovations

With a growing population comes growing demand, which produces growing markets, allowing the maximal utilization of creative talents in the production of technological innovations to solve logistical hurdles created by the need to provide for the masses. Without a growing market most of our factories of mass production would shut down. There would be no need to innovate since the current processes would be sufficient to provide for current needs. There would be no need to increase efficiency because without growth there would be insufficient return on capital to justify investment in larger and more efficient plants. Technological innovations such as steam power, oil and gas power, steel, electrical generation, railroads, automobiles, the electric light bulb, telephones and computers are only viable when there is sufficient market demand to pay for the research and development and the machines to produce them. Without market demand, these innovations would remain forever an idea in someone's head or scribbles on a sketchpad. Further discussion on innovations as a factor of demographics can be found in chapter 7 and in appendix B.

Consumption and
Shifts in Aggregate and Disaggregate Demand

In the short term, economic variables may fluctuate relatively independently of population growth, but in the long term, the economy has reflected the growth and composition of the population. Population growth determines the rate of consumption, which is the driving force behind the economy. The greater the rate of growth of population, the greater the rate of growth of consumption. The slower the rate of growth of population, the slower the growth in consumption. There are five key determinants of consumption or demand, three of which are closely related to the composition of the population, all of which are in some way related to demographics.

- Price of goods
- Availability of substitutes
- Affluence of consumers - usually certain age groups
- Size of the market - such as the baby boom market
- Taste preferences - sometimes varies with age.[2]

The affluence of consumers varies with age group. One would expect that those who have worked for several years would be more affluent than someone just out of school. Each group would have different needs. Different sectors of the economy would be influenced according to these needs. The size of the market also depends on the population. Certain goods would appeal more to teenagers than to adults. If the majority of the Baby Boomers had just reached their teenage years, then the teenage market would be the largest consumer market. Indeed, marketers have been appealing to the Baby Boomers since they were very young and are still appealing to the Baby Boomers now that they are gaining in age. The final determinant is taste preferences — the young and the old have different tastes and different cultures.

As we trace the lifecycle of the average person from childhood to old age, we discover shifts in spending patterns. Children begin learning about the use of money by buying low-cost perishables, such as ice cream, bubble gum, chocolate and chips. When they reach their teens, they have gained sufficient savings from their allowances or part-time jobs to purchase for themselves their first major durable item such as a stereo or a bicycle. Those that have reached their 20s and 30s begin major lifestyle changes. Many move out from their parents' homes to live on their own. Many get married and have children. Major purchases of large durable items such as a house, car, washer, dryer and furniture are made during this stage of the lifecycle, perhaps by taking on large debts. By the 40s and 50s, these major basic purchases are more or less complete. There is now money for luxuries and a rising demand for services, for the adage, "time is money" now becomes wisely revised to "but money is not time." Those that have reached this stage have more disposable income than at any other time. Planning for retirement, saving to invest in a business of their own, or saving for the future of their children are given more priority. Everyone must prepare for the years ahead. The middle-aged tend to be savers more than the young or the old.[3] They invest their money in hopes of getting a better return. The young have a higher propensity for consumption and the middle aged have a higher propensity for saving. The propensity to consume or to save are variables that are more dependant on the age of the population than on economic changes, unless these changes are extreme, such as hyperinflation or depression. The increased propensity to save is deflationary. Since this money is not spent, it seeks higher yields, quite often ending up in the stock and bond market, creating a boom in those markets.

The economic long-wave is a direct reflection of the lifecycle of the large section of the population called Gen-B. As Gen-B is born, comes of age, enters the work force, prepares for retirement, and then retires, the entire economic system of society reflects the changing needs of this generation. First there is commodity inflation caused by the demand for basic material goods such as food. The economic boom broadens to include durable goods such as cars, houses, furniture and appliances as Gen-B enters the work force. This boom is induced in part by the cost of independence and by the establishment of new families. Once Gen-B has attained a lifestyle suitable to income, a greater amount of money is available to be spent on luxuries, services or just saved. As Gen-B shifts from spending to saving, the economy shifts to the production of a greater quantity of luxury goods. These periods include the Roaring 20's or the period that produced the Yuppies of the 80's and the stock market bubble of the hopeful 90's. Suddenly, people find that they need a fourth car instead of being happy with the usual three. Or that breakfast just cannot do without an egg scrambler that scrambles eggs inside the shells, despite the mixer, beater, blender, food processor and fork sitting on the counter top. The propensity to consume drops with age, but corporate expansion continues, unsuspecting of changing circumstances. Spending money is fun after all, when there is money to spend. Surveys heralded shopping as North America's favorite pastime in the 1980's.

Retail Outlets

By the downswing of the long-wave, the baby boom youths have become adults. No longer dependent on their parents, they are now adult consumers themselves. Retailers have responded to the increasing number of customers of increasing wealth and disposable income in different ways. The period between the 1820's and the 1850's is known as a period of the country store or general store.[4] Population growth had allowed the establishment of fixed location stores in many rural areas that were once served only by wandering peddlers.

After the 1860's, on the downswing of the second long-wave, many stores re-organized their merchandise into departments.[5] The department store carried a large variety of goods under one roof so that customers did not have to visit several stores to make their purchases. Unlike the general stores where people went simply to buy things, department stores were built to imitate the opulence of palaces that gave middle-class shoppers the experience of being pampered and served. The purchasing power of department stores and the large turnover of merchandise gave the department stores many competitive advantages over general stores. There was considerable opposition to what many viewed as unfair competition. Many department stores were firebombed, but nevertheless, the department store became a permanent feature of the retail business by the 1870's. Some of the many department stores founded during this era were Bloomingdale's in 1872, May Department Stores in 1877, K-Mart in 1897, J.C. Penney in 1902 and Marshall Field in 1865.

In Canada, Timothy Eaton founded the T. Eaton Company on Yonge Street in Toronto in 1869. Robert Simpson founded R. Simpson, Dry Goods across the street from T. Eaton in 1872. Jas A. Ogilvy was founded in Montreal in 1866. Dupuis Frères was founded in 1868. Woodward Stores was founded in Vancouver in 1892. The term "department store" became a common part of the vocabulary by the 1880's.

Mail-order was founded on the downswing of the second long-wave and became a service offered by many department stores. Among the first to start a mail-order business was a thirteen year old boy named Charley Thompson who made a fortune selling stationery with which he enclosed a free piece of jewelry. He ran his first advertisement in the New York Tribune with borrowed money in 1866. Montgomery Ward started as a mail-order business in 1872 and became the largest of the time. As with the department store, mail-order encountered fierce opposition from opponents. Public burning of catalogues took place in many cities.

John Wanamaker changed the post-office and the nation when he petitioned that the post-office should provide the services of rural free delivery (R.F.D.) and parcel post. He was the first to send a package by parcel post on January 1, 1913. His mail-order business, of course, benefited tremendously. The golden age of mail-order was over by the 1920's and Montgomery Ward had to establish retail outlets in order to survive. Sears, Roebuck, founded as a mail-order business in 1886 and Montgomery Ward's main competitor, entered the retail business first. Montgomery Ward followed two years later. Both began establishing department store chains.[6]

General Robert E. Wood was the vice-president of merchandising at Montgomery Ward in 1919. Demographics and the *Statistical Abstract of the United States* were his favorite hobbies. He saw in the statistics a movement of people from the rural areas to the urban areas and believed that by establishing retail outlets Montgomery Ward would be able to serve the changing demographics better. Unable to convince the board of directors at Montgomery Ward, Wood joined Sears, Roebuck in 1924. He began to establish chain stores for Sears and Sears surpassed Montgomery Ward in growth and sales for the first time.

As a side note, in 1931 Sewell Lee Avery became the chairman of Montgomery Ward. Under his management Ward had almost a billion dollars in annual sales by the end of WWII. But instead of expanding like Sears and other retail operations, Avery let Montgomery Ward disintegrate. He even refused to paint the stores. On his office wall was a chart that he would point to showing how the U.S. economy had fallen into a depression after each war since 1812. If Robert Wood and Sewell Avery could have sat in the same room and discussed their ideas, they may have discovered that they were each looking at the same elephant, and maybe, could have linked the long-wave to demographics at that time.

The 1920's, the downswing of the third long-wave, brought the rise of the chain store and Montgomery Ward and Sears, Roebuck entered the chain store business when almost everyone else was moving in the same direction. Retailers discovered the advantages of opening multiple stores under the same name across the country. In 1919 chain store sales made up approximately four percent of retail sales in America. By 1929, it had become thirty percent of total retail sales. The sales of A & P, one of the earliest and most successful chain stores, increased from $195 million in 1919 to over $1 billion by 1929. F. W. Woolworth had 1,081 stores in 1919 with sales of $120 million. By 1929 it had 1,825 stores with sales of $303 million. Walgreen had 23 stores in 1920 with sales of $2.2 million. By 1929 it had 397 stores with sales of $46.6 million. J.C. Penney had 197 stores in 1919 with sales of $29 million. By 1929 it had 1,395 stores with $210 million in sales. The dominance of chain stores in the 1920's prompted a Senate investigation on whether or not chains were monopolies. The brand name recognition and advertising efficiency gave the chain store many advantages over the single store. Chain stores had more purchasing power over smaller single stores and many operated warehouses of their own. Chains had such large purchasing power and warehousing ability that manufacturers were willing to sell directly to them without going through a wholesaler. In 1933, as a reflection of growing public resentment against the power of chain stores, there were 225 anti-chain store bills in the state legislatures.

In Canada, Canadian Tire was founded in downtown Toronto in 1922. By 1944 there were 116 stores. T.P. Loblaw founded Dominion Store in 1910. It became a chain in 1919 with 16 stores. By 1930 it had 550 stores. T. Eaton Company had become a chain of 65 stores across the country by 1930. The Government of Canada investigated to see whether chains were monopolies but found no cause for concern. The claim to being the oldest chain store in North America belongs to the Hudson's Bay Company founded in 1670. It had trading posts throughout Northern and Western Canada. The first shopping malls were founded in the 1920's and took on tremendous growth after WWII along with the automobile, the bungalow and the flight to the suburbs.

The business expansion of the 1980's and 1990's, on the downswing of the fourth long-wave, will be remembered for the rise of franchises such as MacDonald's, Tim Horton's and Wendy's and warehouse or big-box stores such as Home Depot, Staples' Business Depot and Rona with 100,000 square feet or more of retail space. The franchise has all the advantages of purchasing power, uniformity and brand recognition of a chain, but instead of being managed by a central office, it has the advantage of being managed by a licensed owner. The big-box store came about when warehouses began selling directly to the public. The concept took root when retailers created warehouses just for the purpose of selling to the public. The cost of stocking merchandise in two different areas, in the customer area and in the back warehouse, is eliminated, and the cost for fancy displays and décor are kept to a minimum. The "dollar stores" that began to proliferate in the 1990's are a sign of how retail prices have fallen since the 1970's.

While department stores such as Eaton's were closing their catalogue order departments by the top of the fourth long-wave, just as Montgomery Ward was having difficulties with their mail order at the top of the third long-wave, television home-shopping channels were becoming successful in the 1990's. The Internet arrived just in time for home-shopping. The last time that home shopping was this popular was in the 1940's and 1950's when houses were built with intake boxes for milk delivery.

Mansions, Wealth and Good Feelings

Upswings of the long-waves coincide with idealistic eras. The idealism of the Enlightenment occurred on the upswing of the first long-wave along with the ideals of disinterested benevolence. The rise of perfectionism at usδ carried onto the upswing of the second long-wave. There was the Progressive Era and the ideals of the Social Gospel on the upswing of the third long-wave. On the upswing of the fourth long-wave there was Kennedy's and Johnson's Great Society and the ideals of liberalism. But by the downswing of the long-wave, attention became focused on wealth. Utilizing the vast amounts of wealth accumulated by Baby Boomers, purchases of large furniture, large cars, large homes and mansions continue the long-wave cycle.

The downswing of the first long-wave is known as the Era of Good Feelings associated with the founding of the Second Bank of the United States and the land speculation that followed. One of the examples of the wealth of the era are the high-style houses, such as the townhouses of La Grange Terrace, parts of which still stand on Lafayette Street in New York City.

The downswing of the second long-wave is known as the Gilded Age. The period is remembered for business tycoons and laissez-faire economics. Rich American industrialists married poor English aristocrats for the privilege of being called Lords and Ladies. Andrew Carnegie cornered the steel market and retired in 1901 at the age of 66. John D. Rockefeller cornered the oil market and retired in 1897 at the age of 58. J. Pierpont Morgan, the leading banker of the day who financed the Federal Reserve during the depression of the 1890's was 63 years of age in 1900. Financier Jay Gould was 56 years old when he died in 1892.

Cornelius Vanderbilt was 68 when he began building his railroad empire in 1862. Horatio Alger's "rags to riches" novels became extremely popular. The housing boom of this era created many great mansions still standing today, a large number of which are found in Newport, Rhode Island.

The downswing of the third long-wave is known as the Roaring 20's. A building boom was just beginning when the Great Depression hit. But as soon as peace and prosperity returned after WWII, the housing boom resumed. Figure 5.05 shows that home ownership rates increased by over twenty-five percent from 1940 to 1950.[7] Hundreds of large mansions were built on Long Island's Gold Coast in the 1920's and 1930's, ranging from dozens of rooms to over a hundred and on several hundred acres of land. This was the location of F. Scott Fitzgerald's *The Great Gatsby*. Many of these mansions were owned by the grandchildren of the Gilded Age tycoons. The 1950's is most remembered for the creation of large neighborhoods of suburban bungalows.

With each downswing of the long-wave a new generation of Baby Boomers comes of age, ready to put their newfound wealth to use. The downswing of the fourth long-wave with the stock market boom and housing boom is a reflection of similar wealth accumulation at work. The 1990's was an era of hopes and dreams of workers that their mutual funds and pension plans would provide them with a comfortable retirement. Mansion-size houses of 5,000 to 10,000 square feet became a common part of the landscape. Twenty to fifty thousand square feet homes continue to attract wide media attention. Home ownership rates increased by close to eight percent from 1990 to 2005, the largest increase since the 1940's.

Wealth and Income Disparities

The Gilded Age and the Roaring Twenties are two periods in American history that have been noted by various writers at various times for the great divide between the rich and the poor. We can add to those two periods our current period from the 1980's to the present time. With each downswing of the long-wave there are growing wealth and income disparities. The rich get richer, the poor get poorer. A number of factors may contribute to this condition. One is age. With an ageing population on the downswing of the long-wave, those that are older have accumulated a greater amount of wealth compared to the young. Another contributing factor is the tremendous rise in equity values. Those that are poor can never have sufficient money to risk investing in stocks, nor can they afford a house, so they cannot and do not participate in the area of equity inflation on the downswing of the long-wave. The downswing of the long-wave also has the lowest wage increases. Those most affected are never the top management of companies, but those workers at the very bottom. In the 1930's a downturn in equity prices and a serious depression wiped out some of these disparities. Since a large proportion of the wealthy are older, the redistribution of wealth to multiple heirs contribute to the closing of these disparities also. Taxation helped to reduce these inequalities from the 1930's to the 1960's, but in the 1980's taxes were substantially reduced for the wealthy. That a CEO of a publicly traded company can get paid hundreds of millions of dollars more than the company itself earns speaks volumes about the attitudes of this era.[8]

Inflation, Stagflation, Deflation, Supply-side/Demand-side Economics

Throughout the upswing of the fourth long-wave, in the 1960's and 1970's, the persistence of inflation puzzled many economists. There were food shortages, gas shortages, shortages in just about everything. In attempts to contain inflation, price controls were put into place. With price controls, high interest rates and heavy regulatory controls, businesses found it unprofitable to expand. People were asked to consume less. However it wasn't that a family of two was consuming like a family of five, it was because a family of two became a family of five. Demographics was a misplaced element in economics. The population boom was completely overlooked. The resulting economic situation was termed "stagflation," a period of rising prices and stagnant economic expansion. There was no planning to increase productive capacity in anticipation of the increased demand by a growing population. It was obvious to everyone that there was not enough supply to meet increasing demand, but no one seemed to understand why this was happening. It almost seemed, and indeed many believed, that we had exhausted the earth's natural resources. The demand and supply curve had been slowly shifting since the 1940's and few even noticed.

By the 1980's there was enough disenchantment with Keynesian economics among economists and politicians that the neo-classical supply-side economics came into favor. Taxes on businesses were greatly reduced, interest rates fell and regulatory statutes were disregarded. From the 1980's onward there has been a noted inability for retailers to raise prices. Whether it is for imported goods, cars, groceries, fast food or beer, price pressures tend to be more downwards than up. The upward price pressures no longer aggregate across all goods and services, but disaggregate through selective areas such as oil and housing. The manufacturing capacity has expanded sufficiently on the primary downswing of the long-wave to mitigate the impact of inflationary pressures.

Deflation itself is not all bad. As long as employment and GNP remains stable, the population as a whole experiences a higher standard of living. It becomes a problem when revenue falls faster than costs and debt repayments. Figures 5.06 and 5.07, the percent change per decade in Wholesale Price Index, show the periods of inflation and deflation throughout the history of the long-wave. The year 1999 became the first decennial deflationary year in the U.S since 1940. Price increases have reached the lowest rate in six decades. Along with changing inflation come changes in interest rates. Figures 5.08 and 5.09, interest rates on 10 year bonds, show the rise and decline of interest rates following the phases of the long-wave. Interest rates have fallen to the lowest level in four decades. Low interest rates are beneficial to the housing market, but adversely affect retirement pensions in making benefits payments. Figures 5.10 and 5.11 show wages moving in conjunction with the long-wave. When there is inflation, wages move up. When there is deflation, wages decline. Wage increases have fallen to the lowest level in about six decades in Canada.

A stock and bond market boom follows as Gen-B becomes preoccupied with getting higher yields for their money. Stock values no longer reflect corporate earnings, but the purchasing power of individual savings. By the time Gen-B reaches retirement, another Gen-B is being born to produce the next long-wave cycle. First comes commodity inflation, then comes a boom in durable goods such as housing, then comes growth in the services sector along with a savings and investment boom. Each disaggregate component of the economy receives its turn in consumption demand. These disaggregates, taken together as an aggregate, fluctuate to produce the long-wave cycle. Each economic long-wave of our study has followed a similar sequence of events. With each downswing of the long-wave, a new generation comes of age that wants to enjoy their newfound wealth. As Gen-B is born, comes of age and then grows old, the consumption pattern causes shifts in disaggregate demand, ultimately producing shifts in aggregate demand, generating a complete economic long-wave cycle.[9] With the presence of a large proportion of the population at a similar age group, ageing together through time, economic history is made. The final shift occurs when retirement becomes a reality. The stock market declines as savings are divested for payment to retirees and pensioners. Accompanying the stock market decline is a prolonged economic contraction.

Farm Cooperatives

Inflation has been beneficial to farm prices. The inflated prices do not return to deflated levels for many years, but historically they have been doing so. The primary decline of the long-wave has been particularly pronounced in agricultural prices. Among the first casualties of the long-wave downswing are the farmers. Each downswing has brought farmers to organize to seek government aid. Cooperatives form and farmers unite against other interests.

The first organizational effort on the downswing of the second long-wave in the U.S. was the Grange Movement in the late 1870's. Originally founded by Oliver H. Kelley as The National Grange of the Patrons of Husbandry to give farmers social and cultural stimulation, the Grange became the organization through which farmers gathered to find solutions for their economic malaise. They lobbied politicians, formed cooperative stores, plants and grain elevators, and fought with the railroads for lower rates. In the late 1880's when the economy turned down once more, the Populist movement arose. Two large groups were organized for political agitation, the National Farmers Alliance and the Cooperative Union. When political parties would not listen to their demands, they formed the People's Party, also known as the Populist Party. By the upswing of the next long-wave, as conditions improved, many cooperatives shut down, the political protests subsided, and farmers went back to farming.

The next mass organizational effort of farmers occurred on the long-wave decline of the 1920's. Irate farmers formed groups such as the Farmers Union and the American Federation of Farm Bureaus to seek government aid. Cooperatives flourished and political agitation mounted. With the "New Deal", an agricultural stabilization program was put into place and the agitation came to an end. Farmers did not organize again until the 1980's in the face of declining farm prices. The vast number of family farms going into bankruptcy on the downswing of the fourth long-wave led many to believe that an end of a long tradition had come. Farmers organize into cooperatives during hard times, but when prosperity returns, many of these cooperatives dissolve.

The Acceleration Principle

To understand how Gen-B affects the economy, we will begin by looking at two economic principles. The first is called the Acceleration Principle. This states that in order for the economy to remain prosperous, the rate of production, and therefore consumption, must grow at an equivalent or a greater rate every year. Should the rate of increase in production just level off, then the prosperous period will come to an end.[10] Let us now look at a very simple example of how the acceleration principle works in a jeans factory. Ritzy Genes Inc. produces 100 percent pure cotton gem-washed jeans with spring water. Ritzy Genes has done such a great marketing job that almost everyone between the ages of 5 and 14 wants a pair. And almost all parents who are environmentally minded and who want their children to have the natural best have come to the conclusion that these jeans are great value for their money. Ritzy has dipped into a bonanza. The sales of 100 percent pure cotton gem-washed jeans soar. For the previous 5 years, sales for Ritzy were flat. Ritzy had capital equipment consisting of 20 machines of different ages, with 1 machine having to be replaced every year because of wear. Now, sales have doubled. In order to keep up with demand, Ritzy Genes has had to double the number of machines in the factory. So instead of replacing just 1 machine, Ritzy had to purchase an additional 20 machines. When sales increased 100 percent, Ritzy's annual investment increased from 1 machine to 21 machines, an increase of 2000 percent. This acceleration of investment is passed on to Ritzy's supplier of machines and on throughout the economy. In order for Ritzy's supplier to maintain their sales, the demand for Ritzy's jeans must continue to grow at a pace so that Ritzy will purchase 21 machines every year. Should Ritzy's sales level off at a new level, then Ritzy will no longer have to purchase 21 machines annually to keep up with demand. Ritzy will discontinue its high level of investment and Ritzy's supplier will have a very real drop in sales. This in turn passes through the economy. Each long-wave downturn has resulted in recessions of varying severity. When capital equipment is purchased to meet demand, the curtailment of this demand results in a capital surplus. The acceleration principle cannot take effect again until this surplus is used up. Thus for a long time, the economy experiences very slow growth. The result of fluctuations in population growth is the need to build productive capacity to meet growing demand, which brings in the prosperity of the long-wave upswing. Then as the population ages, demand diminishes, creating a situation of overcapacity and the long-wave decline.

The Multiplier Effect

The second principle that we will look at is the Multiplier. This is the determination of the effect spending has on the economy.[11] Assume that the population, on average, spends 80 percent of its income and manages to save the other 20 percent. If a person spends $10,000 to hire unemployed workers to finish the basement of a home, the workers receiving this money will spend 80 percent of it, that is $8,000. Those that receive this $8,000 from the workers will also spend 80 percent, that is $6,400. As this chain of events continue, the total increase in spending within the economy is given by the formula:

$$\frac{1 \times \$10,000}{1 - MPC}$$

Equation 5.00 - The Multiplier Effect

where MPC is the ratio of the marginal propensity to consume. With a marginal propensity to consume at 80 percent of income, while 20 percent is being saved, then from the above formula, the total increase in spending on the economy would be $50,000. But as Gen-B ages and begins increasing the rate of savings, say from 20 percent of income to 30 percent of income, then the marginal propensity to consume falls to 70 percent. From the above formula, the total increase in spending $10,000 is $33,333. The net effect is a drop of $16,777 or 33 percent. Thus as Gen-B ages, the net effect of spending on the economy decreases. One hundred million dollars in government spending on the upswing of the long-wave does more for the economy than on the downswing.

Figures 5.12 and 5.13 display U.S. and Canadian government expenditures on a logarithmic scale. It can be observed that government outlays fluctuate with the long-wave and that the outlays are much greater on the upswing of the long-wave than on the downswing, except for the current long-wave. For the first time since the founding of the two nations government expenditures have continued to grow even on the downswing of the long-wave. The acceleration principle, the multiplier principle, a youthful Gen-B, an accelerating rate of growth of population combined with high government expenditures produces the prosperity of the upswing of the long-wave. These same economic principles along with an ageing Gen-B, a declining rate of growth of population and a decline in government spending all combine to keep the economy in a gloomy condition on the downswing of the long-wave. These factors are further aggravated by an increase in debt that is barely sustainable with present incomes. These debts are taken with the belief that the economic prosperity will continue on forever.

In agricultural societies, the long-wave of economic swings may not be as extreme as in industrial societies since agricultural societies neither experience the great prosperity that accompanies industrial production nor do they have a large concentration of labor whose employment is dependent upon that growing prosperity. As for unemployment, there is always work on the farm. If the production cannot be sold, at least one can produce to feed the family. Subsistence farming has been a normal part of rural life since the beginning of farming. In industrial societies, once there was unemployment, there was no real means of support until the 1930's when social security was put into place by the government.

Regulation/Deregulation, Savings and Investment Booms, Mergers and Acquisitions, Debt, Depressions

From its earliest times the corporation has been the favored way of doing business in America. In England, early corporations were charters granted by royalty, and later by Parliament, to individuals or groups, bestowing upon them special rights and privileges not given to anyone else. Incorporated entities helped organize groups to build colleges, limited the liability of towns and cities, encouraged foreign trade and other ventures. Because the investors' liability was limited to the amount that they invest, the owners were more willing to make investments that partnerships might not consider. These charters were granted on the provision that they advanced the public interest. In the colonies, the state legislatures claimed the power of parliament in granting special charters. After the Revolution, charters were granted liberally in hopes of stimulating economic growth and by the 1830's corporations were very common. The corporation dominated banking, insurance, mining, transportation and most industrial and commercial enterprises. The large business corporation, with its ability to command enormous capital and human resources in an instant has been the center of much economic and political interest. These interests have varied with the long-wave along with the perception of corporate power. During times of industrial growth, on the rise of the long-wave, regulatory laws are passed and corporations are prosecuted for monopolistic practices. As the long-wave declines, industry deregulation begins and the government no longer concerns itself with regulatory laws. Accompanying each era of deregulation are vigorous activities in corporate acquisitions and mergers attending a spectacular economic boom. Figure 5.14 shows some of these activities on the different phases of the long-wave. As Gen-B makes its way through the system, the economy begins to experience many years of economic decline. Figure 5.15 charts three discontinuous estimates of the number of mergers and acquisitions. Each merger wave peaks on the declining side of the long-wave, where it is also the most spectacular.

WAVE I

The period of prolonged economic contraction in the U.S. on the downswing of the first long-wave had its beginnings around 1833. There the economy was fuelled by high cotton prices due to heavy overseas demand. With the growing prosperity, cotton producers took out large advances on prospects of future sales. Accompanying the prosperity was massive speculation on land. Land that once sold for $1.25 an acre increased by over twenty times in value. English firms came from overseas to invest in the expansion of roads and canals undertaken by numerous states.

Within a few years the speculative activities came to the attention of the Federal government. The United States Treasury ordered its land agents to accept gold specie only for payment in order to restrict the supply of money available for transactions. At the same time the English, who were having financial difficulties back home, ended their investment and attempted to collect their debts. Cotton prices had nearly halved by 1837. Further aggravating a worsening situation, the Federal government decided to release its surplus of Federal Funds to various states at a time when the banks that held these deposits were critically overdrawn. The result was that the banks virtually stopped lending. The panic of 1837 ensued.

As the economy teetered, the Bank of Pennsylvania, formerly the Second Bank of the United States, failed in 1839 and hundreds more banks followed, resulting in the depression of 1840 to 1846. Hundreds of thousands of people became unemployed. Between the years 1841 and 1843, when there was a law enabling the declaration of personal bankruptcy upon the surrender of all property and belongings, 34,000 people applied. Bank loans shrank from $525,000,000 in 1837 to $255,000,000 by 1843 and sale of government land fell from $24,867,000 to under $2 million.[12]

During the panic of 1837 and the depression that followed, corporations came under attack for unfair and sometimes scandalous business practices. Creditors and stockholders who suffered losses wanted the limited liability provisions removed. Those that opposed corporations contended that it was unfair that businesses such as sole proprietorships or partnerships should compete with large capital-based enterprises of limited liability. Under the charter laws of the time, each corporation was granted special privileges, some more than others. Depending on how well they lobbied, with two corporations competing in the same business, one might be severely disadvantaged. Accusations arose that the corporation was a monopoly.

When American industry was still in its infancy, monopolies were not a concern. In colonial times, producers were often given exclusive rights to the manufacture of products or in the use of processes in order to encourage the development of industry. Land, subsidies, interest-free loans and even money were given to those willing to undertake ventures in establishing industries where none existed. The benefits to the colony would have been tremendous if such ventures became viable, for the colony would become independent of foreign sources. In the post-colonial period there may have been local monopolies, but the many rural and dispersed settlements, limited transportation and small markets of the early days vastly limited their influence. Nor were the means for large-scale production available. But in the 1800's, improved transportation had allowed a producer to sell goods from one end of the country to the other profitably. The large amounts of capital necessary for the machinery of large-scale production that came with the advent of the Industrial Revolution also made establishing a competitive business more difficult. The rise of the corporation, with its power to influence markets, was a developing concern.

WAVE II

The complaints against corporations on the upswing of the second long-wave brought reform to state constitutions in their method of chartering. Beginning with the state of Maryland in 1837, a general charter was passed by which all corporations were to be regulated. To prevent legislatures from chartering corporations with special privileges, amendments were put into state constitutions prohibiting the granting of special charters. Of the thirty-seven states in existence, twenty-four had passed similar measures by 1875.[13]

Since each state independently issued its own charter, groups wanting to incorporate would do so in the state where charter laws were to their advantage, and since states did not regulate corporations from other states in interstate commerce, the general charter did not effectively protect public interest. As the downswing of the long-wave proceeded, states began competing against each other in luring businesses and incorporation laws were relaxed. By the 1880's competition among states had become so severe that it became known as an era of "charter mongering."[14] The result of relaxing regulatory laws was a wave of mergers and consolidations. Henry Seager says of this period:

> The trust movement began in the United States with the organization of the first Standard Oil Trust in 1879 and ended as a movement in 1903. There were two distinct phases: 1879 to 1896 was the period of the trust proper; 1897 to 1903, that of the holding company and giant consolidation.[15]

One thousand eight hundred firms disappeared as a result of consolidations. Out of 93 consolidations surveyed, 42 controlled at least 72 percent of their respective industries.[16]

The bankers who provided financing and underwriting of loans and shares benefited tremendously from the consolidation of industry. J.P. Morgan and Company, First National Bank and National City Bank held 341 directorships in 112 corporations valued at $22,245,000,000.[17]

Of the many monopolies that arose in that period, one of the most notable was Standard Oil Trust. With its beginnings in 1865, Standard Oil, in collaboration with the railroads (on which oil producers depended almost solely at that time for transportation) managed to buy a number of small refineries. Through its acquisitions in early 1872, Standard Oil's refining capacity jumped from 1500 barrels a day to 10,000 barrels a day, about one fifth of the nations refining capacity.[18] By means of price fixing practices and buying out or underselling local competitors, Standard Oil became one of the largest oil producers in the nation. It consolidated operations by placing all forty of its companies under nine trustees who appointed directors and dictated the policies of what became Standard Oil Trust in 1879. By 1882 it controlled almost 90 percent of all oil refineries, pipelines and transportation facilities for oil. It continued its practice of lowering prices to the point of taking losses until local firms were eliminated, then proceeding to raise prices as much as the market would bear. Standard Oil even received rebates from the railroads when their competitors transported oil.

In one incidence, the Pennsylvania Railroad and the Empire Transportation Company attempted to challenge the supremacy of Standard Oil and its alliance of railroads. Empire proceeded to acquire refineries of its own in order to produce and sell processed oil. A rate war between the railroads ensued and at one point Pennsylvania was transporting Empire oil at a lost while Empire was giving away refined oil in markets controlled by Standard. By the autumn, Standard took control of Empire for $3 million.

Standard Oil Trust was eventually prosecuted under the Sherman Anti-Trust Act and was ordered dissolved by the courts. But it did not do so until seven years after the court order. Control of the companies was then passed to Standard Oil Company of New Jersey, a holding company. The holding company enabled minority shareholders to control several levels of corporations with minimal investment. Under this arrangement, the shareholders of Standard elected its own board of directors which in turn elected the directors of the operating companies controlled by Standard. It was ensured that there would be no competition amongst themselves.

Standard Oil was a national monopoly. Others developed into regional monopolies because of the restrictive nature of their business. The railroads were of this nature, their markets being limited by the number of tracks laid.

In the 1870's the railroads dominated the nation's transportation system, taking business away from barges, canals, turnpikes and steamboats because of their increased efficiency and capacity. Early railroad companies began small and built their rails locally. Mergers of companies meant better and extended services with more interconnecting routes. The public widely welcomed these moves. However as the downswing of the long-wave progressed, the mergers began to gain monopolistic overtones. Where an area was once served by two or more lines competing for business, the lines were now owned by a single interest that could raise prices as it pleased.

In areas where competition existed, rate wars were fiercely waged. Companies that could not withstand the competition sold out, went bankrupt or were forced to join pools and fix prices. Large shippers were often given lower than published rates or rebates to help them drive smaller companies out of business.

When some states attempted to regulate prices, the courts ruled that it was out of their jurisdiction to influence interstate commerce, whether directly or indirectly, by regulating intrastate pricing. Interstate commerce belonged to the Federal government. By the 1880's, it was difficult to find a railroad company that was not a member of a pool.[19]

With the concern about monopolies, the Interstate Commerce Act of 1887 was passed to regulate the rates the railroads were to charge, and which sought to end rebates and pooling and disallowed varying charges for different commodities; but the railroads soon found loopholes in the law and as a result the Act was not very effective. The Sherman Anti-trust Act of 1890 further strengthened the provisions of the Interstate Commerce Act to bring an end to pools. When pressure was brought to bear on the railroads, interlocking directorships developed and cross ownership of stocks emerged as a way of escaping competition.

Along with the wave of mergers came market speculation and two depressions, a set of activities that were not unlike those of the first long-wave downswing. Of the speculators, Jay Gould and James Fisk managed to gain lasting notoriety for their exploits that scandalized the Grant administration. In 1869 their attempts to corner the gold market resulted in the collapse of gold prices, on Black Friday, September 24, destroying many businesses in New York.

A more serious economic consequence came with Jay Cook and Company. A respected financier, Jay Cook bought the bankrupt Northern Pacific Railroad with dreams of building a railroad empire. When it failed in September 1872 it brought down with it 57 other firms. Stock prices tumbled and the exchange had to be closed for ten days. In the ensuing depression that lasted from 1873 to 1879, Europeans withdrew their investments from the U.S., over 10,000 businesses failed and millions were without jobs.

After a recovery in the 1880's, the stock market took its largest one-day drop in nine years in May of 1893. The National Cordage Company went into receivership followed by three brokerage houses. By June of 1894, 192 railroads were in receivership involving one quarter of the nation's tracks. Over 700 banks closed and 15,000 businesses went under. The result was the depression of 1893 to 1898.

The word depression has changed in meaning over many years. It once had the same meaning that the word recession has today. But after the Great Depression of the 1930's, depression came to have severe connotations, and a much softer word had to be found. Thus when historians use the word depression to refer to a historical period, it may not be indicative of or comparable to other periods without first examining the statistics.

WAVE III

It was not until the upswing of the third long-wave that the public was once again alerted to the problems of monopolies. Under the administration of President Theodore Roosevelt, the prosecution of monopolies began. Legislation was passed to strengthen the provisions of the Interstate Commerce Act and to give it power over parcel post, telephone and telegraph, and oil and gas pipelines. The Northern Securities Company, which controlled several large railroads, was ordered dissolved. Under the Taft administration, the Standard Oil Company of New Jersey was ordered dissolved and the American Tobacco Company, the United States Ship Building Company, United States Steel Corporation, International Harvester Company and many others were prosecuted for monopolistic practices. When Woodrow Wilson was elected president, he wanted the total elimination of trusts and to prevent them from ever forming. It was Wilson's belief that if large corporations were prevented from unfair practices, small businesses would be able to establish themselves competitively and add further growth to the economy. Under his administration the Clayton Act was passed, forbidding interlocking directorships and the cross-ownership of stocks of competing companies. The use of holding companies and other methods that may lessen competition or give rise to monopolies was forbidden and the Federal Trade Commission was created to prosecute violators. But the efforts to keep industry regulated were nullified by the downswing of the long-wave when the antitrust laws were relaxed and the nation pursued a philosophy of less government and more business. We read from Robert Russel:

> During the Golden Twenties, with the country generally prosperous, the general public was apathetic about trusts. The administrations in Washington were friendly to big business and indisposed to anything which might disturb it... Holding companies were formed by the hundreds most notably, but by no means only, in electric light-and-power and banking fields, and interlocking directorates were not interfered with. Practically all the holding companies were in violation of the Sherman Anti-

trust Act as it had been interpreted by the courts before World War I and in violation of the clear intent of the Clayton Act.[20]

The threat of monopolies was no longer a public concern by the 1920's. As expressed by President Calvin Coolidge, "the business of America is business." Mergers and consolidations took place across the country. At its height, over 1,200 mining and manufacturing firms were swallowed up in one year. Between 1919 and 1930 the net number of firms disappearing due to merger activity totaled 8,003.[21]

It became difficult to get the courts to rule against corporations for monopolistic practices. Size or monopolistic capabilities, the courts decided, were not a violation of the Sherman Anti-trust Act. In 1921 the Supreme Court held that competitors sharing pricing information were in violation of the Sherman Antitrust Act. But by 1925 it had reversed its decision. The Secretary of State Herbert Hoover encouraged trade associations to develop, the main functions of which involved consumer education, the sharing of pricing information and union busting. Commercial banks, which were not allowed to engage in investment banking, to use deposits as risk capital, by now had organized subsidiaries for that purpose. The petroleum industry, in light of the perceived energy shortage, had convincing arguments that pooling would end wasteful practices and help conserve energy.

At the same time, there was a great investment boom, first in the housing market, then in the stock market. During the summer of 1928, Westinghouse rose from $151 to $286, General Electric rose from $268 to $391 and AT&T rose from $209 to $303. With just ten percent down, anyone could own the stock of a great company. The value of loans made by banks for stock purchases increased from $3.5 billion in 1927 to $8 billion in 1929. The banks were not the only ones lending money for the purchase of stocks; major corporate loans for such purposes almost equaled that of banks just prior to the market collapse.

With the great investment boom came the development of the investment trust. The purpose of the trust was to invest in stocks of other companies. The person who could not afford to pay for a high price stock could purchase shares in an investment trust that owns the stock.

The added advantage is that the investor's money is well diversified to keep it safe from the sharp fluctuations of the market. The trusts could hold shares in several hundred to several thousand companies; they did not limit themselves to investing in stocks. Some were set up just for the purpose of investing in other investment trusts. With less than 40 trusts before 1921, the number grew to approximately 300 by 1928. In 1928 another 186 were formed and in 1929 a further 265 were added to the list.[22] The trust that invested in other trusts utilized leverage, by borrowing against its equity, for the greatest possible gain. With its ability to leverage, the American Founders Group, which began with a $500 investment in 1921, became a group valued at over $1 billion by 1929.[23] Since the propensity to consume was leveling off by this time, the investment by savers was not used to purchase capital equipment, but to bid up the price of stocks to valuations unprecedented by earnings or by the state of the economy.

Consumer loans reached record levels as thousands of people bought large homes, cars and appliances, even though they were barely able to make payments with their income. With the growing prosperity, the taking on of debt was hardly given a second thought.

When the stock market crashed on October 29, 1929, marking the beginning of the Great Depression which lasted until 1939, few could believe that a depression was beginning. During the market decline from October 23, 1929 to the end of the month, heavy liquidation reduced brokers' loans by $1 billion. When President Hoover met with the nation's leading businessmen, union leaders and farmers, they impressed upon him their views that prosperity would continue like never before. Celebrated Yale economist Irving Fisher is often quoted as saying that he believed that stock prices had reached a "permanently high plateau" just before the market crashed. Afterwards he was celebrated no longer.

By 1933 industrial production was about half that of 1929. Figure 5.16 shows the unemployment rate for the past 100 years. Over 13 million people were out of work in 1933, comprising approximately 25 percent of the work force, a figure that did not include the millions who held part-time jobs and were barely making a living. Over a quarter of the nation's banks failed and the decline in public confidence jeopardized even the healthy banks as large sums of cash were being withdrawn by people forming seemingly endless lines. Farmers were hit even harder when agricultural prices fell a further 30 percent, and the wholesale abandonment of farms in the Midwest and Southwest led to dust storms that literally turned them into deserts. Typical of most investment trusts, the stock of the United Founders, which belonged to the American Founders Group, dropped from a high of $75 in 1929 to 75 cents by 1935.

The downswing of the long-wave is sometimes known for growth in average real wages, which could be interpreted to mean that with growing wealth disparity there is a growing divide between the rich and the poor. This may be advantageous to the wealthy and to those who have jobs, but with the severe economic decline that is endemic to the decline of the long-wave, it is of little consequence to the masses that become unemployed.

WAVE IV

Under the "New Deal" promised by President Franklin Roosevelt with his election in 1933, the Social Securities Act made unemployment insurance, disability insurance and retirement pensions available to the poor. Farmers benefited from the Agricultural Adjustments Act which helped to stabilize farm income so that farmers would not be vulnerable to market prices. To revitalize the economy, several make-work and work improvement acts were passed to create public works projects. Under the Wagner Act, the National Labor Relations Board was established. Labor was given the right to organize and bargain collectively and it became illegal for employers to interfere with union activities. For the first time, people would be able to look to the government for help in times of need. And bank deposits were federally insured so that the catastrophic effects of massive withdrawals could be avoided and depositors could be protected.

A new economic theory began to gain acceptance as propounded by John Maynard Keynes. The theory provided another piece to the economic equation. During times of economic downturns, the government must stimulate the economy. What was known as classical economics began to lose its grip as the accepted economic theory. The acceptance of the new Keynesian economic theory was not a response of the seasoned economists, but that of a new generation of young economists at Harvard. In writing about the structure of scientific revolutions, Thomas Kuhn quotes Max Planck as saying, "A new scientific truth does not triumph by convincing its opponents and making them see the light, but rather because its opponents eventually die, and a new generation grow up that is familiar with it." Scientific revolutions do not always happen this way, but sometimes they do. This generational change in perspective is found not only in the sciences, but on enough occasions in theology and economics also.

With the upswing of the fourth long-wave the vigorous prosecution of monopolies began once more. The Temporary National Economic Committee, formed in 1937 by members of government, concluded that monopolies were a cause of the depression. The Federal Trade Commission was revitalized to carry on its role. The Securities and Exchange Commission was created to regulate stock and bond transactions and to prevent practices that were believed to have led to the stock market crash. The Securities Act of 1933 and the Securities Exchange Act of 1934 required the disclosure of relations between business firms and the promoters of mergers. It was believed that one of the greatest contributors to the depression was the irresponsible practices of banks. The Glass-Steagall Act of 1933 prohibited banks from engaging in investment banking, the promotion of new securities and the use of depositors' funds to acquire them. Banks, brokerage houses and insurance companies were to remain as separate entities and to be independent of each other.

President Roosevelt appointed Thurman Arnold of Yale Law School, who was, just a short time earlier, an ardent opponent of antitrust regulations, to be Assistant Attorney General and head of the Antitrust Division of the Justice Department. As the long-wave moved up, the general consensus among economists became that there was a need for strong antitrust enforcement. By 1950 the Celler-Kefauver Act was thought to have brought a halt to any future waves of mergers.

When signs of new mergers began in 1967, more regulatory laws regarding acquisitions were introduced. The Williams Act of 1968 required disclosures before a takeover could proceed so that shareholders could make informed decisions about the future and direction of their firm and whether or not to sell. The Tax Reform Act of 1969 erased the tax advantages corporations once enjoyed from making acquisitions. By 1976 it was necessary to consult with antitrust agencies before mergers. But the seemingly strong attempts to enforce antitrust legislation were undermined by an eroding consensus as the downswing of the long-wave approached.

In 1968 the assistant attorney general for antitrust had put forth stringent guidelines for the Justice Department to evaluate mergers. At about the same time, the presidential Task Force on Antitrust Policy headed by the dean of the University of Chicago law school, Phillip Neal, had recommended new and stronger antitrust legislation. These reports were barely evaluated before the underlying sentiment about trusts had changed. Kenneth Davidson of the Federal Trade Commission observes:

> Almost before the ink was dry on the Justice Department's "Merger Guidelines" and the Neal Report, President-elect Richard Nixon appointed George Stigler to chair a Task Force on Productivity and Competition. The report cast doubt on the need for the deconcentration and antimerger legislation advocated by the Neal commission and for the enforcement of antitrust laws against conglomerate mergers. By 1974 academic consensus on antitrust had collapsed. At the same time scholarly opinion was shifting, the antitrust bureaucracies were moving from enforcement policies supported by political theory to theories based on economic theory. And by the end of the decade claims were being made for a new consensus that greatly reduced the role of antitrust. Certainly by the 1980's in the administration of President Ronald Reagan the Department of Justice and the Federal Trade Commission have adopted much less aggressive enforcement policies.[24]

Economists who were once cited as proponents of regulation could now be cited as proponents of deregulation. Schools that once drew up plans for government regulation were now opposing government interference in business. And economic theories that had as their basis a regulated economy were now shown to be even more effective under an unregulated economy.[25] The consensus in general was that the economy was over-regulated. The airlines, it could be pointed out, could not even change their passenger meal plans unless they had received approval by a regulatory body. No new airlines were created in over thirty years. During the Carter administration the airlines and trucking industries were deregulated. During the Reagan administration, lawsuits against the monopolistic practices of AT&T, IBM, the nation's eight largest oil companies and other corporations were dropped. In the railroad industry, the Chessie System bought Seaboard Coast Line for $1 billion to form the CSX Corporation in 1980. Union Pacific bought Missouri Pacific for $900 million in 1982. Norfolk and Western merged with Southern Railway the same year to form Norfolk Southern Corp. And in 1983 Santa Fe Industries merged with Southern Pacific in a deal worth $2.3 billion.[26]

The non-enforcement of regulatory statutes in the financial sector enabled financial institutions to venture into previously forbidden areas. Financial institutions such as Citicorp, Bank of America, Merrill Lynch and American Express are among the many that have expanded their services. By the 1980's even department store retailers could offer under one roof, services which were once limited to different industry groups such as insurance, savings and loans, mortgages, stock brokerage, real-estate and credit cards. Many have diversified into previously restricted areas. Before the 1990's were over, virtually every depression-era statute for the regulation of corporations had been repealed.

The number of mergers and acquisitions over $100 million went from 14 at a total value of $12.5 billion in 1974 to 200 at a total value of $122 billion in 1984. By 1989 they had reached over $250 billion. More than a third of the Fortune 500 Industrial and Fortune 500 Service companies were swallowed up or went private. The cost of the merger activities was estimated at over $1.5 trillion.[27]

Firms attempting to thwart hostile takeovers had several lines of defense. One was to find a "White Knight," that is a firm willing to merge on friendly terms, making them too large for the hostile firm. Another was to make the firm undesirable to the acquiring company by taking on billions of dollars in debt. Such a method was dubbed "the poison pill." Alternatively money would be paid to the acquiring firm to drop its bid. This sum, which sometimes amounted to tens of millions of dollars, was labelled "Green Mail." Whatever actions were taken, the target firm would be left in a financially weakened position.

The wave of merger activities and speculation moved the stock market up in leaps and bounds. The number of mutual funds, reminiscent of the investment trusts of the 1920's, grew substantially during the rapid market rise. In the 1940's, there were less than 100 mutual funds in existence with assets of no more than $2 billion. In 1980, that number grew to 564 with assets of $135 billion. By 1990, the number of mutual funds had grown to 3,106 while the assets grew to over $1 trillion. In one decade, the number of funds had grown more than five-fold while the assets had grown eight fold. There were 12 million fund accounts in 1980 and by 1990 there were more than 62 million.

By comparison, on the New York Stock Exchange, there were 2,228 stock issues in 1980 and 2,284 stock issues in 1990. On the NASDAQ, there were 3,050 stock issues in 1980 and that increased by 50 percent to 4,706 issues in 1990. In the case of personal savings, in 1980 it was valued at $154 billion. By 1990, that grew to $176 billion. It had long been taught that the stock market was a place for corporations to raise risk capital. Seemingly overnight it became a haven for retirement savings. Clearly the mutual fund has become the favored vehicle of savings and investment. The growth of the mutual fund has surpassed the growth in the number of stock issues and its value has surpassed that of estimated personal savings. As society ages, pension funds have become major economic forces, being influential corporate shareholders and landlords. And mutual funds have even attempted to dictate the policies of countries in which they invest.

Figure 5.17 charts the percent change per decade of per capita savings. While the rate of population growth is declining, the rate of savings continued to grow on the declining side of the long-wave. In the 1870's, savings went into banks and savings institutions. But by the 1900's, investment trusts, the stock market, and later, mutual funds have been getting a greater share of the money. From figures 5.18 and 5.19, we find that the savings rate for the fourth long-wave peaked around 1980 and turned negative by 2005. Whether overall savings peaked in 1980 or peaked with the stock market peak of 2000 or whether people are saving by investing in real-estate or people are just starting to save, or people are not saving at all has been an open debate.

What has changed is that North America has become a credit society where credit and debt have gone through phases of eroding taboos. Before, getting a loan meant a formal meeting with a banker and showing that one was an upright and responsible citizen. Now, anyone opening a new bank account is begged to accept a credit card, offered a line of credit and asked to sign for overdraft protection. Those that refuse are pestered several times a year with pre-approved lines of credit and credit card offers. Before, buying groceries on credit was considered a taboo. Now grocery stores offer their own credit cards along with rewards as inducements to use them. Before, American Express felt that they were so exclusive that their charter stated that banks were not allowed to offer their cards to customers. Now that credit is abundant, American Express has had to change their charter to allow banks to offer their cards in order to stop eroding their market share. Exclusivity has its disadvantages.

Following the great market rise and brief collapse of the 1980's was the failure of hundreds of banks and Savings and Loans institutions due to bad loans and land speculation. Their liability was taken over by the federal government. The junk-bond boom came to an end with the failure of numerous mergers and with the prosecution of brokers for illegal practices. Yet the economy remained resilient, the economic downturn not being as severe as many had anticipated. When the scandals and controversies subsided, the stock market continued its upward course to ever dizzying heights. There was every confidence that the disaster of 1929 could not happen again because stock margins, the collateral required to purchase stocks, had been raised to fifty percent as compared to ten percent in 1929.

When the Internet was made available to the public in the mid 1990's, a large number of new technology companies began issuing stocks on the Nasdaq stock exchange. The internet was perceived as the technology that would bring about a revolution in the way we work, the way we shop, the way we conduct our business and even in our daily lives similar to the industrial revolution. Bidding frenzies became the order of the day since no one wanted to miss out on the ground floor of this new economy. Some of these new companies with few workers and no revenue gained higher capitalization than profitable companies with tens of thousands of employees world-wide and hundreds of millions in revenue. From October of 1998 to the top in March 2000, the Nasdaq index increased by over 400 percent. Given the duration and magnitude of the price gains, even the most conservative of investors could hardly avoid being drawn into the new economy companies. Unfortunately, the immediate promises of the new economy, as it turned out, were still virtual-reality. Increasing volatility became characteristic of the stock market on the course of its run. A growing number of stock market gurus managed to garner the trust and respect of a large number of investors over the years because of their uncanny ability to predict the market rise. Each time they proclaimed that the market would go up, it would eventually come true. But when the market finally turned and headed down, they were gurus no more. History has shown time and again that in the transitional eras in which youthful populations become mature populations, vast sums of wealth are generated. Periods in which there are vast sums of newly found wealth are subject to episodes of investment euphoria. From figure 5.20 we can see that the stock market is another economic activity that follows the long-wave.

The stock market top in 2000 was followed by a three-year decline. As usual with each episode of spectacular booms, when the stock market boom ended, many scandals were brought to light, such as the $187 million compensation package of the chairman of the New York Stock Exchange, the failure of Enron and WorldCom due to illegal accounting practices, and the insider trading practices in the mutual fund industry which began with Putnam funds and involved the investigation of approximately a dozen firms, raising concerns about possible effects on corporate and personal pension plans. Indictments came against Arthur Andersen, Adelphia Communications and Tyco International, among many, for improper business conduct. Fraudulent research by stock brokerage firms, used as a method to help unload overpriced stocks to unwary investors, came to the surface. With so much concentration on the accumulation of wealth, financial scandals were bound to happen in greater numbers.

In the aftermath of a three-year decline in stock valuations, corporations and pension funds began to realize that there were growing gaps in their pension obligations. With some companies and funds supporting a retired force of former employees more than three times the number of their active employees, the ability to pay the benefits promised and to keep the company viable and competitive becomes more difficult. The health care benefits alone for some companies have become a significant burden. The pension landscape has begun moving away from defined benefits to that of defined contributions, or doing away with pensions altogether.

Coinciding with each period of deregulation has been the tendency for corporations to decentralize their work environment. Projects no longer have to be rubber stamped as often by the chief executive as long as each section or individual fulfils certain quotas.

International Debt

Deficit accumulation is reflected on the international level as well as on the individual level. Governments, as a reflection of the people that they govern, not only spend what they have, but also what they do not have. Investigations by Ulrich Pfister and Christian Suter reveal that clusters of default in international debt have correlated with the downswing of each long-wave. On the downswing of the first long-wave, from 1826 to 1842, the Latin American Republics, Greece, Portugal and Spain failed to make payments and repudiated their external debt. On the downswing of the second long-wave, from 1875 to 1882, several Latin American republics, Egypt, Greece, Liberia, Spain, Tunisia, Turkey and eleven southern U.S. states repudiated their external loans. On the downswing of the third long-wave, from 1932 to 1939 seventeen Latin American countries, Austria, Bulgaria, Germany, Greece, Hungary, Poland, Romania and Yugoslavia defaulted on their loans. And the most recent surge of loan problems began in the second half of the 1970's. On the downswing of the fourth long-wave from 1983 to 1985 there were 96 multilateral reschedulings.

Trade Tariffs and Protectionist Policies

Before the introduction of personal income tax, governments depended on tariffs as one of their major sources of revenue. Each downswing of the long-wave has brought with it an increase in protectionist sentiment and the raising of trade barriers. The downswing of the first long-wave culminated with the Tariff of 1828, also known as the "Tariff of Abominations," bringing calls of secession from the southern states. On the downswing of the second long-wave McKinley was elected as president by campaigning for prosperity and protectionism. The Dingley Tariff of 1897 raised taxes on imported goods to an average of fifty-seven percent. The downturn of the third long-wave culminated with the Smoot-Hawley Tariff of 1934. With each increase in trade tariffs on the downswing of the long-wave, retaliatory moves are made by other nations creating significant reductions in the movement of goods between countries. Figure 5.21 shows the impact that wars, inflation and depressions have had on the value of imports to the U.S.

Labor Union Membership

The sharpest increase in union membership occurs near the trough of the long-wave with union affiliation reaching its greatest extent near the top of the long-wave. The number of violent strikes increases and member militancy seems to have no limit by the long-wave peak. The energies that induce an increase in union membership are similar to the energies that induce an increase in membership in the social movements.

Early labor organizations were formed by highly skilled wage earning tradesmen. These organizations, called "trade societies," protected the workers interests and the quality of work. The first ones to organize in America were the Federal Society of Journeymen Cordwainers and the Typographical Society of New York in 1794. Most of these societies limited their organizational efforts to one locality and concentrated on negotiating better wages for themselves. By the 1830's the many scattered societies of similar interests began organizing under some form of federation. Thirty years later there were about 26 national trade unions with a total of 300,000 members. The National Labor Congress was held in 1866 and the National Labor Union was formed to give general direction to unions of different trades. But as the downswing of the long-wave progressed, these organizations quickly disintegrated.

On the upswing of the third long-wave union membership increased from 2.5 million in 1915 to just over 5 million by 1920. The American Federation of Labor, which was founded in 1886, took an active part in organizing skilled labor. A more radical group called the Industrial Workers of the World, founded in 1905, organized unskilled labor and advocated sabotage and other violent means to meet their objectives. As the long-wave declined union membership fell to about 3 million in 1933. A similar rise in union membership occurred near the upswing of the fourth long-wave and by the downswing of the long-wave, membership has fallen throughout the 1980's and into the new millennium.

Oil Crisis

As Gen-B moves through the system generating intense inflation, deflation and other economic fluctuations, society reacts to cope with these changing situations. Accompanying each period of long-wave inflation has been a national concern over the shortage of energy. On the upswing of the second long-wave America experienced what may be its first oil crisis. Scientific American reports in 1857 that:

> The necessity for inventors applying their genius and skill to improved means of obtaining light and heat is constantly becoming more and more urgent. The whale oils, which have hitherto

been much relied on in this country to furnish light, are yearly becoming more scarce, and may in time, almost entirely fail, while the rapid increase of machinery demands a large portion of the purest of these oils for lubricating. Hence, good inventions, in any way connected with these two great subjects, can hardly fail to reward the inventor.[28]

Where sperm whale oil once sold for below fifty cents a gallon, its price increased by more than fourfold. The invention of the kerosene lamp and stove eventually replaced whale oil in lighting and heating and as petroleum came into greater use, the dependency on whale oil was greatly reduced. By the downswing of the long-wave the shortage of oil ceased to be.

By the time these concerns were all but forgotten, cries of an oil shortage on the upswing of the third long-wave agitated the nation once more. These concerns prompted the American Institute of Mining Engineers, which represented over 90 percent of the petroleum engineers at that time, to search for methods of conserving gas and oil supplies. In their meeting in 1917, the New York Times reports:

> W. G. Matteson, a geologist and mining engineer of Houston, Texas, urged that the government should take steps to conserve the country's oil and gas supply by passing laws requiring all oil and gas well drilling to be done under Federal supervision, so as to avoid wastage. "Various experts have calculated that with the current consumption and production our present oil fields will be exhausted in 25 to 50 years," he said.[29]

In January 1918, the U.S. Fuel Administration, established in 1917, ordered all plants east of the Mississippi to shut down for 5 days to conserve coal. This was followed by nine Monday closings. In February, Broadway theatres were closed. During the summer, the Fuel Administration ordered four lightless nights per week from July 24 until November 22 to conserve fuel for winter.[30] As in the previous oil crisis, the fears evaporated and the memories faded when oil continued to flow in abundance.

After the Organization of Petroleum Exporting Countries (OPEC) was formed during the upswing of the fourth long-wave and the price of oil went above thirty dollars a barrel in the 1970's, petroleum engineers were warning once again of dangerous shortages, and predicted that the world could be left dry in about thirty years.

These predictions influenced government policies, the allocation of valuable public resources and billions of dollars in investments. The crisis predictions prompted investment in oil mega-projects in anticipation of higher prices, investments that were not considered profitable at lower oil prices, only to face bankruptcies when the price of oil tumbled. Projects as diverse as research into new energy sources, to the building of smaller cars to the designing of more fuel-efficient homes have been affected. Yet by the late 1980's, Saudi Arabia was more concerned about the shortage of fresh water than it was about running out of oil. One day the world may run out of oil, but when a science is not an exact science, it is difficult to distinguish between analysis and emotion.

Service Sector Growth

Throughout the last two decades people have been lamenting the lack of growth in the high-paying industrial production sector and that most of the jobs being created were in the low-paying service sector. That is looking at only half the equation. As the GDP figures reveal, the shift in disaggregate demand has moved demand towards the service sector. More service sector jobs are being created because there is a greater demand for services. No business would open a factory for the sake of opening factories if there is no demand. This is the same for services. Along with the shift in disaggregate demand, the growth in the service sector is also the result of considerable growth in the labor force as a percentage of population. As more people enter the work force, they have less time to do their own chores. Table 5.01 shows that from 1970 to 1999, the number of families where both parents worked increased by fifty percent. Also, as Baby Boomers grow older and wealthier, they value their time more. Time is money, but money is not time.

Year	Single (never married)	Married	Other
1970	53.0	40.8	39.1
1980	61.5	50.1	44.0
1985	65.2	54.2	45.6
1990	66.4	58.2	46.8
1995	65.5	61.1	47.3
1996	65.2	61.1	48.2
1997	66.8	62.1	48.7
1998	68.1	61.8	49.4
1999	68.1	61.6	49.4

Table 5.01 - Participation Rate of Women in the Work Force (U.S.)

Source: (SAUS year 2000 no. 653) Employment Status of Women by Marital Status and Presence and Age of Children: 1970 to 1999

Where We Stand

As indicated in various places in this book, many factors were suspected of contributing to the economic downturn of 1929. Even the closure of the Ford automotive plants for retooling was considered culpable since Ford had grown to be a substantial part of the economy by 1929. Other theories point to the over-tightening of monetary policy by the Federal Reserve, the loss of business confidence, and a drop in consumption. Several depression-era economists attribute a drop in consumption to the decline in population growth. There continues to be no consensus about the cause of the Depression among economists.

For nearly two and a half decades after the Great Depression, economic policy's central theme was one of preventing depressions. After the inflationary bout of the 1970's, fighting inflation has been the priority of economic policy for nearly three decades. Currently the inflation rate, interest rates and wage increases are at the lowest level in many decades. From figures 5.22 and 5.23 we can see that the GNP of both countries is increasing at the lowest levels in decades but remain healthy. The unemployment rate remains healthy also. As long as wages and the economy retain the current growth rates, those that are employed will continue to have a rising standard of living.

But what is not healthy are government and personal debt. North Americans have no savings at a time when Baby Boomers are entering retirement. Many pension funds are in shortfall and some funds will not be able to meet pension payments as promised. From figure 4.14, the percent change per decade of population over 65, we see that those in retirement age have been increasing at the lowest rate in decades. It is because of this demographic situation that the economy has remained as resilient as it has. This is expected to change by 2007 when the rate of baby boomer retirement will begin to escalate. By 2011 the number of people over 65 will expand rapidly. That is when the real economic challenge will begin.

In the United States, because of the enormous deficit, the ability to meet the challenge of demographic shift has become more limited. If the government cannot stabilize the economy, government bonds and foreign exchange will lose their appeal. The Federal Reserve will be more limited in its ability to control monetary policy. There is a high probability that the downswing of the current long-wave will eventually be accompanied by monetary inflation. But it is unlikely that monetary policy alone will be able to reverse a demographic economic decline for as people retire poorer, their needs are more defined, their means are more limited and they move further from the reach of monetary manipulation. This has been the situation in Japan for the last two decades, from which many lessons could have been learned.

The Canadian deficit situation is the best among the G8 nations. However the U.S. is the world's largest economy and the economic changes there will affect Canada. Canada currently has a similar demographic situation as the U.S, Japan, China and most of Europe. The population is ageing and barely growing. Many pension funds are in shortfall. If the Canadian government takes a conventional response to the changing demographics, as previous governments have, then there is a high probability that the long-wave downswing will continue to be deflationary. In order to create a working economic model, we must give sixty percent of the economy at least sixty percent of the relevancy. We must realign our perspectives and move to a population-centric model.

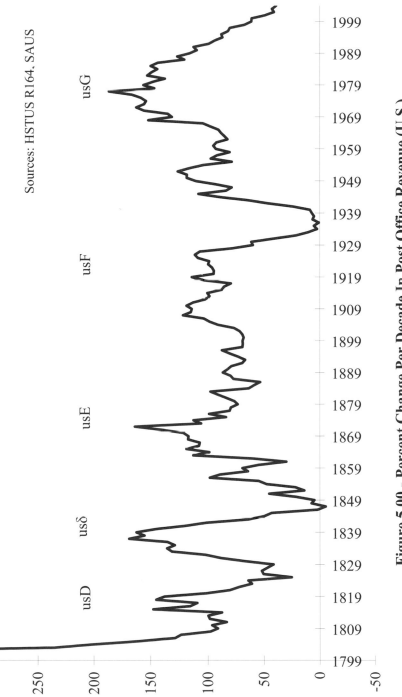

Sources: HSTUS R164, SAUS

usG

usF

usE

usδ

usD

Figure 5.00 – Percent Change Per Decade In Post Office Revenue (U.S.)

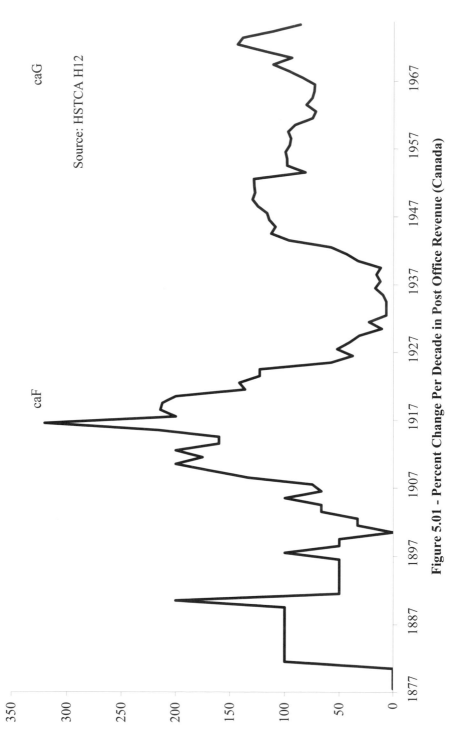

Figure 5.01 – Percent Change Per Decade in Post Office Revenue (Canada)

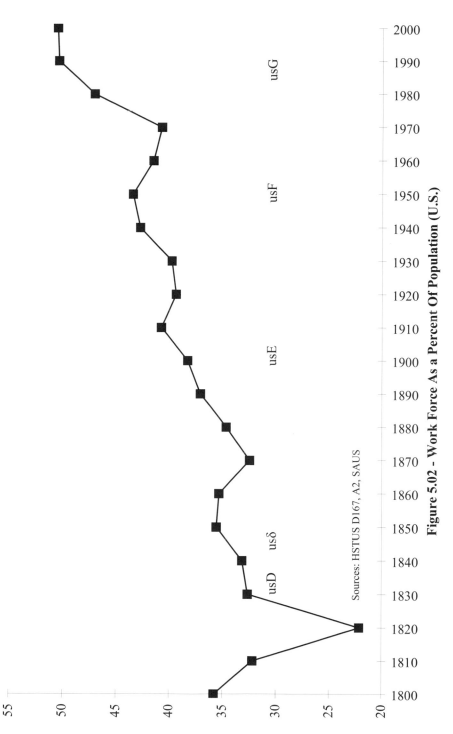

Figure 5.02 - Work Force As a Percent Of Population (U.S.)

Sources: HSTUS D167, A2, SAUS

usG

usF

usE

usδ

usD

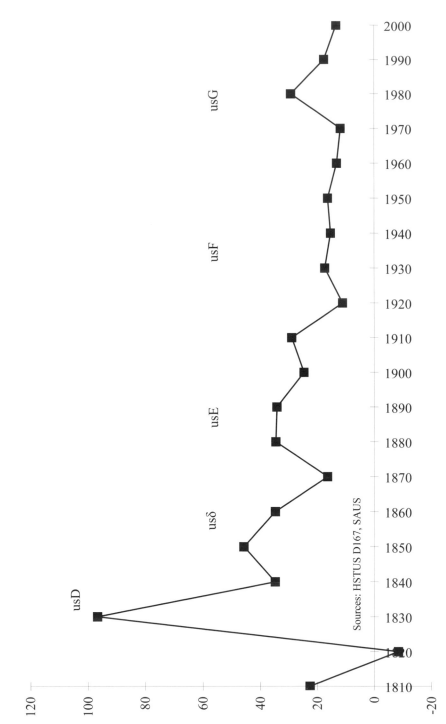

Figure 5.03 - Percent Change Per Decade in Work Force (U.S.)

Sources: HSTUS D167, SAUS

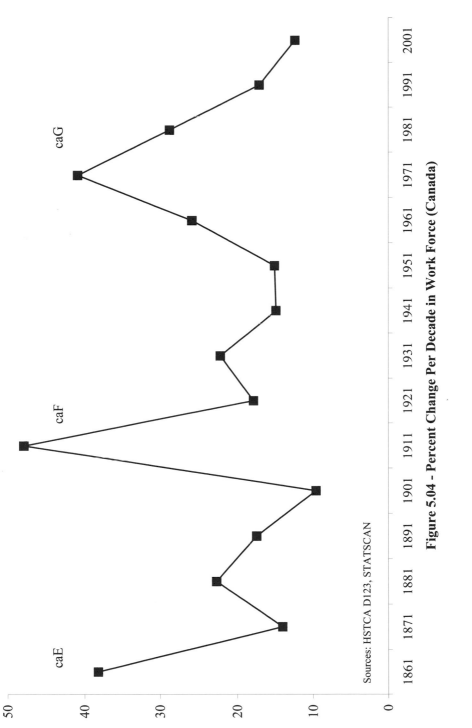

Sources: HSTCA D123, STATSCAN

Figure 5.04 – Percent Change Per Decade in Work Force (Canada)

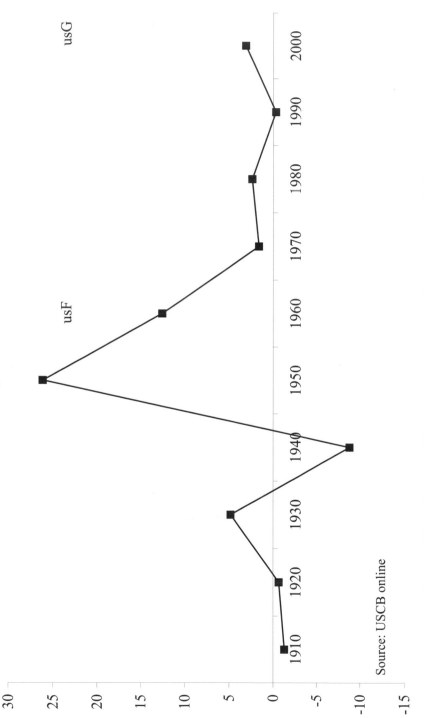

Figure 5.05 - Percent Change Per Decade in Home Ownership Rates (U.S.)

Source: USCB online

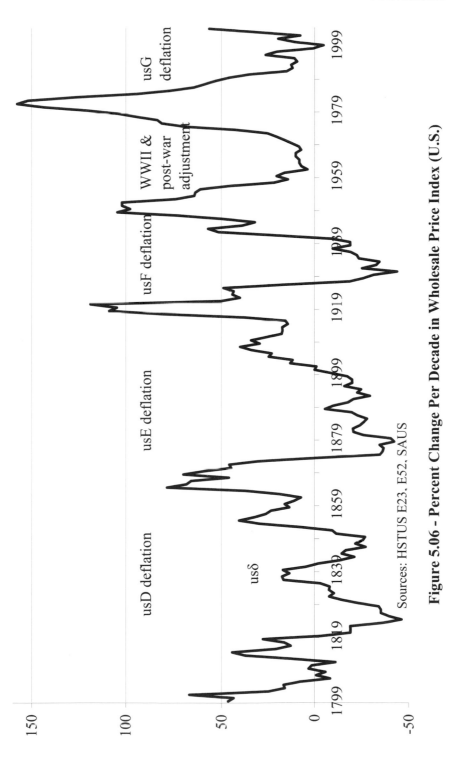

Figure 5.06 – Percent Change Per Decade in Wholesale Price Index (U.S.)

Sources: HSTUS E23, E52. SAUS

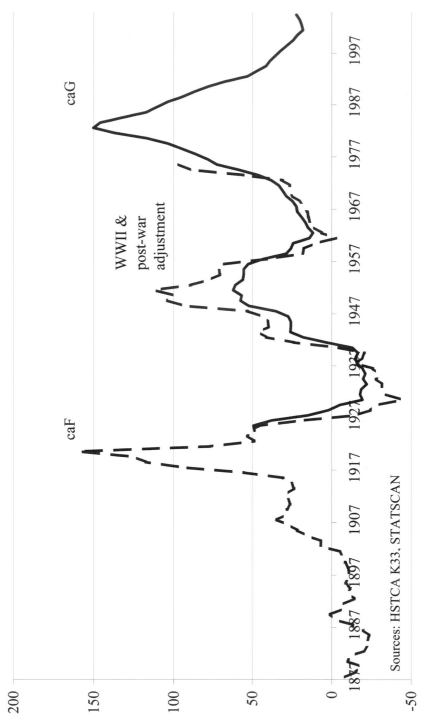

Figure 5.07 - Percent Change Per Decade in Composite Price Indexes (Canada)

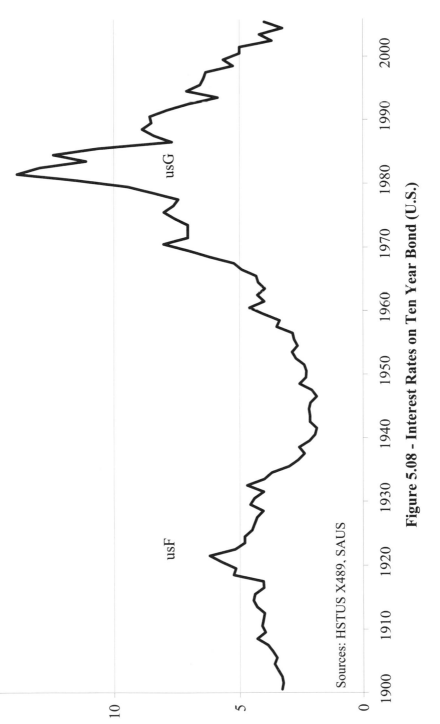

usG

usF

Sources: HSTUS X489, SAUS

Figure 5.08 - Interest Rates on Ten Year Bond (U.S.)

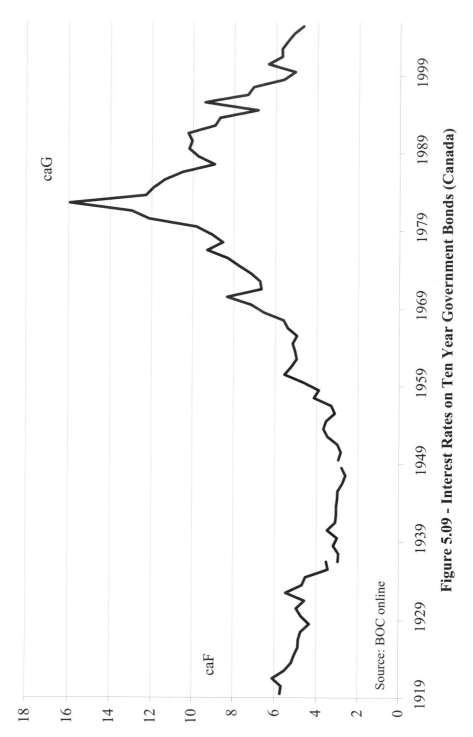

Figure 5.09 - Interest Rates on Ten Year Government Bonds (Canada)

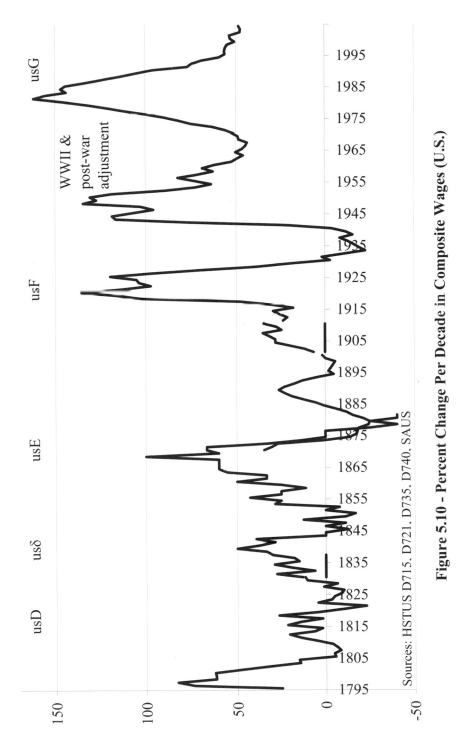

usG

WWII &
post-war
adjustment

usF

usE

usδ

usD

Sources: HSTUS D715. D721. D735. D740. SAUS

Figure 5.10 - Percent Change Per Decade in Composite Wages (U.S.)

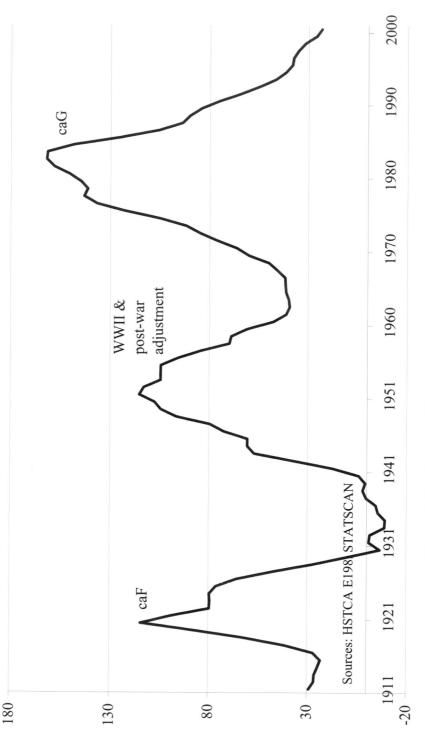

Figure 5.11 - Percent Change Per Decade in Wages (Canada)

Figure 5.12 - Total Federal Government Expenditures (U.S.)

Sources: HSTUS Y457, SAUS

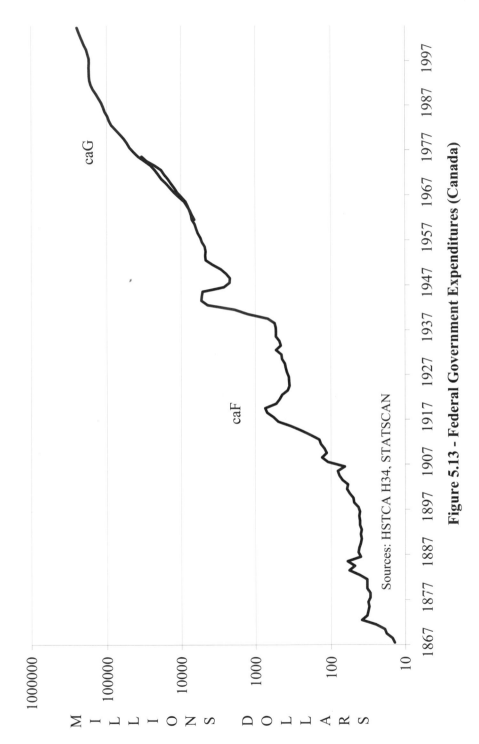

Figure 5.13 - Federal Government Expenditures (Canada)

Sources: HSTCA H34, STATSCAN

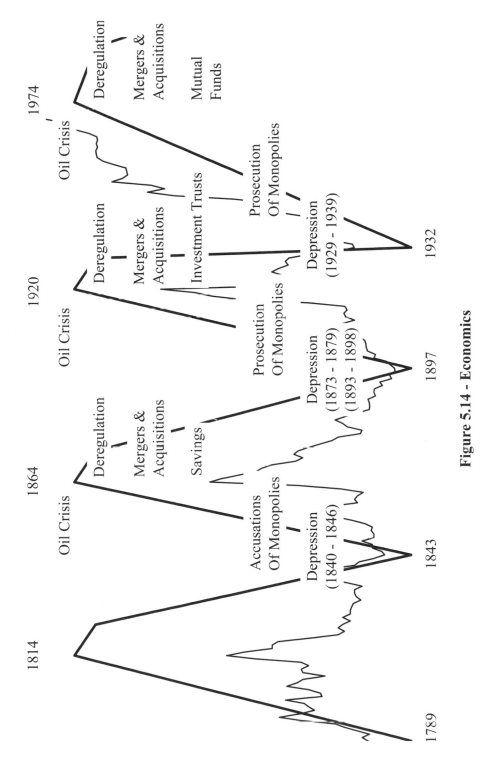

Figure 5.14 - Economics

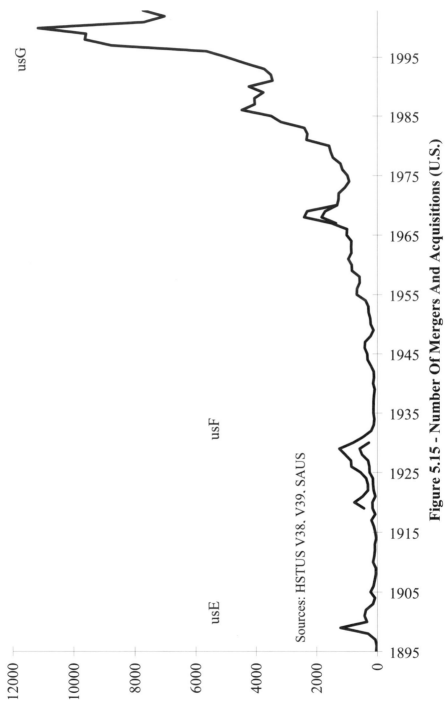

Figure 5.15 - Number Of Mergers And Acquisitions (U.S.)

Sources: HSTUS V38. V39. SAUS

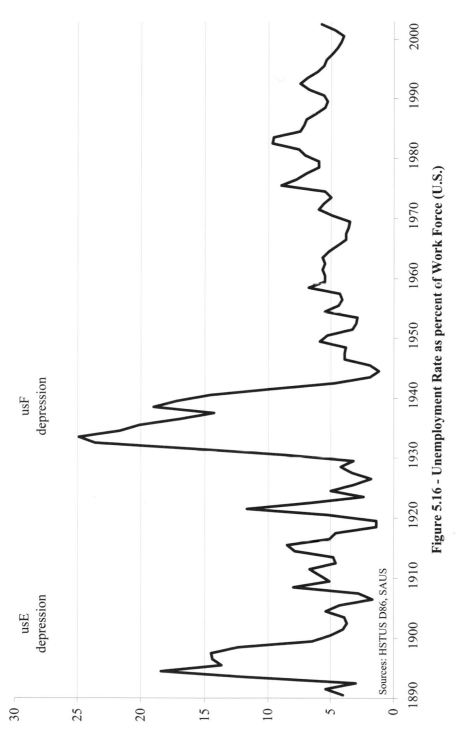

usF
depression

usE
depression

Sources: HSTUS D86, SAUS

Figure 5.16 - Unemployment Rate as percent of Work Force (U.S.)

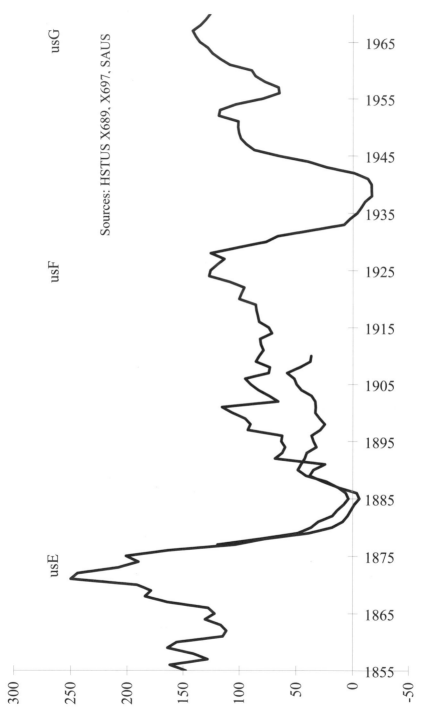

Figure 5.17 - Percent Change Per Decade in Per Capita Savings And Time Deposits (U.S.)

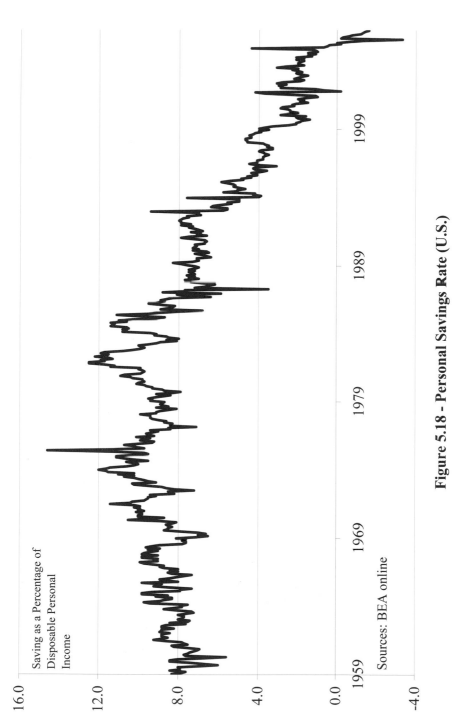

16.0

12.0

Saving as a Percentage of
Disposable Personal
Income

8.0

4.0

0.0

-4.0

1959

1969

1979

1989

1999

Sources: BEA online

Figure 5.18 - Personal Savings Rate (U.S.)

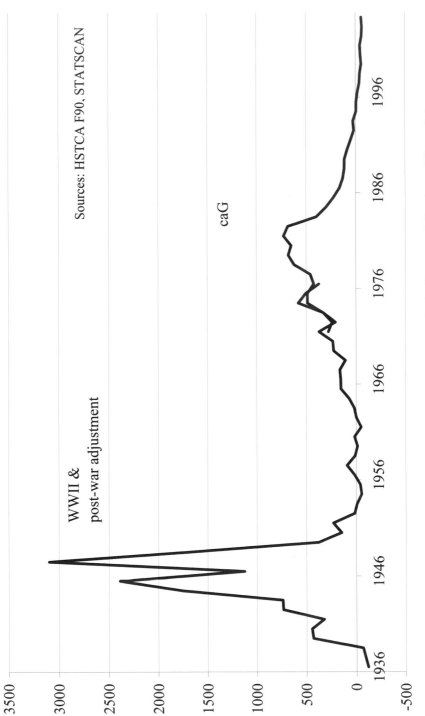

Figure 5.19 - Percent Change Per Decade in Personal Savings (Canada)

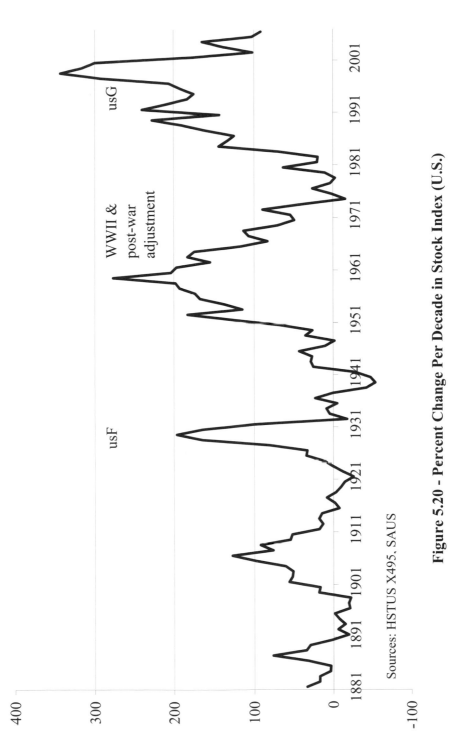

Figure 5.20 - Percent Change Per Decade in Stock Index (U.S.)

Sources: HSTUS X495, SAUS

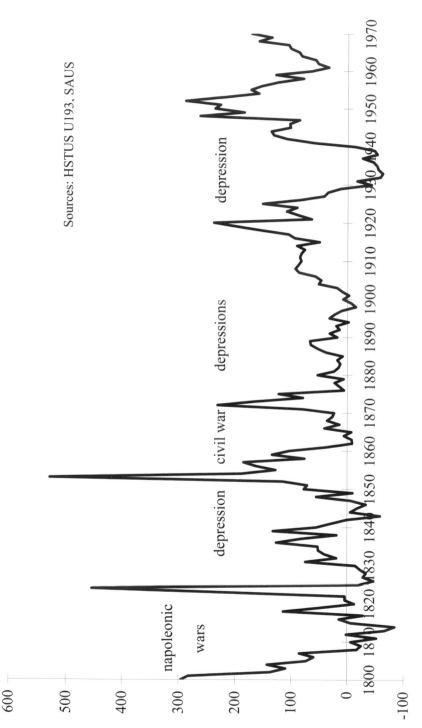

Figure 5.21 – Percent Change Per Decade in Imports (U.S.)

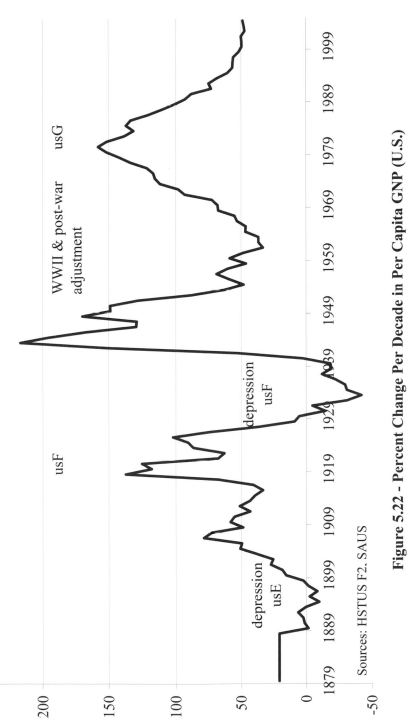

Figure 5.22 - Percent Change Per Decade in Per Capita GNP (U.S.)

Sources: HSTUS F2. SAUS

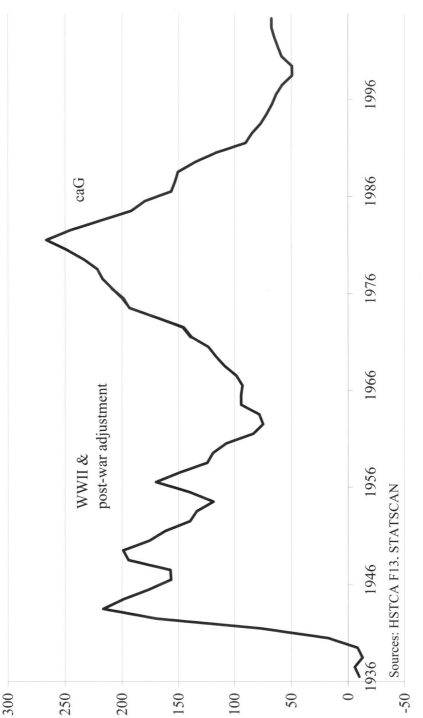

Sources: HSTCA F13. STATSCAN

Figure 5.23 – Percent Change Per Decade in Gross National Product (Canada)

6 MORE WAVES OF SOCIAL CHANGE

Demographics affect all aspects of our lives, whether we are aware of it or not. From birth to death all our beliefs and all our activities are a reflection of our society. We create the society in which we live; in turn our society provides us the context with which we understand our surroundings. There are few islands that can withstand the tides of social change.

Marriage and Divorce

Having children has been one of the activities traditional to the institution of marriage. Since children born out of wedlock made up five percent of births in 1950 and ten percent of births in 1970, increasing birthrates would suggest that there were increasing marriages also. When we compare figure 6.00, the marriage rate per 1,000 population to figure 4.00, the birth rate per 1,000 population, we find that they increase and decrease together. The marriage rate began increasing in the middle of the depression, marking 1933 as the period when the birth rate stopped decreasing and began to reverse. With an increase in common-law relationships, children born out of wedlock made up about thirty percent of births by the 1990's. However birthrate and marriage rate continued to move in tandem.

With a higher rate of marriage, one might expect more mismatches also, resulting in divorce. Figure 6.01, divorce rate per 1,000 population shows that the divorce rate increases and decreases in conjunction with the marriage rate. In the 1940's the divorce rate was about one quarter of the marriage rate. By 1980 it was half the marriage rate. When comparing figure 6.02, the percent change per decade in married couples to population ratio with figures 4.00, 4.02 and 4.13, we can see that as the number of married couples increase and decrease, so does the birth rate. The marriage rate was greater in the 1950's than in the 1980's and so was the birth rate. Marriage and divorce for Canada can be compared in figures 6.03 and 6.04, the percent change per decade in marriage and divorce. Comparing figure 6.05, the percent change per decade in married couples to population ratio with figure 4.17, percent change per decade in population under 5, we find similar peaks and valleys. Everything that we believe and everything that we do are related in the interwoven fabric of society. The birthrate and marriage rate are currently the lowest in recorded history in North America, which does not bode well for our future or our economy.

With the changing attitudes toward marriage and a changing birth rate, there is a change in attitude towards children. On the one extreme, should children be left alone to explore and learn on their own, without any guidance, or on the other extreme, should they be raised in a strict and disciplinarian fashion? These changing attitudes about children are not only reflected in popular child rearing books, but in ongoing debates within the educational system as well.

Education

The education of children is important to the future of any society. How that is to be done and what resources should be allocated for that purpose is the subject of constant debate. In North America educational policy is known to be like a pendulum that swings between a traditional educational philosophy and a progressive and practical educational philosophy. Like all other activities of the long-wave, educational philosophy swings towards the progressive on the upswing of the long-wave and towards the traditional on the downswing.

A traditional education is usually based on a structured curriculum with emphasis on the three "R's" – "reading, 'riting and 'rithmetic." The teacher is expected to lead the class and the students are expected to follow a set curriculum. A liberal arts education, a back-to-the-basics education, an academic education and a classical education are traditional educations. A subject-centered curriculum with testing to ensure that what was taught was learned is a part of a traditional education. There is a tendency for curriculum to be set centrally and uniformly throughout the school system.

A manual education, industrial education, agricultural education, commercial education and career education are practical educations. Practical educations aim to teach a skill useful for getting a job while a traditional education aims to teach skills in abstract thinking and problem solving.

A progressive education is much less structured than a traditional education and gives the students and teachers greater choices in the subjects to be studied and in the roles that they play. A progressive education aims to be child-centered and is more open to using experimental methods of teaching. The teacher does not necessarily have to set the agenda for the class. Often the students get to decide what they want to pursue. A progressive education is usually advocated at the same time that a practical education is called for. Since a progressive education is child-centered, it has a greater tendency to create streams to accommodate children of the same grade but at different levels of ability. Testing is demoted to a minor role in a progressive education. The upswing of the long-wave brings calls for a secular education also, while the downswing brings calls for a return to a religious morality.

United States

The swing from practical to traditional is exemplified by Noah Webster, known for the Webster's Dictionary and a compendium of works and textbooks that he wrote for the purpose of education, for which he is sometimes referred to as the "Schoolmaster to America." In writing the American dictionary, one of Webster's goals was to simplify the spoken and written language. When Webster was young he rallied around the ideas of the Enlightenment and the Revolution and supported a separation between church and state. He believed in a practical education that would train students in whatever business or trade that they may enter. But later in life he would give up those ideas and call for a return to a religious morality and traditional teaching methods. At the laying of the cornerstone of Amherst College in 1820, Webster announced his belief in a liberal arts education for ministers of the gospel.

Some of the early advocates of a practical education were the poet John Milton and Benjamin Franklin. In his *Proposals Relating to the Education of Youth in Pennsylvania* published in 1749, Franklin proposed that an education should include gardening, planting and grafting with field trips to plantations. Benjamin Rush believed that a practical education was suitable for most people because very few actually go on to university. Schools such as Yale and Harvard were originally founded for engineering and geological training where a classical education was not required. But when the issue of a practical curriculum was brought before Yale in 1828, the faculty rejected the idea because a classical education trained students to think for themselves. If students could master difficult and abstract subjects such as Latin and Mathematics, they would be able master simpler subjects if they needed to. Difficult subjects disciplined the mind, which was what was required to master any subject. For Yale, the classical education had become the most practical education.

WAVE II

The early education reformers believed that a formal education would be beneficial to society not only in the acquisition of skills but also in the prevention of crime and in the development of moral character. Education was necessary for the survival of the democracy which demanded informed and educated participants. At usδ common schools, now known as elementary schools, were being established and began to receive tax funding. Beginning with the state of Pennsylvania in 1834, a bill was passed for the use of tax money to support a public school system. There were those who resented paying taxes for the education of someone else's children but the movement continued to spread. Three years later, Massachusetts passed a similar law. Many other states followed. The era became known as the age of the common school revival because it revived the demand for universal education that once existed during the colonial period. It was felt that education was a basic right of every citizen and should not be reserved only for the elite. Education was viewed as the great equalizer of society. Schooling was the means by which every member of society could climb in social and economic status if given the opportunity. The prominent common school reformer, Horace Mann, derived his educational philosophy from Johann Pestalozzi who believed in learning by doing, stimulating the curiosity of children, and making the learning process interesting and pleasurable. He believed that the teacher should be able to govern the students through love rather than corporal punishment. Catherine Beecher championed schools for girls. She founded the Hartford Female Seminary in 1823 and helped to establish women's colleges in several states.

The first high school was initially opened as the English Classical School in 1821 in Boston and then changed its name to the English High School in 1824. Most of the students were boys who did not plan to continue to college. As such it offered a practical education. Throughout the 1840's to the 1860's, the upswing of the second long-wave, there were calls for more practical curriculums in higher education. The Morrill Act of 1862 granted public land to states to support military, mechanical and agricultural training in colleges.

By the downswing of the long-wave there was a steady movement away from a practical education. With a substantial flow of endowment funds from wealthy families to institutions of higher learning, a large number of universities were established. Cornell was founded in 1868, Harvard was changed from a college to a university in 1869, John Hopkins was founded in 1876, Stanford in 1891 and the University of Chicago in 1892.[1] In the last two decades of the nineteenth century, over 130 new colleges and universities were founded. The education reform at us8 and on the upswing of the long-wave attempted to make education available to everyone. But on the downswing of the second long-wave, universities were established as elite institutions requiring as a prerequisite high academic achievements, usually graduation from a traditional academic or classical school. University programs were more advanced than colleges and the course loads were heavier. There was a rise in scientific research and graduate programs. Preparatory schools were founded for the children of wealthy families in preparing for university life.

In trying to determine admissions standards to university, the National Education Association appointed a Committee of Ten to investigate. The report that was released in 1893 stated that the "best education for life" is the best education for entry into college. Students that show that they are "properly prepared for life" are prepared for college and are ready for membership into the elite. The Committee's report held that every student should be given the "best education for life" in the event that a decision is made later to continue on to college. The high school's function was to prepare that small proportion of students that will go on to play important leadership roles in the welfare of the nation. The best education for life was one that disciplined the mind rather than imparted a vocational skill.[2] Schools should not create a class-based education. Since 75 percent of students did not continue on to post secondary education, the prime beneficiaries of an academic education were the 25 percent who did. Approximately 15 percent went on to some form of post secondary education and less than 10 percent of students went on to university. The Committee of Ten report reflected the general movement of high schools that was already taking place throughout the downswing of the long-wave, towards acting as feeders to universities.

The American Herbartian Association, in following the philosophy of Johann F. Herbart, developed a rigid five step educational program of preparation, presentation, association, generalization and application. Herbart's work had a great influence on the educational system and provided a uniform method of teaching throughout the country. The Herbartians believed that these concepts extended the ideas of Pestalozzi. Others believed that school curriculum became more rigid and uncompromising.

WAVE III

Between 1893 and 1918 the high school changed from being an elite institution for entry into university into an institution that shared the goals of a common school and was referred to by the same name. While the Committee of Ten's report stated that secondary schools should be "training the powers of observation, memory, expression and reasoning," by the top of the third long-wave the Commission on the Reorganization of Secondary Education of 1918 directed that the Cardinal Rules of Secondary Education were, "health, command of fundamental processes, worth of home-membership, vocation, citizenship, worthy use of leisure, and ethical character." With the rise of social work, the Commission recommended that schools take on a social service approach.[3] Schools were re-focused on teaching vocational subjects such as business, agriculture, fine-arts, industrial skills and clerical skills.

By 1907 the acceptance of industrial education was becoming widespread. It was seen as a direct way to prepare students for life. The Vocational Bureau and Breadwinner's Institute was established in 1909 to help children select school subjects that supported their vocational choices. The 1912 Report of the Committee on Industrial Education stated that for half the youth of the land, the educational system had become "horrible, unmindful, uninformed and inconsiderate," and recommended that continuing education be made available to youth that had left school to work.[4] Streaming students into different courses could be viewed as aiding students that would not be attending university, or it could be viewed as creating a class society. The Commission on National Aid to Vocational Education in 1914 believed that vocational training was the democratization of education. The Commission's report became the basis of the Smith-Hughes Act of 1917 that provided federal funds for the salaries of teachers who were involved with vocational training. Matching funds were expected to be contributed by the states.

John Dewey, an advocate of learning by doing and a leader of progressive education, rejected Herbartianism because a child's individuality was lost in the method. Progressives believed that education should be child-centered rather than subject-centered as the rigid Herbartian system had become. Before Dewey, school desks were nailed to the floor to minimize disruptions. Dewey wanted children to do group work and be involved in student activities. The nails were removed from the desks to allow students to move around. Dewey did not believe in teaching abstract ideas but in teaching practical subjects that had application in real life. He believed that learning was not just sitting down with books but should be a part of daily living.

Progressive education continued into the 1930's. Open classrooms, team teaching, individual instruction, schools without walls, work-study programs, competency-based programs and other experimental programs were tried. But by the 1930's, as the downswing of the long-wave progressed, even John Dewey was complaining about the direction that people were taking progressive education.

By the 1940's, schools were going "back-to-the-basics" as it was felt that there was a need for a subject-centered education and an intellectual discipline. In order to compete against the threat of Russian scientific progress as manifested by the advances of the Russian space program, along with the Cold War, elite schools were seen as a necessary development. Science professionals were summoned to testify that a return to a traditional education was necessary to get society back on course. Critics held that an education meant more than obtaining a skill, getting a job and spending money. Students must become intelligent citizens with a sense of social value. Academics such as historian Arthur Bestor spoke

out against streaming and believed that there should be an equal education for all. He started a petition to bring intellectual disciplines back to
the classroom. James B. Conant, a president of Harvard, a founder of
the National Science Foundation and a member of several commissions
on education, believed that schools should be sorting through students
so that those of intelligence could be trained for leadership roles and to
join the ranks of the elite. Admiral Hyman Rickover, sometimes known
as the father of America's nuclear navy, testified that education was important to national security and that strong subject matter experts were
needed to help fight the Cold War. With that testimony, the National
Defense Education Act (NDEA) was passed in 1958 placing emphasis
on subject-centered disciplines of science, technology, mathematics and
foreign languages. President Eisenhower called for standardized testing
and the encouragement of talented students to enter science programs.

WAVE IV

By the 1960's, as the upswing of the fourth long-wave progressed,
the focus of schools shifted from a role in national security back to a role
in social service, in helping to resolve the issues of poverty and racial dis-
crimination. The Economic Opportunity Act of 1964 created the Head
Start program for the children of the poor. The following year 560,000
children were enrolled. The Elementary and Secondary Education Act
of 1965 provided financial assistance to poor children and funding for
libraries, text books and educational research. School curriculum became
child-centered rather than subject-centered. The Supreme Court banned
prayer in public schools in 1962. The reading of the Bible as a religious
text was banned in 1963.

The Civil Rights Movement spawned busing, desegregation, alternative schools for integration and cultural centric schools. The Nixon
administration brought in career education because it was thought to re-
store law and order to campuses. The administration felt that education
should be made meaningful to students. Students completing grade 12
should either be ready for a career or for higher education. For a period in

the 1970's, programs such as open classrooms, team teaching, individual instruction, schools without walls, work-study programs, competency-based programs and other programs could be seen reappearing in schools.

By the 1980's, on the downswing of the long-wave, education was moving back to the basics again. Both the Reagan and Bush administrations supported school prayer and a return to moral values. The report "A Nation at Risk" blamed education as the reason for the declining competitiveness of American industries. The Bush administration believed that there should be voluntary national achievement tests. In the 1990's the privatization of school administration allowed commercial interests to manage and operate educational institutions. These commercial interests were paid based on meeting academic and financial objectives. With the No Child Left Behind Act of 2001, standardized testing became mandatory, attempting to ensure that there was a uniform core curriculum across the country. The popularity of the spelling bee is reminiscent of the era of the 1950's. In the cycle of changing educational philosophy, John D. Pulliam observes that:

> modern educational history describes a pattern of back to basics movements followed by liberal responses like team teaching and non-graded schools, followed again by back to basics. Sometimes the cycle is fostered by comparison with foreign schools as was the case with Admiral Hyman Rickover and James B. Conant following the Soviet success with Sputnik in 1957. More recently, the cycle was initiated by education secretary T. H. Bell and his National Commission on Excellence in Education which produced "A Nation at Risk" in 1983.[5]

Ontario, Canada

When Upper Canada's first Lieutenant-Governor John Graves Simcoe addressed the issue of education in 1795, he expressed that only the children of a few select "Principal People" should be given a proper education since they would be the future leaders of the colony. He called for a grammar school for teaching classical studies and a university also for that purpose. However, when Bishop John Strachan became master of the first grammar school in Cornwall in 1803, Strachan realized that the residents of Upper Canada would not appreciate a liberal education but would be better served with a practical education. Youngsters reaching the age of seven or eight were far more likely to wield an axe than a textbook. Few would have a chance to go on to university.

This difference in philosophy is seen again when Bishop Strachan went to England to negotiate a charter for King's College in York in 1826. The Colonial Office, the Archbishop of Canterbury and the Society for the Propagation of the Gospel all held that the charter would be too liberal without the stipulation of a religious test. The Charter was issued in 1827. One of the additional outcomes of the negotiations was the creation of Upper Canada College in 1829 modeled on the English classical school.[6]

When King's College finally opened its doors in 1843, Robert Baldwin, a Reform politician, introduced a bill to create the University of Toronto as a non-denominational degree granting institution. Baldwin's efforts would not meet success until the upswing of the long-wave in 1849. King's College became the University of Toronto as a secular institution where the clergymen were forbidden to hold the post of chancellor and there were to be no religious tests or denominational worship. Affiliated denominational colleges were restricted to granting divinity degrees only. Appointments to the Senate and faculty were to be the responsibility of the government.[7]

The Methodist minister Egerton Ryerson, the first Superintendent of Schools for Canada West and Horace Mann's counterpart in Canada, concluded that a practical education would be best when he drafted the Common School Act of 1846. A classical education would be of little use in a rural, agrarian commercial society. Some of the subjects that he advocated were book-keeping, nature study, agriculture, history, geography, arithmetic, hygiene and music.[8] However when grammar schools were brought into the public system on the downswing of the second long-wave by the Act of 1871, he divided the secondary schools along two institutional lines. One was a "high school" for more practical subjects such as commerce and agriculture and the other was a "collegiate institute" for the study of the classics that would lead to university. Legislative grants were provided based on the examination results of students in each school. The practice of linking grants to test results would be discontinued after 1882 but the effects would be long-lasting.

As we can see, in these early years of British North America there were constant debates about the type of education that should be made available to the population. The alternation in educational philosophy, the need for examinations and the role of religion in school curriculum have consistently accompanied the swings in educational policy in Ontario in conjunction with the swings of the long-wave.

Between 1871 and 1875, as the downswing of the long-wave progressed, the teaching of Christian morals became a requirement. Although religious exercises and prayers became optional after 1875, over four thousand schools continued to include religious exercises and prayers as part of their daily routine while over three thousand schools included the Ten Commandments also.

The entire school curriculum was used to reinforce moral principles. English literature was viewed as "the greatest moral power on earth." Mathematics and foreign languages were used to demonstrate the value of rules. History was interpreted to show the importance of bravery and honesty. Many other subjects were taught with the reinforcement of moral values in mind. In 1883 there was pressure to return Bible reading to the school curriculum again. A special reader was introduced for that purpose. The teaching of moral principles became a legislated requirement by 1896.

Throughout the 1880's and 1890's there were debates as to whether a traditional or practical curriculum was most appropriate for Ontarians. In the end, courses that were considered suited to a practical education were removed from the list of core subjects and made optional. In the view of the Education Minister George Ross, the three R's should be the limits of education.[9] There was little movement away from the academic tradition of education during this period.[10] Teachers and principals were required to adhere to strict regulations and guidelines. Education became uniform throughout Ontario and to serve one purpose from kindergarten through to high school; that was in preparation for entry into university.[11]

Yet in the 1880's and 1890's there were emerging in Ontario new ideas about education. Influenced by educationalists such as Friedrich Froebel who originated the kindergarten, Johann Pestalozzi and John Dewey, the New Education Movement began in 1895 followed by the Industrial Education Movement in 1905. The "Old Education" was seen as a study of books and the memorizing of useful and useless information, only incidentally training the mind. The "New Education" was promoted as a study of more than books. It trained the mind and made the acquisition of knowledge incidental to the process. Education began moving away from a subject-centered curriculum to a child-centered curriculum.

As early as 1886, Toronto's public school inspector James Hughes called for a move towards a more practical education. But parents objected to a practical education because they believed that it was inferior to an academic education. Unions objected to a practical education because they believed that it would compete with their apprenticeship programs.

Ontario's public schools began offering manual training programs towards the upswing of the long-wave in 1896. The Macdonald Manual Training Fund, established in 1899, provided funds for three years to local school boards to develop new courses in practical education. By 1903 the fund was operating in 21 Canadian cities, paying the salaries of 45 teachers and training 7,000 boys. Domestic science courses were introduced for girls. When the funds expired, it was proposed that the new courses be funded as a regular part of the curriculum. Examinations for promotions were abolished.

One school principal told a meeting of the Ontario Education Association in 1901 that "the day for arguing the importance of mathematics, classics, English, Moderns and Science has long ago vanished."[12] By 1904 there were seven different high school programs. The Industrial Education Act of 1911 provided the resources for the expansion of industrial education. Central Technical School of Toronto was opened in 1915 at a cost of $2 million dollars, the most expensive school in the province. The following year the Central High School of Commerce moved into its own building. By 1919 there were sixteen technical and commercial high schools with 7,000 full-time students.

As the long-wave began to decline in the 1920's, schools re-oriented themselves back to a traditional academic curriculum. The high schools re-focused their courses on the fifteen percent of students who would go on to some form of post-secondary school education. There was a re-emphasis on the examination to allow universities to sort through qualified students and schools to compare their results with those of others in their promotion of excellence.[13]

When progressive education was re-introduced in 1937, the re-action from the public was swift. The lack of basic skills, the lack of discipline, the seemingly effortless ways of learning with the belief that something would be learned and the lack of testing all came under heavy criticism. By 1941 the movement continued towards a back-to-the-basics education. Ontarians wanted rote learning over experiential learning. Religious education was legislated back into schools in 1944. Only 40 of Ontario's 5000 school boards asked for an exemption. When the opposition party in the Ontario Legislature passed a confidence motion against religion in schools, the minority governing party won the Provincial election that followed by a landslide by representing itself as a defender of Christian values.

In 1945 the Royal Commission on Education was appointed under a justice of the Supreme Court of Ontario John A. Hope. The report that was released five years later reflected the traditional approach to education that was already taking place. The report endorsed subject centered learning over student centered learning. Honesty, Christian love and reward for hard work were the values that exemplified the report. In 1954, C. C. Goldring, the director at the Toronto Board of Education who introduced progressive education in 1937 stated that "there is not in Canada today a publicly supported system of education taught along progressive educational lines for the simple reason that parents and tax-payers would not approve of it."[14]

The move to a practical education on the upswing of the fourth long-wave was prompted by the Federal government in 1960 when it passed the Technical and Vocational Training Assistance Act believing that it must help shape the economy to become more competitive internationally. In its first year, 124 new vocational schools or composite vocational/academic schools were approved. By 1967 there were 335 new schools and 83 additions to existing schools. Under then Education Minister John Robarts the Reorganized Program of Studies was introduced in 1962, dividing the school curriculum into three streams of Arts and Science, Business and Commerce, and Science, Technology and Trades. In theory universities were to accept graduates from all three programs. But in practice, they preferred students who graduated from the Arts and Science academic program.

The Provincial Committee on Aims and Objectives of Education had been studying education in Ontario for three years. Co-chaired by Justice Emmett Hall and elementary school principal Lloyd Dennis, the result was the Hall-Dennis Report of 1968, *Living and Learning*. The report reflected the progressive tendencies of society already taking place. It opposed traditional approaches to education and advocated a child-centered education. There was no more emphasis on hard work or traditional values. Experience and discovery learning were more important than acquiring bodies of arbitrary knowledge. Corporal punishment, after-school detention and other forms of punishment were deemed unacceptable.

For three years the Mackay Committee, chaired by former Lieutenant-Governor Keiller Mackay, a person recognized as the pillar of the establishment, studied the issue of religion in education. In keeping with the times, the report produced in 1969 recommended that religious education as set out in 1944 be removed from the school curriculum. The Bible stories did not encourage objective evaluation of evidence, did not stimulate natural enquiry and did not teach children to think for themselves. Religious education, the report concluded, was a total failure and did not reflect the principles of modern education. The report recommended that children be taught to make their own value judgments.

Two years after the publication of his report Lloyd Dennis could look back and reflect "The days of established order, propriety, virtue and hard work, when schools are institutions of solemn purpose and moral admonition are gone."[15] For those that agreed with the direction that education was going, it meant freedom and individuality. They saw in children an enthusiasm for learning, self confidence and freedom from fear. The critics saw it as unbounded permissiveness and an attack on the pillars of civilization. Progressive education, a teaching philosophy, came to be viewed by some as the source of a medical condition, dyslexia. The Calvinist work ethic was replaced by bohemian listlessness. Some schools seemed to be no more than an extension of Yorkville, a communal haven for hippies just 10 minutes walk from the Ontario legislature. Students from the more experimental schools, such as Everdale Place, had difficulty integrating back into mainstream society and into jobs. Everdale Place had no fixed curriculum and the students were free to come and go as they wished. It had been believed that the freedom would allow students to self-educate.[16]

By the mid 1970's, the downswing of the long-wave, there was a steady move away from progressive education. The Ontario Secondary School Teachers Federation announced that "The present demand for a core curriculum can no longer be denied. There are subject disciplines that are keys to the preservation of our civilization and these should be studied in some depth."[17]

In the 1980's those that were in the basic stream of education had a dropout rate of 79 percent, those in the general stream had a dropout rate of 62 percent and those in the advanced academic stream had a dropout rate of 12 percent. It became clear, as it was clear to educators more than a hundred years earlier, that those who did poorly in school came from the lowest social-economic backgrounds, the very ones now enrolled in the basic and general streams.[18] The wide variety of courses that these students could select from was interpreted to mean that the courses were not fundamental to any education. It was perceived as a disservice to the poor that they should be streamed into a program that was meaningless to them and their future. It was unjust that the poor were not given an equal opportunity to a first class education and that possibly neither they nor their parents understood the implications of streaming. The education system began a move towards a de-streaming process.

There was also a call for greater accountability and a need for assessments. The Provincial Standards Program that was introduced utilized an "outcomes-based" education model. The program required that objectives be defined that were achievable by all children; then tests were instituted to measure the achievement of the objectives. The education system began a move back towards standardized testing. As the long-wave downswing progresses, we have been returning to a traditional education with a uniform core curriculum.

As an expression of changing demographics, over the years, the area known as Yorkville changed from a hippie hangout, to a trendy dining and shopping area for yuppies, and then to an area of exclusive shops, high-end real-estate and expensive art galleries, reflecting the changing lifestyle of Baby Boomers from youth to age.

Linguistic Changes

The work of sociologist Zvi Namenwirth reveals that there was an increasing use of "power words" on the upswing of the long-wave. Profanity, for example, was once controlled by fines and censors and by what is considered civility. The upswing of the fourth long-wave saw an increasing use of profanity. In the 1970's, children were given scripts with interjections of profanity for their acting roles in movies and the audiences would view it with hilarity. By the late 1990's television stations were allowing profanity uncensored, and now it has come into common use almost everywhere. At the same time on the downswing of the long-wave, two new phenomena have entered the English language. The first was concerned with the difference between asking a question and making a statement. The difference between the two began disappearing when people were finishing their sentences with inflexions, elevating the tones of the last few syllables as if asking a question, even when there was no question being asked. The second is "politically correct" speech, such as saying the appropriate things at the appropriate time. Socialization has changed from one of bold assertiveness to one of measuring social consensus.

Hollywood Movies

In recent cultural activities there was a noticeable return to the events of a previous era. The downswing of the long-wave is known for its romanticism, sentimentalism and escapism. The romanticism of the 1940's and 1950's was seen in the countless movies with love stories such as Casablanca and Gone with the Wind and the popularity of actresses such as Doris Day. As the 2000's began, Hollywood has been producing almost countless romantic comedies. The Hollywood formulas of the day dictated that romance was comedic and sex should be accompanied by a combination of drugs, violence or coarse language. The moral theme has returned to the movies. Whereas the upswing brought in numerous movies where the good guy didn't always win, the downswing has brought back the traditional ending where the bad guy gets his just desserts. There are consequences to one's actions. Some even border on moralizing activist messages.

The *Famous Funnies*, published in 1934, was the first comic book to be sold in the U.S. The artistic style and layout were taken from Chinese and Japanese art prints and cartoons. The escapism of the period is seen in the number of superhero comics that were created in the 1940's such as Batman, Spiderman, Wonder Woman and Superman. The 2000's has opened with the X-men, Spiderman, the Hulk and other superhero escapist movies making the blockbuster list. The recent return of structured dancing such as Latin and ballroom is also reminiscent of the long-wave downswing of the 1940's and 1950's.

Censorship and Morality

With an ageing population on the downswing of the long-wave there is a return to a conservative moral society. While each upswing of the long-wave increased sexual freedoms and introduced sexual revolutions, each downswing has reverted to increased levels of censorship with an increasing willingness of the population to comply. The downswing of the second long-wave resulted in the Comstock Act of 1873 that declared information about contraceptives to be obscene and outlawed its distribution. Many people were jailed for contravening this law.

From the 1930's to the 1950's, the downswing of the third long-wave, the movie industry and the comic book industry, fearing government fines and regulations, embarked on self-censorship. The Motion Picture Producers and Distributors of America (MPPDA) put together a Motion Picture Production Code that lasted from the 1930's to 1966. The Comics Code Authority (CCA) was set up as part of the Comics Magazine Association of America, organized in 1954 by twenty-four of the twenty-seven comic book publishers. A stamp was put on all approved comic books whose publishers subscribed to the CCA's code of ethics. This allowed the comics to be distributed on newsstands open to public view. From the 1960's and into the 1990's censorship was increasingly relaxed.

On the downswing of the fourth long-wave, when singer Janet Jackson exposed her breast during the half time show of Super Bowl XXXVIII in 2004, in what she termed a "wardrobe malfunction," there were calls for increased fines and censorship for such conduct. Broadcasters voluntarily put in five second delays on live broadcasts so that they can catch and censor inappropriate materials. Fines imposed jumped from $400,000 in 2003 to $8 million in 2004 for violations of broadcast standards. In 2006 the U.S. House of Representatives voted 379-35 to pass the Broadcast Decency Enforcement Act, increasing the FCC (U.S. Federal Communications Commission) fines from $32,500 to $325,000 per incident.[19]

Crime

With the youthfulness of the long-wave upswings, along with the tensions generated, there were increases in violent crimes. Figures 6.06 and 6.07 show that homicide rates increased in both Canada and the U.S. on the upswings of the third and fourth long-waves. Violent crime was a greater problem on the upswing of the long-wave, yet there exists a great fear of crime on the downswing of the long-wave, even though the crime rate has actually fallen to the lowest level in decades. The reason for this fear may be that as Baby Boomers age, they become more aware of their own mortality. Whereas in youth they had the options of fight or flight, in age neither option is viable for ensuring safety. Another factor is that the upswing of the long-wave produces more issues and events to occupy the newspaper headlines and to divert attention, whereas on the downswing, with fewer issues and events in the headlines, crime garners more attention. The downswing of the long-wave is accompanied by a greater awareness of crime.

The population of prisons today is a reflection of an ageing society. A large proportion of the inmates, now advanced in age, were incarcerated for the crimes of their youth. Youth crime is a major social problem and society must make a greater effort in understanding the problem in order to play an effective role in prevention for the benefit of both youth and society.

Vacation Cruises

As consumers mature and their earnings increase, there is a rise in the consumption of luxury goods. Retail outlets grow in size to respond to the larger group of consumers. Larger houses and furniture are built and larger cars are purchased. The increase in wealth is also reflected in the increase in expensive vacations. Ocean cruises were once the vacation of the wealthy. Now cruise lines cater to a very broad range of incomes. With each downswing of the long-wave, vacation cruises gain in popularity. During a period when the waters are at peace, the ease of travel provided by these hotels on the sea is an ideal way for older, wealthier people to visit multiple destinations in comfort and in luxury. For the cruise line industry, except for during the Great Depression, the most difficult periods have been towards the peaks of the long-wave.

Before pleasure cruises got their official start in the 1920's, we have several glimpses of ocean travel, not for the purpose of passage, but for pleasure and discovery. On the downswing of the first long-wave, writers William Makepeace Thackeray and Charles Dickens both gave accounts of their excursions by ship just for pleasure and discovery in the 1840's, at a time when the Victorians were beginning to discover the joys of tourism. The Peninsula and Orient Line (P. & O.) began offering sightseeing tours around the Mediterranean and by means of a free trip, recruited Thackeray to help promote the excursions. The Thomas Cook travel company is credited with organizing the first cruise in 1841. This first cruise did not have a dedicated ship. Instead passengers had to disembark and change ships at various ports of call to get to their destination and back again.

On the downswing of the second long-wave, Mark Twain in *The Innocents Abroad* describes a year long "pleasure excursion" to Europe and the Holy Land in 1867. He had expected the occasion to be an exciting and joyous affair, but by the end of the year he was barely speaking to many of the passengers. He did make a few new friends and recommended it as a prescription against "prejudice, bigotry and narrow-mindedness." Thomas Cook is also credited for organizing the first "world cruise" from Liverpool to New York to Cairo in 1872. Most of the passengers began to abandon the cruise soon after leaving port and by the time they reached their destination, only a few people remained. In 1891 the Hamburg-America Line began offering pleasure cruises around the Mediterranean and by 1910 was offering a "cruise around the world." This world cruise had over 600 passengers.

The modern cruises as we know them today began on the downswing of the third long-wave in the 1920's. These cruises were lavish affairs for the few who could afford them. It was not uncommon, indeed it was expected, that first class passengers bring a couple dozen pieces of luggage with them. Unlike the previous cruises where ships were allocated when they were not scheduled for other uses, ships were now being built specifically for the purpose of cruising. Since migration to North America was slowing during this period, what had been labelled as the steerage class was converted to the new tourist class. Even into the 1930's, the United States, Britain, France and Germany competed in building the largest and finest of the luxury liners. In 1922 Cunard Lines began offering a world cruise leaving from New York and travelling around the world in four months. During prohibition short cruises became very popular, for once the ships left U.S. boundaries, the passengers could drink all the booze that they wanted. These cruises had a battalion of sailors stationed on deck to ensure that all those that left with the cruise returned with the cruise, no matter if they were dry, wet or waterlogged.

While ocean liners provided cruises, the major part of their business remained passenger transport, but by the late 1950's the commercial jet became the dominant means of transport for world wide travel. It took just over six hours to cross the Atlantic by jet. It took six days to cross the Atlantic by ship. As costs for flying came down, ocean crossing by ship became less desirable. In the early 1960's, over a million people crossed the Atlantic by ship; by the early 1970's, only a quarter of that number did so. Many ocean liners went bankrupt or were sold off. Many of the ships were converted for other uses, sold for low prices or brought to the scrap yard. With the decline of ocean liners, pleasure cruises declined also.

For the few cruise lines that survived, the transportation of vacationers to Caribbean destinations, (which did not have airports at the time), along with some transatlantic crossings, became the new business. By the late 1970's the modern vacation cruise was reborn. Beginning with much smaller ships, by the downswing of the long-wave in the 1990's, cruise ships coming out of the dock yards have surpassed the size of luxury liners of the previous long-wave.

Samuel Cunard was the son of a German immigrant who left the U.S. after the Declaration of Independence and went to Canada. The company that became known as the Cunard Lines was incorporated in 1839. The history of Cunard Lines is the history of the changing influences of the long-wave.

For the first six years Cunard Lines monopolized the transatlantic crossing, being contracted as a mail carrier between England and North America from Liverpool to Halifax. Competition arose in 1845 when the American Ocean Steam Navigation Company began a new mail route from New York to Southampton. Further competition arose in 1852 when the Collins Line entered the transatlantic business with bigger and faster ships. When the Crimean War started in 1854, fourteen vessels were requisitioned by the British admiralty and Cunard was left unable to compete on the transatlantic routes. When the peace treaty was signed in 1856, Cunard Lines looked forward to re-establishing its business but the American Civil War caused a severe drop in migration to the U.S. The Collins Line went bankrupt in 1858.

When passenger travel returned to normal by the downswing of the second long-wave, competition arose from the Inman Line, the White Star Line and from German companies. German ships dominated the transatlantic crossing for about ten of those forty years.

With the onset of WWI the Cunard ships were requisitioned again by the British Admiralty. Twenty-two ships were lost during the war. After the war a massive rebuilding program ensued with stiff competition from several countries, most notably from German companies. The Great Depression hit the Cunard Lines hard and a loan from the British government was required to keep the company afloat. When WWII began, the ships of Cunard Lines were once again requisitioned for the war. The downswing of the third long-wave was known as the Golden Age of Ocean Liners until the upswing of the fourth long-wave, the age of jet travel, marked the decline of ocean travel. With the downswing of the fourth long-wave, Cunard Lines re-emerged again as one of the world's largest cruise lines.

Health and Alternative Medicine

As the downswing of the long-wave continues and the population grows older, we discover that our bodies no longer function like they used to. We get more aches, pains and chronic diseases and naturally there are greater demands for health resources. With growing demand there are responses to meet these demands. The first downswing of the long-wave saw a great influx of people entering medical practice.[20] The downswing of the second long-wave saw the health sector increase its efficiency by forming hospitals.[21] The downswing of the third long-wave saw the rise of different types of health insurance. In the U.S. the insurer Blue Cross began in 1929 with 1500 schoolteachers. By 1945 it had over 19 million members. Twenty percent of the population had hospital insurance in 1942, but by 1954 this figure had grown to sixty percent.[22] Since WWII, medical research and health care costs have expanded rapidly. The fourth long-wave decline is seeing the amalgamation of hospitals into hospital networks, hospital chains and multi-hospital systems. Many of these systems are conglomerates or are vertically integrated to maximize efficiency, and if privately owned, to maximize profits.

Some of the medical specialties founded on the downswing of the long-wave as separate practices were dentistry and optometry, for the simple reason that mainstream medicine did not adequately provide for these needs. With the increasing demand for health care, there were more and more groups of people purporting to have cures for all sorts of ailments. Each downswing of the long-wave gave rise to new forms of alternative medicines. These alternative practitioners made up between ten and twenty percent of total health practitioners, and although the number is relatively small, there is an impact on society and on health practices. Adages such as, "an apple a day keeps the doctor away" and "drink eight glasses of water a day," all have their origins in alternative medicines. Whether or not these alternative medicines work has been difficult to prove since the human body, to some extent, has the natural ability to heal itself, and pain and disease do recede from time to time. The definition of disease also differs from one medical philosophy to another. A large number of the alternative cures that exist today had their beginnings on the downswings of the long-wave. If these alternatives had appeared at any other time in a younger healthier demographic, it would have been more difficult to garner a significant following and most would not have survived. These alternative cures were founded primarily in two periods, the 1820's to 1840's and the 1870's to 1890's.

The period from the 1790's to as late as the 1850's was known as the age of heroic medicine. It was a period when conventional medicine dictated that bloodletting, purging and the ingestion of calomel — mercury oxide — were the scientific means of treating disease. The more that calomel caused the gums to swell, the teeth to fall out, the face to disfigure, sometimes permanently, and the tongue to hang out and drool, the more effectively calomel was believed to be working.

The early alternatives to conventional medicine were herbs used by native populations or traditional remedies practised mainly by women because, and some say fortunately, there were no doctors around. From diverse unorthodox beginnings, some alternative medicines have changed so significantly that they have been accepted into the mainstream fold. Whereas many of the leaders of the social reform movements became active in their youth on the upswing of the long-wave, the founders of these alternative medicines came into prominence on the downswing of the long-wave when they were either past middle age or had personally experienced an extended period of illness.

The Botanical movement was one of several alternative medical movements that began on the downswing of the first long-wave. Beginning at an early age Samuel Thomson (1769 – 1843) followed an elderly woman around collecting herbs and plants and learning about their medicinal value. As far as Thomson could recall there were no doctors in rural New Hampshire. At least he had never met one. Those that looked after the sick were mostly women who made use of herbs passed down through tradition and through the knowledge of natives. When Thomson grew older he tried his hand at farming but found that he had no affection for the work. In 1805 Thomson decided to become an itinerant botanical doctor. He developed a system of treatment which consisted of the application of a sequence of six numbered remedies. The botanical movement, known as Thomsonism, brought Thomson into national prominence in the 1820's and 1830's when he was in his fifties.

The botanical movement went through several transformations after Thomson. The most popular movement to emerge was called "Eclectic Medicine." John King of the Eclectic Medical Institute managed to concentrate botanical medicine into a more palatable form that heralded great commercial success. By the time of the upswing of the long-wave in the 1850's, it was no longer believed that these medicines had any therapeutic value and the movement went into a drastic decline.

The leadership of the movement was passed to John Scudder, one of the students of the Eclectic Medical Institute. By the downswing of the second long-wave, during the 1870's and 1880's, the EMI became the largest medical school in Cincinnati. By 1900 there were thirty state societies in the National Eclectic Medical Association and twenty-two schools throughout the country. On the upswing of the third long-wave, these societies and the schools teaching Eclectic medicine began closing their doors until by 1920, only the Eclectic Medical Institute remained. The Institute was finally closed in 1939.

Hydropathy, or the cold-water cure movement was started by a European peasant by the name of Vincent Priessnitz who, in the 1820's, treated his two broken ribs by drinking lots of cold water. He began treating farm animals and then people with his methods. This therapy emerged in America with great popularity in the 1840's.

Homeopathy began with a German physician named Samuel Christian Hahnemann who had given up traditional medicine because of his inability to cure his patients. Hahnemann became a translator who translated foreign medical texts into German. It was through his experimentation based on one of these texts that he formulated his homeopathic principle that "like cures like." That is, a substance that produces the same symptoms as the disease would cure the disease. Homeopathy was brought to America by the physician Hans B. Gram when he set up his practice in New York in 1825.

Mesmerism or animal magnetism began in France in the 18th century with Franz Mesmer who thought that he could cure sicknesses with magnets. When he discovered that the same effects occurred even when he didn't use magnets, he explained that every animal had a magnetic force within them. People would faint, convulse, dance and do all sorts of unusual things under his influence that mesmerism became not just a healing process, but a great entertainment spectacle as well. The French medical establishment, along with their guest Benjamin Franklin, denounced animal magnetism as a fraud but in 1835, Charles Poyen brought the concept to the shores of America.

Mesmer's explanation about what he had uncovered about human response may have been unsatisfactory to the scientific community at the time, but its effects continued to reverberate well after he left the scene. The methods that he used were modified and incorporated into the areas of psychology and hypnotism on the one hand and into spiritualism and séances on the other, and can even be traced to faith healing in religious services.

Although not considered a founder of an alternative form of medicine, Sylvester Graham became famous as an advocate of good hygiene and the vegetarian diet during this period. He is remembered through the Graham Crackers that bear his name, although the recipe today may not be the same.

The decline of the second long-wave saw the emergence of still more alternative cures. Daniel David Palmer (1845–1913) a Canadian-born schoolteacher, grocery store owner and then a practitioner of magnetic healing, founded Chiropractic medicine in 1895. It was in that year, as one half of the story goes, that he had cured a patient's deafness of 20 years by manipulating a vertebra that he noticed had been misplaced. From there Palmer began developing his theory of chiropractic technique, "chiropractic" meaning "done by hand."

Andrew Taylor Still (1828–1917) founded Osteopathic medicine in 1892. A self-taught medical practitioner, he believed that he could bring about cures by skeletal manipulation. Osteopath literally translates as "bone disease," but Still liked how it sounded, and as with a few other branches of alternative medicine, called his medical practice a disease.

Naturopathy was founded by Benedict Lust (1872 – 1945) in 1901. Lust was a German immigrant seeking his fortunes in America when he contracted tuberculosis. He went back to Germany where he believed that he was healed by using water therapy. He returned to America to open the American School of Naturopathy in Manhattan conferring the N.D. degree of Naturopathic Doctor. His therapies included just about anything that could be considered natural medicine such as herbs, magnetism, sunshine and water.

Christian Science Healing was founded by Mary Baker Eddy (1821 – 1910) when she first advertised herself as a healer in 1868. Having all sorts of ailments but without any success in finding a doctor who could help her, she started her own faith healing service.

While most alternative cures required a potion or manipulation of some sort by the practitioner, a new breed of healers began appearing that claimed that they could call upon divine intervention. Even though the Catholic Church had promoted faith healings and other miracles throughout its history, the early leaders of the protestant reformation regarded them as no more than Christian lore and legends. But all this had changed in America by the 1900's. The likes of William J. Seymour were vaulted to fame with a potent mix of revivalism and faith healing on Azusa Street. Another with claims of miracles of divine healing was John Alexander Dowie. He bought 7000 acres of land in Illinois and built Zion City which soon claimed a population of over six thousand. He died insane and paralyzed.

By 1900 most of what are known as alternative medicines had been founded. During the 1950's, near the trough of the third long-wave, faith healers such Oral Roberts of the Pentecostal movement and other ministers saw a revival. New alternative forms of medicine were kept in check by the expansion of hospital and medical insurance, the Food and Drug Administration's stringent guidelines on what could be considered medicine, and the prosecution of practices that were not considered acceptable to established medicine. Faith healing alone remained a growth frontier because it was considered religion.

In 1971 an American journalist went to China to report on the renewal of relations between the two countries. He fell ill with appendicitis, was operated on and received acupuncture for the relief of pain. His article describing his experience was printed on the front page of the New York Times and attracted considerable interest. Paul Dudley White, the former physician to President Eisenhower, visited China two months later to investigate. When President Nixon visited China in 1972, his personal physician Walter Tkach investigated acupuncture also. Patients were operated on while still conscious yet they exhibited no feeling of pain or discomfort. Immediately after surgery the patients were able to step off the operating table with little or no difficulty, a rare sight at that time for practitioners of Western medicine. Following these accounts, Eastern medicine and health practices began to receive a considerable amount of attention.

With the decline of the fourth long-wave in the 1980's there was another surge in many alternative forms of medicine such as therapeutic touch, visualization, faith healing, holistic medicine and herbal and folk remedies. Naturopathy and homeopathy, facing extinction in the 1970's, were revived as the fourth long-wave declined.

That people still look for alternative cures today is a statement about the difference between the needs of the people and what mainstream medicine can provide. Whereas in the past governments were eager to prosecute alternative medicines as quackery, the high cost of health care has led them to re-think their position. If patients believe that they are benefiting from therapy, then there may be a benefit after all.

In Canada, the progressive publicly funded medicare system faces a foggy future as a provincial court ruled recently that a person has the right to pay for private health care. Clearly the dynamics of what is considered best for society have changed from a time when families with many children could not afford proper health care to the present time when Baby Boomers are older, and some are wealthier, and want to be able to use their wealth to their personal benefit before others. The fear with the opening of private health care is that there would be an abandonment of the public system by doctors. When the public system has to compete with a private system for resources, costs will increase. In 1990 healthcare cost 9 percent of GDP in Canada while in the U.S. it is 12 percent of GDP.[23] Health care in Canada covers all Canadians while in the U.S. tens of millions are without coverage. Whereas inflation has been generally less than three percent, annual increases in health insurance premiums in the U.S. have been above ten percent, setting the stage for a health care crisis. The unfunded post-retirement non-pension benefits offered by government entities in the U.S., such as medical insurance and drug benefits, could exceed a trillion dollars for the current wave of Baby Boomers, potentially sending some of these entities into bankruptcy.

Diseases

Human diseases have many causes. Some are attributed to genetics, some are caused by environmental pathogens, viruses and bacteria, others are caused by the degenerative process of ageing and yet others are related to social pathology. Diseases are related to our general health and our general health is related to our age and the activities in which we engage. As the long-wave moves from a generally younger society to a generally older society, we find that the rise and decline of lifestyle diseases align closely with the social pathology of our age.

Figure 6.08 shows the death rates due to liver disease. Notice that cirrhosis increases on the upswing of the long-wave and decreases with the downswing. It is known that the consumption of alcohol causes liver disease. Compare figure 6.08 with figures 6.09 and 6.10, the per capita consumption of alcohol, and note the matching slopes and turning points. Cirrhosis mirrors the consumption of alcohol very closely.

Temperance historian Jack Blocker gives the following assessment of the consumption of alcohol. From 1830 - 1840, the consumption of absolute alcohol dropped from 4 gallons per capita to 2 gallons per capita. Consumption rose sharply for a few years in the early 1870's after which it declined again and settled at between 1 and 1 1/2 gallons in the 1890's. In 1873, there were 4.8 liquor dealers per 1000 population. This number declined to 3 per 1000 in 1890 and by 1900 there were only 2.6 dealers per 1000. Between 1906 and 1917, consumption of absolute alcohol peaked at 1.7 gallons per capita and dropped to 3/4 of a gallon in 1921 - 1922 after prohibition set in. Once bootleggers became organized, consumption recovered to 1.1 gallons per capita between 1927 and 1930. After the lifting of prohibition, the consumption of alcohol increased until the 1980's, when it faced a period of decline again. Figure 6.10 shows the per capita consumption of three alcoholic beverages, beer, wine and spirits. The rise and decline follows that of the long-wave, with hard liquor topping out first in 1978, then followed by beer in 1981 and wine in 1985. Wine consumption began increasing again after 1995 possibly due to an increasingly popular belief that wine is good for the cardio-vascular system, a belief propagated by reports that claim that drinkers are healthier than non-drinkers. There are other reports that dispute the claim however, stating that those that don't drink as cited in these reports were not long term abstainers but were too sick to drink wine.

Since different concentrations of alcoholic beverages were consumed at different periods in history, in order to understand liquor consumption patterns, historians have collected statistics on the consumption of absolute alcohol. Figure 6.09 shows the per capita consumption of absolute alcohol from 1785 to 1975. There appears to be variances of between seven and thirteen years between Blocker's consumption peaks and Rorabaugh's consumption peaks in the graph. In either case, it can be seen that the peaks and troughs follow closely to that of the long-wave. The heaviest drinkers in the population are males between the ages of 20 and 29 with an average age of 24.[24] Consumption declines to its lowest point after the age of 45. This graph is a reflection of the proportionate number of 24 year olds and the general youthfulness of society. Notice the steep decline in per capita consumption from 1830 to 1845. Compare this change with the steep decline in the number of children under 5 years of age per women 20 to 44 in figure 4.02 and table 4.00 starting from 1820 to 1850. The slope is much steeper from usD to usE than it is from usE to usF. This proportionate drop in the number of children in society is reflected years later in a steep decline in the consumption of alcohol. The baby-boom peak in 1957 is followed by an alcohol consumption peak in 1981 some 20 years later also. Carrying this correlation to other parts of the graph, the consumption peak in 1810, 1910 and 1860 (Blocker: 1917 and 1872) reflects a proportionately large number of drinking age men at that time. The consumption of alcohol peaked in 1910 (Rorabaugh) with the beginning of state prohibition in Georgia. The steep drop in the consumption of alcohol from 1917 (Blocker) onwards took place when a large number of these drinking age men were shipped overseas to fight a war. When they returned, prohibition was in effect. Looking at the overall graph, the consumption of absolute alcohol dropped from a high of 7 gallons per capita in 1810 to fluctuate between 1 and 3 gallons per capita currently. Taking a longer-term view, this is a general reflection of an ageing society. Those under 17 years of age once composed 50 percent of the population, but now they compose only about 25 percent of the population.

Our mental health changes with the long-wave also. Figure 6.11 shows that suicides increase with the long-wave upswing. With greater social stress, there is greater mental stress; some of the more publicly known suicides of the fourth long-wave were committed by rock musicians. Suicides also increase with increasing economic stress, during economic depressions.

Diabetes is known as the disease of the affluent. In poor countries where the diet is basic, the rate of diabetes is very low. In wealthy countries where people indulge in a diet of rich foods, the diabetes rate is high. As our diets have changed and our age increased from the upswing of the long-wave to the down-swing, diabetes has been growing at an alarming rate. In the 1960's and 1970's with food shortages and inflation, when a bottle of pop became a half bottle of pop and a candy bar shrank to half the size while its wrapper grew, when a burger was a more meaningful name than hamburger because people had to look to find the patty, young, growing, active boys and girls could not seem to get enough to eat. "Where's the beef?" one franchise asked, implying that it had all but disappeared from everyone else's burgers but theirs. In the 1990's when food was cheap and plentiful, fridges grew to twice the size, shopping was twice the pleasure, restaurant portions contained twice the calories and people could not seem to eat enough to clear their plates. As the population ages it is much less active and at a greater risk of diabetes. Figure 6.12 shows that deaths due to diabetes were increasing throughout the third long-wave well after insulin was discovered by Drs. Frederick Banting and Charles Best at the University of Toronto in the 1920's. The death rate began to decrease in the late 1940's, reached the lowest level in the 1980's and has begun to move up since. The treatment of diabetes is among the top medical expenses in Canada. As the population ages, there is a danger that diabetes deaths will continue to increase.

Retirement and Pensions

On the downswing of the long-wave, there is an increasing number of people entering retirement. With retirement comes an increase in the disbursement of pension benefits and it is on the downswing of the long-wave that pension issues become critical. During times when there are a growing number of elderly people, it should not be surprising to find a clustering of activities to support their needs.

Canada

The Hudson's Bay Company is North America's oldest company. Chartered in 1670 to engage in the fur trade, its history is a reflection of the history of North America. When it amalgamated with the North West Company in 1821 it was already over 150 years old and had employees with lengthy terms of service. The amalgamation agreement was one of the earliest records to contain clauses stipulating the terms of employee retirement, pensions and the rights of retired employees and their dependants. Both active and retired employees were entitled to shares in the company and profit sharing payments. In 1826 the company increased the incentives for retirement by increasing the share of profits for retirees. By 1840 the Benefit Fund was established for those at retirement age but who were "in limited circumstances." Pensions were given to those over sixty years of age whose conduct was shown to "merit such consideration" and subject to the "pleasure of the Governor and Committee." Employee contribution rates were established for all employees.[25]

For members of the British Civil Service, including those living and working in British North America, the pensions were not as well managed as those of the Hudson's Bay Co. On the downswing of the first long-wave from the 1820's to the 1830's, the British Civil Service retirement age was raised from sixty to sixty-five, pension payments were reduced and employee contributions were made mandatory. Employees reacted unfavorably to mandatory contributions, but that provision would not be changed until 1857, on the upswing of the next long-wave.

On the downswing of the first long-wave, as the general population was getting older, the Hudson's Bay Company found that they had a correspondingly large number of older people who could no longer handle the rigours of the outdoors that the fur trade demanded. The pension became the means of removing these older workers from employment and an inducement to compliance. For the British Civil Service on the other hand, inadequate planning to meet the needs of an ageing staff created pension problems that required resolution. As we view pensions through the lens of the long-wave, we find that pensions were created to assist corporations in keeping their staff young and active and also to provide a means of support to employees in their advance years. Yet at the most critical periods of mass retirement, there were unexpected economic changes and actuarial miscalculations that caused pension shortfalls and payment reductions. Contribution rules, pension qualifications and payments were changed to meet more stringent economic conditions on the downswing of the long-wave until the bulge of retirees had passed through the system before the rules were relaxed again.

The first pensions in North America arose from paternalism, disinterested benevolence or business considerations and were given to a very fortunate few. Pensions were not always bestowed with the needs of employees in mind. Most people were left on their own, depended on charities such as almshouses, or depended on their children to support them through the last years of their lives. Approximately three quarters of those that had reached 65 years of age or older continued to work in order to support themselves. Many others were in no condition to work, and due to the state of medical sciences at that time, did not live long thereafter. Considering that life expectancy was less than 50 years for most of the 19th century, few people lived long enough to retire.

The next downswing of the long-wave from the 1870's to the 1890's saw an emerging awareness of the ageing society. Whereas youth once made up more than half the population, by the downswing of the second long-wave, the large number of people of advanced age initiated the development of the modern pension.

After Canadian Confederation in 1867 the Superannuation Act of 1870 was passed in the House of Commons to purge the civil service by getting "rid of officers who are no longer capable of discharging their duties in an efficient manner." Those who were sixty years of age or had the required minimum years of service were entitled to a pension if they were incapable of performing their duties. The pension amounted to a maximum of 70 percent of salary based on the average of the last 3 years of service and 2 percent entitlement per year of service, with a minimum service of 10 years. This has become the basis of the modern pension calculation. The contribution rate for those that earned over $600 per year was 4 percent of salary and those under $600 per year was 2 percent of salary for a maximum of 35 years. The program was funded solely by employees.[26]

Government contributions into the fund started in 1906 when a two-tier pension system was created. Those who entered the civil service before 1893 would continue as before, but those that entered after 1893 would benefit from the new funding structure.

What is considered the first modern private pension was introduced by the Grand Trunk Railway of Canada in 1874 with a 2.5 percent
employee contribution rate and matching contributions from the employer. Many railways and banks followed the lead of the Grand Trunk
Railway. The Canadian banks felt that their pension plans should be
protected by legislative authority. Parliament passed the Pension Fund
Societies Bill in 1887 on their petition. In 1889 Sir John A. Macdonald
ordered the Royal Commission on the Relations of Labour and Capital.
Some of the recommendations of the Royal Commission were that the
government should encourage individual savings for retirement and create and administer a pool for those savings that would accumulate with
interest. Retirement could start as early as age fifty, but definitely by age
sixty-five. These contributions were to be locked in to protect the workers from themselves, for the report noted that the working man passes
more taverns to and from work than savings banks. Thus began the concept of annuities that was adopted by the government twenty years later
and the concept of locked-in contributions that was adopted by pension
legislation in the 1960's.

Under pressure for a national pension plan, the government of
Canada stated that it was not in the business of charity and that a national
pension plan was the first step towards socialism. Even though cabinet
ministers, judges, civil servants, military servicemen, railway workers and
bankers had pensions, the government's response was that these were
deferred wages rather than pensions. With that argument, the pension
took a step toward being viewed as a right. What was finally passed in
1908 was the Government Annuities Act that allowed workers to save
for themselves. The first public pension plan would not be introduced
for another twenty years when there would be even greater pressure for
government intervention, on the downswing of the third long-wave.

It is on the downswing of the third long-wave that we come upon
statistical data to help us see what has been happening in demographics
to bring about the recurring attention to pensions. From figures 4.14
and 4.18, the percent change per decade in population ages 65+ and 70+
(Canada) we can see that the number of people reaching over 65 years of
age was increasing rapidly from the 1920's to the 1960's, encompassing

the complete downswing of the third long-wave. As this rapid growth compelled a response to increasing health care needs, it also compelled a response in pension plans and government legislation towards a retiring population. The War Tax Act of 1917 and other legislation which followed gave special tax treatment to pension contributions. James Shaver Woodsworth, a Labour MP and former Methodist minister brought up the issue of old age pensions in Parliament in 1926. The Old Age Pension Act was passed in 1927 as a national pension plan. In the 1930's there was renewed interest in government annuities in which corporate and private pensions invested their funds. From 1908 to 1930 an average of 524 annuity contracts were issued per year. But from 1930 to 1939 an average of 4,400 contracts were issued per year.[27] There was also a sharp increase in the creation of pension plans. Between 1900 and 1939 there were 1,065 plans created, but between 1940 and 1947 there were 2,340 plans created. In a survey of companies offering pensions, only 60 percent of the 1.2 million workers had pension entitlements by this time.[28] Government annuities became the main funding instruments for pension plans. When insurance companies introduced group life and pension plans in the U.S. to reduce administrative costs, the Canadian government followed suit and introduced group annuities also. The growth of group annuities peaked sometime in the late 1950's when there were 966 group contracts covering 236,145 employees in 1955 and 1,556 group contracts covering 185,000 employees in 1960.[29]

The Old Age Security Act (OAS) was passed in 1951 and the Canada and Quebec Pension Plans (CPP/QPP) were set up in 1965. Both were available only to those over seventy years of age. The age was not lowered to sixty-five until 1970, when the growth rate for that age group was slowing.

In the aftermath of the stock market crash of the 1930's, pension plans avoided investment in stocks for almost two decades, but by the 1950's, U.S. pension plans began re-entering the stock market and in the 1960's Canadian pension plans re-entered also. Holdings of assets in stocks in 1960 were only ten percent but rose to forty-five percent during the 1970's and 1980's.[30]

The growth rate of the number of people with pension plans began to slow in the 1960's and 1970's and even declined in the early 1980's. With the unexpected rise of inflation in the 1970's and a rise in those over sixty-five years of age, many plans were facing deficiencies but by the 1980's, surpluses became common.

Throughout the 1980's and 1990's there was a great amount of optimism about the promise of pensions in retirement. With the stock market moving up by leaps and bounds, pension plans were making tremendous gains on investment. For those two seemingly short decades, any suggestions that there could be future short falls were kept from the public eye. Again referring to figures 4.16 and 4.20, the growth rate for the number of retirees declined in the 1960's, rose in the 1970's and declined from the 1980's onward. Pension surpluses made possible generous pension contribution holidays and early retirement packages.

United States

In the United States the American Express company, affiliated with the railroads, was the first to introduce a private pension plan in 1875 on the downswing of the second long-wave. The Baltimore and Ohio Railroad (B. & O.), the Pennsylvania Railroad and many other railroads followed. For the railroads the pension plan was a means of removing employees who were unable to work. The many railroad accidents of the period were seen as a signal to railroad management that they needed to reduce employee errors that were blamed on ageing employees. In 1900 the Pennsylvania Railroad retired all employees over the age of 70 by giving them one percent of the average of the last ten years salary for every year worked.

It has been a tradition for governments to offer their military servicemen pensions. The Civil War pension bill was passed in 1862 in keeping with that tradition. By 1880 the federal government was making pension payments to over 100,000 claimants. When the 1890 Pension Act lowered eligibility requirements, over 600,000 applications were received. By the mid 1890's the Civil War pension made up over forty percent of federal expenditures. The Confederate states provided a pension to their soldiers also.

As the number of seniors began to increase in the 1920's as seen in figure 4.16, pensions began to face mounting pressures. When the Morris Packing Co. failed in 1923, it left a pension fund that was unable to cover pension benefits for 400 retirees and 3500 participants. U.S. Steel had offered a very generous pension in the early years with 20 years service plus age 60. In 1915 the qualifications were increased to 25 years service and age 65 and then again in 1918. The Pennsylvania Railroad did not operate its pension in a separate fund and found that by the end of the 1920's, it was paying its 9,500 pensioners eight percent of payroll.

During the depression approximately ten percent of all pension plans were discontinued or suspended. Other plans reduced benefits or required that employees and retirees share the costs. Companies in financial difficulties tried to shift costs by moving people into retirement. The number of people drawing pensions doubled during this period.[31] The average age of railroad workers increased from 32 years in 1920 to 42 years in 1930. As the railroads reduced their work force by forty percent, approximately 700,000 workers were laid off and the number of railroad pensioners increased from 34,000 to 56,000. While older pension plans ran into financial difficulties, younger companies continued to establish new ones. Between 1927 and 1932 the number of new pension plans created rivaled the numbers that came into existence during WWI.

With mounting pressure to provide for an ageing population, ten states had old age pensions by 1930. Nineteen more states added pensions by the end of 1934. That same year Francis Townsend, a California doctor, claimed that he had the support of 25 million voters when he called for a nationwide old age pension program. Social Security became a reality in 1935.

Between 1932 and 1938 almost 300 employers began new pension plans, approximately the total number that was in existence in 1929. Pension contribution payments became tax deductible and pension trusts were exempt from taxes on investment, which gave employers the incentive to create new plans. Employers found that pensions were useful in retaining employees. Considering that young employees did not care much about pensions, and during WWII many of the able young men were shipped off to fight the war, pensions attracted more experienced employees. In 1938 pensions covered 2 million employees but by 1945 they covered 6.5 million employees. From 1942 to 1944 four thousand new pension plans were created. From the 1940's to the 1950's pensions became a major negotiation concern with unions. With the large amount government spending during WWII and the post war era fueling the economy, along with the rapid population growth of the baby boom years, pension plans were able to meet the needs of retirees.

Wave Four: Canada and U.S.

With a keen memory of the stock market crash of 1929, pension plans generally avoided the stock market altogether. As the downswing of the fourth long-wave continued the stock market was rediscovered. When pension plans began moving money into stocks, investment returns for everyone grew by leaps and bounds. The appearance of pension surpluses made pension contribution holidays and early retirement possible for many workers. The market moved even higher when mutual funds were promoted for widespread public investment. If there was ever a time that workers owned the means of production, it was now; not through revolution, nor through the ideology of communism, but through the savings in their pension plans in a free enterprise system. Within a generation workers and retirees, through their pension plans, became the largest owners of stocks, bonds and real-estate in the world. A large segment of the population also had individual holdings of mutual funds and stocks.

After the stock market correction from 2000 to 2002 many pension plans found that they were in a funding shortfall. The Ontario Teachers' Pension Plan valued at $96 billion, for example, estimated that it was under funded by $32 billion in 2006 even though earnings increased by 17 percent and the Toronto Stock Exchange was at new highs. There are currently 1.6 teachers for every retiree. The ratio would be reduced to one to one in coming years.[32] An estimated 72 percent of Canada's private pension plans were under funded in June 2005, up from 53 percent six months earlier.

Concerned with future liabilities, companies moved away from defined benefit pension plans guaranteeing a fixed income at retirement, to defined contribution plans providing no guarantees at all. In 1980 approximately 38 percent of Americans had a defined benefit pension plan. By 1997 only 21 percent did so. Currently the worker to retiree ratio for these plans is almost 1 to 1, down from 3.5 to 1 in 1980. Companies such as General Motors, with over 100,000 active employees, have about three times more retirees than workers. In the 1960's General Motors had about eleven employees for every retiree. As the worker to retiree ratio shrinks, a shrinking number of workers will have to contribute more of their earnings to support a growing number of retirees.

Retirement Benefit	Shortfall
Corporate Pensions	$140 Billion
Corporate Post Employment Benefits	$280 Billion
State Pensions	$284 Billion
Federal Pensions (Civilian & Military)	$4500 Billion

Table 6.00 U.S. Pension Shortfalls
(S&P Predicts Widening Gap in Pension Under-funding for Companies, Federal, State and Local Governments, June 6, 2006, www.standardandpoors.com).

Even before the Baby Boomers have begun to retire en masse, pension shortfalls have become a liability issue for many companies and for society as a whole. With no wartime spending or post war reconstruction as in the previous downswing of the long-wave, and with population growth rates at their lowest in modern history, the ability to pay for the future needs of a large retiring population has become a looming crisis. In San Diego for example, approximately a quarter of the city's budget is used to make pension payments. Pensions have again become a major negotiation issue with unions. In many countries mandatory retirement at age 65 has been overturned, either because there is not enough money to fund the large number of retirees, the employees themselves have no desire to retire, or the employees do not have enough savings to retire.

Table 6.00 shows the estimated pension shortfalls calculated by Standard and Poor's. Whether these shortfalls must be made up by the companies, taxpayers, or in default to pensioners, the scenario does not bode well for the future of the economy. It is estimated that if these shortfalls are allowed to materialize, the deficits needed to pay the retirement bill will overwhelm the economy.

Philanthropy

As people enter retirement, there is a greater tendency to be involved in charitable works and a small proportion of people make monetary contributions to philanthropy. Some of these monies go to causes which many agree are beneficial to society such as the building of schools, libraries, hospitals and scientific and medical research facilities. Some monies go to alleviating the conditions of poverty. Others support arts and culture. Still others go to purely ideological causes such as influencing the outcome of elections and promoting regional instability. As Baby Boomers enter retirement, many charitable organizations are anticipating a wave of philanthropy.

Some people begin their philanthropy early in life while others wait until they retire; still others contribute to philanthropy only in their will. This is a very large time frame over which philanthropy can start in peoples' lives. The period from retirement to death alone could encompass a period of thirty years, which makes philanthropy a widely dispersed activity. Even so, Waldemar Nielsen's work on the history of philanthropy follows the long-wave well. He selects three groups of philanthropists to represent successive generations of donors. Each generation of each group also represents the successive generations of the long-wave. Although large donors currently contribute approximately fifteen percent of the total charitable donations, large donors exert a greater influence on the direction of philanthropy.

Representing the philanthropists of the second long-wave are the Baby Boomers John D. Rockefeller and Andrew Carnegie. When they retired on the downswing of the second long-wave, they were the two greatest philanthropists of the time. Both were reputed for their astute and sometimes ruthless business practices, but both gave a substantial proportion of their earnings to good causes when they were in their youth and into their retirement. Rockefeller tithed from his first pay-check. This was before personal income tax existed and giving had no tax advantage.

At the time that Carnegie sold his shares in Carnegie Steel for half a billion dollars to J. P. Morgan in 1901, he was the richest man in the world. He wanted to die a poor man, so he devoted the rest of his life to giving his money away. Carnegie came from an impoverished family, started work at the age of thirteen and married at the age of fifty-one, after his mother died. He was mostly self educated, was an avid reader and borrowed books from a private library that was made available to the local community of his youth. Among his many philanthropic endow-ments, he helped to establish over 2500 libraries in the U.S., Canada and in many other countries.

John D. Rockefeller was the oldest of five children. His father was a patent medicine salesman who often abandoned the family. When John was 16 years of age, the family depended on him for support. His education consisted of a three month course in bookkeeping after which he got himself a job as a clerk. By the start of the Civil War Rockefeller was a partner in a wholesale produce company. His venture into the in-fant oil business made him the richest man in the world after he retired. The major foundations of endowment created by Rockefeller were the General Education Board, the Rockefeller Sanitary Commission, the Rockefeller Foundation, the Laura Spelman Rockefeller Memorial and Rockefeller University, which has produced a number of Nobel laureates in medicine.

Julius Rosenwald represents Generation 'X' of the second long-wave. Rosenwald came from a poor immigrant family. He completed two years of high school and then went to work in a relative's clothing business. Eventually he started a clothing business of his own. In 1895 he bought into the struggling Sears, Roebuck and under his management the company prospered. Within 15 years his shares were worth $200 million. Rosenwald's charities included Hull-House and Booker T. Washington's

Tuskegee Institute. His funds helped to create 5300 schools for black children in the Southern States.

Representing the philanthropists of the third long-wave are Albert and Mary Lasker, Arnold Beckman and Walter Annenberg. The Albert and Mary Lasker Foundation helped revitalize the American Cancer Society when it was struggling for funds in the 1940's. The Lasker Awards in Medical Research anticipated many Nobel Prize winners. Approximately forty-nine Lasker winners went on to claim the Nobel honor. Arnold Beckman invented a meter that could measure the acidity of lemon juice. He created a company that became one of the largest manufacturers of scientific and medical instruments. He provided grants of tens of millions of dollars to many universities. Walter Annenberg was a media mogul who owned many newspapers, television stations and magazines including TV Guide and the teenage fashion magazine Seventeen. His endowments included hospitals, universities, public broadcasting and a donation of a billion dollar art collection to the New York Metropolitan Museum.

Representing the philanthropists of the fourth long-wave are Warren Buffet of Berkshire Hathaway, Bill Gates of Microsoft, Leslie Wexner and George Soros. Both Buffet and Soros, being born in 1930, belong to the very tail end of the Generation 'X' of the third long-wave, but have enjoyed all the economic advantages of the Baby Boomers of the fourth long-wave. The Bill and Melinda Gates Foundation is the world's largest foundation, being endowed by the world's richest man, Bill Gates, and by Warren Buffet, the world's second richest man. As the Baby Boomers of the fourth long-wave begin to retire, Robert Avery of the Federal Reserve estimates that approximately 10.4 trillion dollars will flow into philanthropic causes between 1990 and 2040.

Funeral Services

With the short life expectancies of the past, very few people lived long enough to enjoy retirement. But whether or not we retire, we all meet death some day and funeral services have altered to meet changing needs.

With an ageing society comes the development of a variety of funeral services.

Prior to the downswing of the first long-wave, the burial of a body was taken care of by family and neighbors. They would wash and lay out the body and dig the grave. A local carpenter or cabinet maker would be asked to build a coffin.

Only on the downswing of the first long-wave was there sufficient work to enable the role of the undertaker to become a full time occupation. This is the first time that advertising for undertakers as a primary occupation is found. The role of the undertaker was to clean and lay out the body, provide a coffin and transport the body to the grave site. Previously family or neighbors had to make all these arrangements because no single person provided this range of services.

The downswing of the first long-wave brought in several innovations for funerals also. Coffins made from stone, marble and "hydraulic cement" were patented in 1835. The first American patent was granted for a metal coffin in 1836. In 1843 a "corpse preserver" was patented and in 1846 a patent was granted for a "refrigerator for corpses." This "refrigerator" would be used for over two decades before a better one would be invented on the downswing of the next long-wave. Eventually embalming would reduce the need for such devices.

The downswing of the second long-wave continued to bring many changes to the funeral service. The period from 1875 to 1900 was a time of tremendous growth for trade organizations and funeral services were no exception. Between 1865 and 1880 most of the major cities had organized associations for undertakers. By 1882 undertakers began organizing under the name of Funeral Directors. It was the first step in moving from an occupation that provided mainly products for a funeral to being an occupation that provided professional services.

Cremation, once rejected as being pagan, began gaining acceptance. Dr. F. Julius Le Moyne constructed the first crematory in his home in 1876 for himself and his friends. Between 1876 and 1884 there were 41 cremations. From 1885 to 1900 those numbers increased to 13,281. Although cremation was gaining acceptance, it was used in less than one percent of deaths. By 1900 there were twenty-four crematories in the U.S.

In 1881 the New York Cremation Society was founded. Numerous other cremation societies were established for the purpose of disseminating information about cremation between 1881 and 1885.

The placing of flowers at funerals was once rejected as pagan and a waste of money. The traditional way of signifying death was by hanging a black crepe on the door. But the turning point of acceptance came with the death of Reverend Henry Ward Beecher in 1887 when a sea of flowers filled his funeral.

Embalming was done extensively during the Civil War to enable the transport of bodies back home. By the bottom of the second long-wave, it became the accepted way of preserving the body. At first embalming met with opposition because it was seen as a mutilation of the body, the temple of God. But with the invention of the embalming needle and good advertising, objections disappeared. By 1900 most of the traditions of the modern funeral service were established but further refinements and developments in licensing, regulation and education would continue.

In the 1920's the funeral home became the place to house the remains of the dead awaiting interment rather than the home. As there was an increasing number of elderly from 1920 and 1950 (the downswing of the third long-wave), who would eventually need funeral services, this period also saw growing complaints against funeral homes. Objections arose about embalming and the public display of bodies as being pagan. The expensive wood, cloths and other materials used in making a casket were criticized by those who wanted to have simpler funerals. The costs of funerals were seen as outrageously high. The flowers and other ornamentation were seen as a waste of money, and the need for funeral clothes and jewelry were viewed as being overly extravagant. As we move down the fourth long-wave and the use of funeral services begin to escalate, we can expect the work of funeral directors to move back into mainstream awareness.

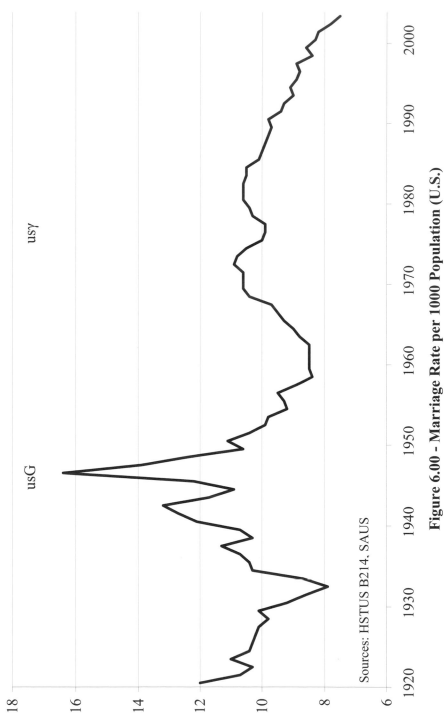

Figure 6.00 - Marriage Rate per 1000 Population (U.S.)

Sources: HSTUS B214, SAUS

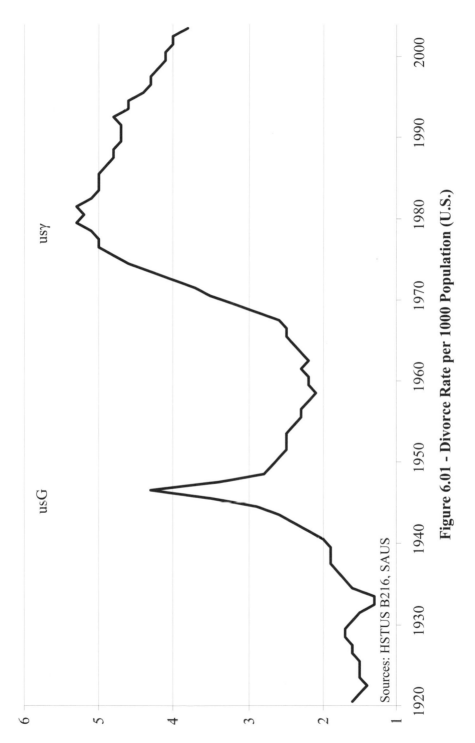

usγ

usG

Sources: HSTUS B216, SAUS

Figure 6.01 - Divorce Rate per 1000 Population (U.S.)

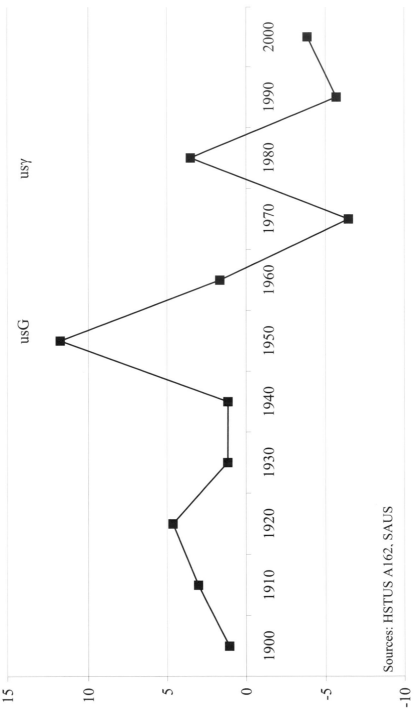

Sources: HSTUS A162. SAUS

Figure 6.02 – Percent Change Per Decade in Married Couples to Population Ratio (U.S.)

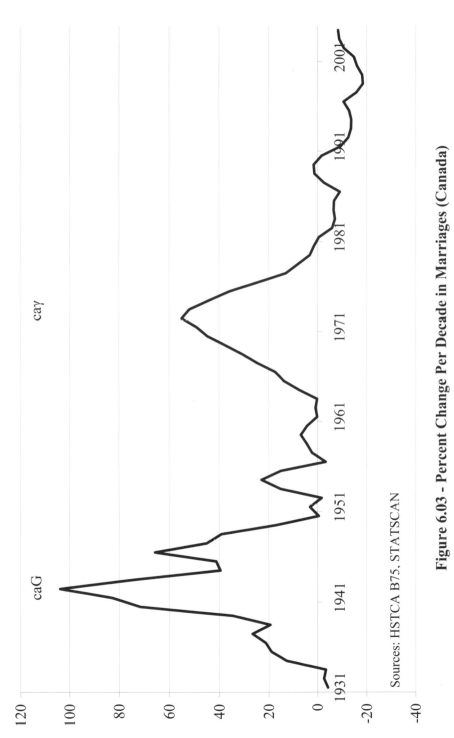

Figure 6.03 – Percent Change Per Decade in Marriages (Canada)

Sources: HSTCA B75, STATSCAN

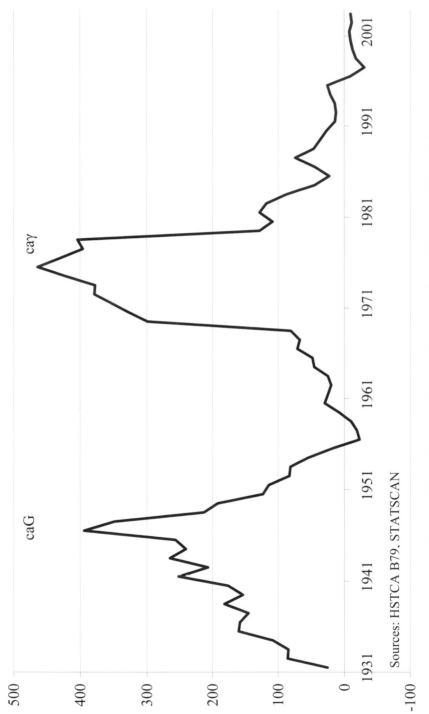

Figure 6.04 – Percent Change Per Decade in Divorces (Canada)

Sources: HSTCA B79. STATSCAN

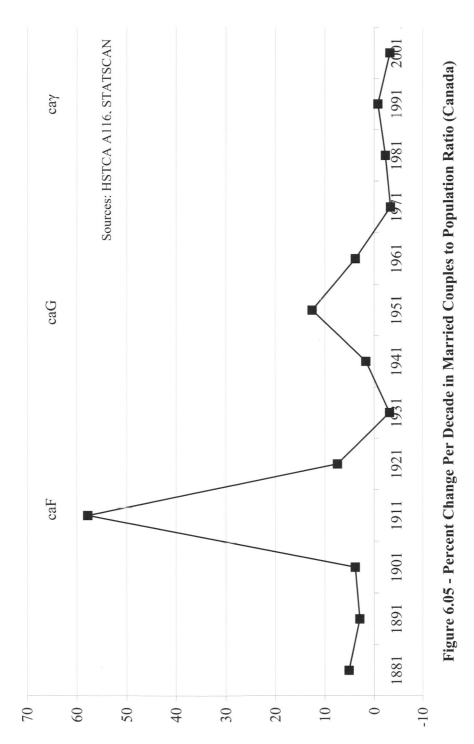

Figure 6.05 - Percent Change Per Decade in Married Couples to Population Ratio (Canada)

Sources: HSTCA A116, STATSCAN

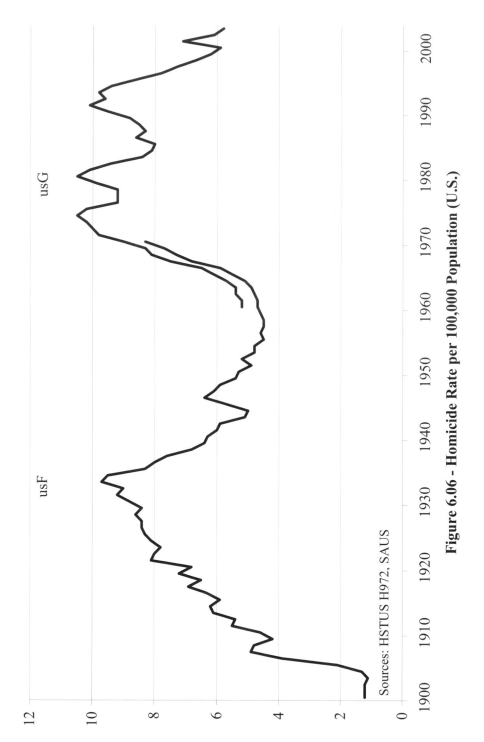

Sources: HSTUS H972, SAUS

Figure 6.06 – Homicide Rate per 100,000 Population (U.S.)

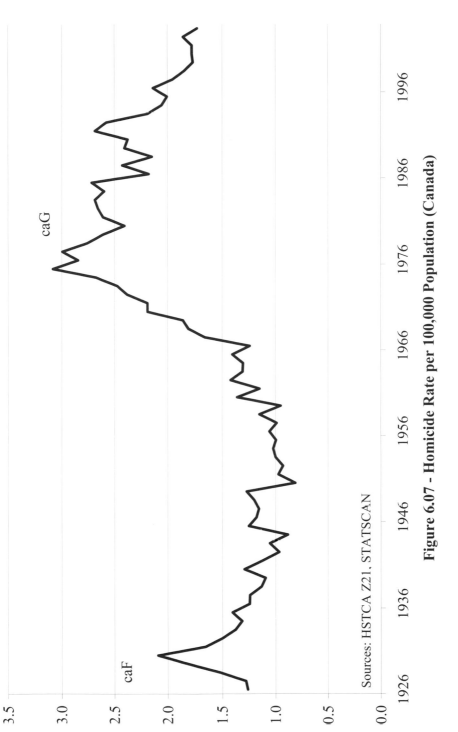

Figure 6.07 – Homicide Rate per 100,000 Population (Canada)

Sources: HSTCA Z21. STATSCAN

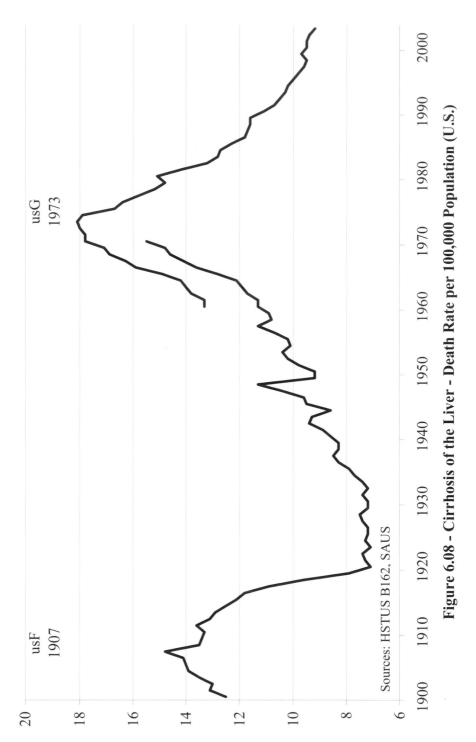

Figure 6.08 – Cirrhosis of the Liver – Death Rate per 100,000 Population (U.S.)

Sources: HSTUS B162, SAUS

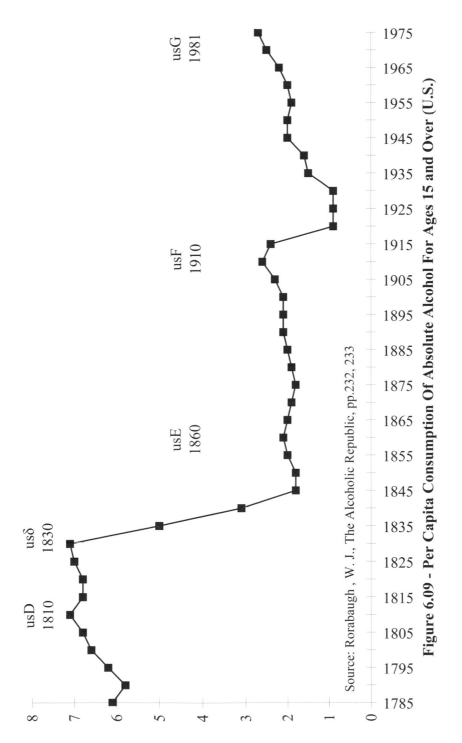

Figure 6.09 - Per Capita Consumption Of Absolute Alcohol For Ages 15 and Over (U.S.)

Source: Rorabaugh , W. J., The Alcoholic Republic, pp.232, 233

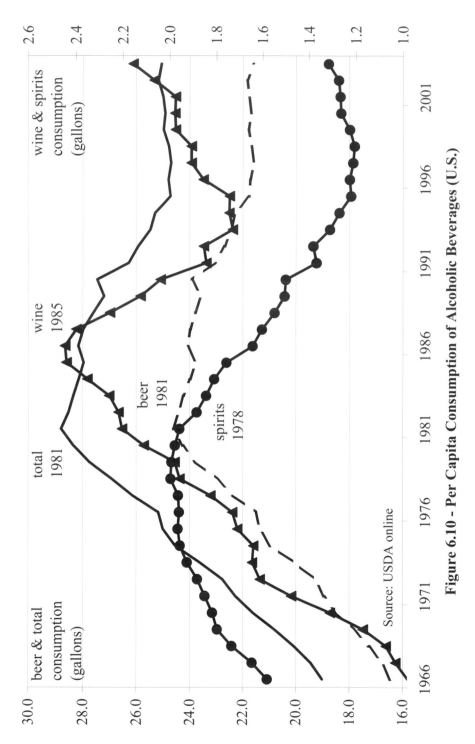

Figure 6.10 - Per Capita Consumption of Alcoholic Beverages (U.S.)

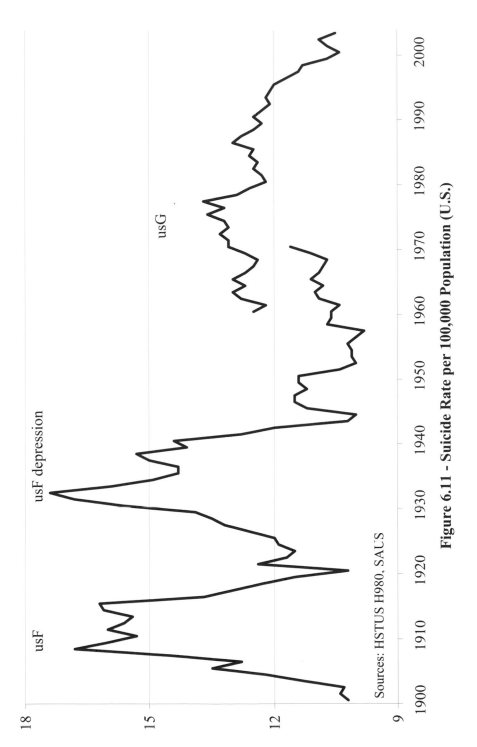

Figure 6.11 - Suicide Rate per 100,000 Population (U.S.)

Sources: HSTUS H980, SAUS

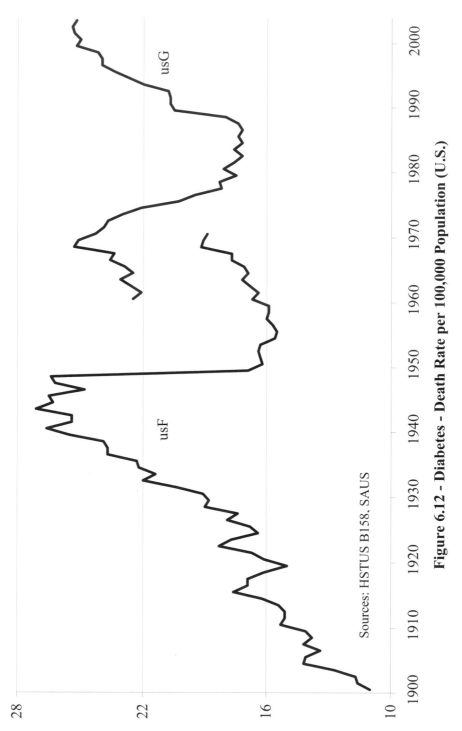

Figure 6.12 – Diabetes – Death Rate per 100,000 Population (U.S.)

Sources: HSTUS B158, SAUS

7 MALTHUS AND LONG-WAVES

In 1798, at a momentous time in British history, the beginning of the Industrial Revolution, the Anglican clergyman Thomas Robert Malthus released a book entitled, *An Essay on the Principle of Population*. Malthus reasoned that population grows exponentially while food supply only grows arithmetically. Since the two rates of growth are dramatically different, population would soon outgrow the nation's ability to produce enough food to sustain itself. In a period of growing inflation, Malthus blamed Britain's 'Poor Laws' for providing social assistance to the poor, enabling the poor to bid up the price of grain. Taking a cue from the plant and animal worlds, he reasoned that populations tend to grow to the limits of food and land. These 'Poor Laws', which he opposed, were encouraging population growth. When we endow animals with human characteristics, we get a warm and fuzzy feeling and call it anthropomorphism. But when humans are endowed with animal characteristics, it is more likely to be regarded as a science. The influence of Malthus' book induced even liberal parliamentarians to call for the sterilization of the poor so that England would not be overrun by a starving and landless population.

Mathematical pronouncements aside, Giovanni Botero had said the same thing about population and the limits of food and land about two hundred years earlier. And there were others that followed him. But Malthus' book appeared at a most propitious time. Unbeknownst to Malthus he was living at the beginning of a period of tremendous population growth in Britain, a period also, when Britain began to take the census.

Sitting in the midst of the Industrial Revolution, Malthus did not realize that technological improvements would enable farming techniques and food supply to meet growing demand, but his theories would be revived whenever there was a period of sustained population growth, as happens cyclically with the long-wave.

By the 1820's Malthus had observed a period of falling prices, drops in marriages and birthrates and a population that was not growing as he had anticipated. To that he contended that moral restraint was being practised more than he had realized.

Before Malthus population growth was perceived as both a result and a cause of prosperity. Population growth was equated with the growth, power and progress of the state. But Malthus' writing had sufficient influence to cast doubt onto the old belief.

A few contemporaries were opposed to Malthus' theories. Alexander Everett surveyed Europe and noted only "two or three small spots, such as England, Holland, and Switzerland, that can be fairly considered as populous; and these are precisely the most flourishing and prosperous parts of the whole region."[1] Everett's arguments against Malthus are particularly interesting because within these arguments are illustrated some of the dynamics of the long-wave. Writing in the early 1800's, he states:

The economical effect of an increase of population, is an augmentation in the supply of labor and in the demand for its products. The wants of the new comers create the new demand, and their labor furnishes the new supply. These principles are too obvious to require any development;

...

...an increase of population on a given territory is followed immediately by a division of labor; which produces in its turn the **invention of new machines, an improvement of methods in all the departments of industry, and a rapid progress in the various branches of art and science.** The increase effected by these improvements in the productiveness of labor is obviously much greater in proportion than the increase of population, to which it is owing. The population of Great Britain, for example, doubled itself in the course of the last century, while improvements in the modes of applying labor, made during the same period, have increased its productiveness so much, that it would probably be a moderate estimate to consider its products as a thousand times greater than before.[2]

Everett's writing reveals remarkable insight into the human character at a time when statistics were still sparsely collected. Inventions follow demographic changes very closely. The relationship between growth in inventions and population growth is found in the percent change per decade in patents issued in Appendix B.

While Malthus' ideas were falling out of favor in the 1830's, they found new life in the hands of John Stuart Mill by the 1840's. Malthus' ideas gave Mill cause to advocate birth control as a method of population control. Although Malthus himself believed that birth control was immoral, his ideas would be called upon for support on each upswing of the long-wave.

Charles Darwin and A. R. Wallace were each inspired by Malthus as the basis for their evolutionary theory published in 1859. British philosopher Herbert Spencer would use "survival of the fittest" in his social theory that became the justification of laissez-faire capitalism on the downswing of the long-wave. Darwin co-opted Spencer's terminology "survival of the fittest" for his evolutionary theory, and Spencer transferred the theory of biological evolution into his theory of social evolution that became known as Social Darwinism. Spencer's selective definition as to what is the fittest sided him with the rich and powerful over the poor and the politically unorganized. He believed that those who were considered fit should be given more power to exercise their will. His theory became the justification for the oppression and exploitation of workers. He considered many of society's infrastructures such as charitable societies, philanthropic organizations, public schools, public health and public sanitation as obstructions to progress. These organizations only served to benefit the weak that should be left to die. He believed that the government should let industry compete unfettered by regulations. Survival of the fittest would ensure the progress of society. The government's roles were to fight wars and eliminate criminals. By the 1880's Britain was lamenting the possible decline of its empire because of the low birth rate and Malthus' theories were more or less abandoned.

Even in our time there continue to be practising Social Darwinists. At the energy company Enron, for example, survival of the fittest permeated the corporate culture. It held employee evaluations where a quota of 15 percent of its employees were declared unfit every year and fired. It held the state of California hostage with rolling blackouts, unconcerned that it disrupted the state's economy and jeopardized the health and safety of its citizens, all in the name of profit. It lied to shareholders and legislators telling them that the corporation was better than ever while the top executives liquidated their shares. In the end it collapsed under the scandals of its own making, proving itself the least fit of all. In its path it destroyed the livelihood of tens of thousands of workers along with their hard earned pensions. Enron was the largest and fastest collapse in U.S. corporate history.

For the Progressives on the upswing of the third long-wave, the misery and suffering caused by the depression, the rise of monopolies and the wholesale destruction caused by World War I made Spencer's theories of Social Darwinism unacceptable. They rejected the nature of biological determinism believing that they could create an environment that would nurture the progress and well being of society. The sociology of those such as Lester Ward made more sense to the Progressives. The Progressives saw that people did not live naked in the environment so that only the strong survived. Instead they made comfortable homes, furniture and clothing so that both the strong and the weak survived. They did not let disease plague their communities and their cities so that only the strong survived. Instead they trained doctors and built hospitals so that their friends and families, both weak and strong survived. They did not let bullies take over their schools and criminals take over their cities so that only the strong survived. Instead they organized the police so that both the weak and the strong survived. They did not allow a violent overthrow of their governments by the strong. Instead they established and followed laws of governance for the orderly transition of power. Survival of the fittest contradicted every ideal of an egalitarian and democratic society where both the weak and the strong have an equal voice. The Progressives recognized that all had different strengths and weaknesses and that they were not necessarily able to predict who the weak and who the strong were. Different skills are necessary for the progress of society. The definition of strength and weakness came only with hindsight. For many that were considered weak have made great social contributions and many that were regarded as strong have become utter failures. There were no means of judging the fittest until after the fact. The progressives saw the survival of the fittest as the law of the jungle. It contradicted every law, ethic and principle for the progress and survival of civilization. Progressive sociologist Lester Ward objected to Spencer's "survival of the fittest," especially when Spencer, having lived a privileged life under the pretence of being a self-made man, admitted that the only reason he was able to write and to publish his ideas was because of the inheritances from his two uncles and his father.

In the 1910's Margaret Sanger and Planned Parenthood would revive the arguments that Malthus had made over a hundred years earlier in their advocacy of birth control. Even John Maynard Keynes was caught up in Malthusianism at that time. After the 1920's, Malthus' ideas fell into relative obscurity once more.

As the earth's population increased on the upswing of the fourth long-wave, from 2.5 billion in 1950 to 3.6 billion by 1970, with some especially alarmed by the rate of population increase in the third world countries, Malthusian ideas were revived again. The shortage of food and basic commodities along with rampant inflation were putting strains on economies everywhere. There were calls for a zero population growth policy. Books such as *The Population Bomb* in 1968 and *The Limits of Growth* in 1972 predicted problems that would be induced by what was labelled as the population explosion. Population control measures were implemented around the world. Even as late as 1992, *Beyond the Limits* and another sequel in 2002 continued to warn of the dangers of population growth. Drowned out by the overpopulation proponents were economists such as Simon Kuznets, a director at the National Bureau of Economic Research, who believed that Western prosperity was due, in no small part, to its tremendous population growth.

In the late 1980's, on the downswing of the fourth long-wave, there was a small but growing body of work that investigated the possible impact of slowing population growth following the baby boom. After year 2000 there was a growing realization that a stable or declining population meant that there would be no economic growth, even perhaps there would be an economic decline. The Green Paper, "Confronting demographic change: a new solidarity between the generations" was published by the Commission of the European Communities in 2005. While Kuznets, four decades earlier, could not find any cases in history where large increases in population growth coincided with declines in per capita income, the report was even more affirmative, stating unequivocally, "Never in history has there been economic growth without population growth."[3] Many European and Western countries are facing the prospect of an ageing and declining population and have only just begun to address the issue. Society must come to the realization that population growths and declines do occur in civilization. Society must make a greater effort to understand the processes and consequences of population change and develop the ability to adapt to the challenges.

8 THE LONG-WAVE LIFE CYCLE

Throughout our lifetime we all experience change. Our bodies grow from young and flexible, to mature and strong, to old and fragile. As children, we are often told that we must be older before we can do many things. As adults we can do as we please. In age, what we please to do is limited again by what our bodies are able to do. When a generation comprises a significant proportion of the population, the activities of that generation overshadow the activities of all others. That generation is Gen-B. As Gen-B is born, comes of age and grows old, the general population shifts from being proportionately young, to middle age, to proportionately old, and all the undertakings of society have reflected these changes. Gen-B is the maker and the mover of society.

The young begin their life exploring the world around them. The sights, the sounds, the smells all bring a different sense of delight and anticipation. From the elders, the young learn to interpret their observations and feelings, giving them an understanding of their surroundings. The young accumulate knowledge from the experience of others. But this is second-hand knowledge and often insufficient knowledge. The experiences of the young are different from the experiences of the old and so are the interpretations. Thus the young must re-confirm that knowledge with their own experiences and decide whether to accept what they were taught or dispose of the old truths and reformulate new ones. The long-wave is often the catalyst for ideological change.

As the young reach the age of awareness and attempt to deal with the complexities of life, they bring with them an awakening. The young have a desire to know who they are and why they live under the circumstances that they do and what their role is in the world. The search for an identity and an understanding of life has traditionally been in the areas of philosophy or theology. On the emotional level, it spurs on the anxious revivals of religion. The recent long-wave has seen the search expand into the areas of psychology and extraterrestrial beings.

Youth is a time of experimentation and discovery. In their exploration of the world around them, the young discover their own abilities and inabilities. They discover the nature of their surroundings, the rules of conduct, the pleasure of play and the allure of achievement. Among the many discoveries of youth is the discovery of sexuality. Each long-wave upswing has been accompanied by a re-discovery of sex and sexual revolutions.

When the population is young, the pursuit of ideological matters takes precedence. The young are idealistic and adventurous. The great social movements to reform the world, to bring justice to the oppressed and to help the needy are a matter of great urgency with the young. The old may be reform in thought, but the young are reform in action. Then comes a time when there is a need for the type of companionship and intimacy that groups cannot provide. Social justice is eventually given up for individual pursuits. The concerns for establishing and providing for a family becomes greater than the concerns of the community. The tensions generated by a youthful population disappear. As Gen-B moves into the establishment, Gen-B brings in a new set of values. These values are adjusted with age. The sexual revolution ceases to be revolutionary. With age comes a development of savoir-faire. The sentimental and the refined are preferred over the rustic and the spontaneous. With the population ageing and the rate of growth declining, a new conservatism develops. Gen-X, being born later and in following the change in attitude of Gen-B, act in a more conservative manner.

The old bring experience and stability. The young bring vision, vigor and discovery. Youth is the amplification of humanity.

Each period of youthful prosperity is a period of new innovations, for youth is a great adopter of new ideas and technology, and with each baby boom, an expanding new market is created that is ready to put to use new ways of doing things. During these booming markets more profits are available for research and development. Innovations become necessary to serve a growing population more efficiently.

As the economic long-wave moves from baby boom to baby boom, the general expenditures of society are reflected in the spending patterns of Gen-B. When a large proportion of Gen-B reaches adulthood the purchases of major durable items such as cars, furnishings and houses bring a boom to the economy. Businesses expand, debt increases, hiring grows and expectations rise to take advantage of an ever prosperous economy. The social movements end by the peak of the long-wave, the economy continues to be prosperous, and for a time, it appears that the nation is back to normal. But when Gen-B has completed major material acquisitions and begins to retire, the industrial economy begins to decline. Sales go down, business profits shrink and workers are laid off. The upswing of the long-wave brings in new business. New houses and new cars are purchased by a growing population. The secondary downswing is mostly replacement business, replacement of clothes, roofs and fences according to the wear and tear experienced by an ageing population.

Accompanying the changes in the composition of the population are changes in all forms of artistic expression, creating trends in industrial and commercial designs. Businesses that manage to catch the new design trends do well; businesses that don't are left to wonder why their products have no appeal, flounder, and go bankrupt.

With all the savings that Gen-B are accumulating, the stock market moves to record highs and mutual funds grow to record numbers, not necessarily reflecting corporate profits or the economy. The ageing economy becomes more pre-occupied with the movement of monetary assets than the production of material goods. These shifts in disaggregate demand from perishables to durables to services to instruments of savings and investment have produced shifts in aggregate demand, generating the economic long-wave cycle.

The 1920's was known as the Roaring 20's, and the 1980's had their yuppies. The New Era of the 1920's promised an era of peace and prosperity and so did the New World Order of the 1980's. Demographics permeate all aspects of our lives, every minute of every day, yet the causal relationships occur over such a long period of time that they have passed for thousands of years with only anecdotal awareness. Our knowledge is highly specialized and our memory of the details of history is limited and everything seems to be different. Our lifespan is sufficiently short and the long-wave is sufficiently long that we generally fail to recognize the causal connections. In order that we not repeat history, not only must we know history, we must understand it.

Since the 1930's, the government has taken an active role in the economy with monetary policies, public works and social welfare programs. The development of a global economy has been influenced by shifts in regional economic expansion. The distribution of income on the international level has been improving. In that more people are able to purchase goods and services, the world economy has grown that much larger. There are also growing government deficits. As a result of these changes, more inflation was possible, making the current period of inflation the most prolonged in our study. Government expenditures also, which have traditionally increased on the upswing of the long-wave, continue to increase on the downswing of the fourth long-wave as seen in figures 5.12 and 5.13 and have come to play a greater role in the economy. The U.S. expenditures have increased from more than $300 billion dollars a year in 1975 to over $1 trillion dollars a year in 1991. All these factors have contributed to the rising level of prices in recent years and have had their effect on the economy. It is even possible that as the federal government attempts to keep this economy going, monetary inflationary pressures will keep escalating the wholesale price index. But the decline in social movements and the ageing Gen-B are symptoms of a long-wave decline.

What this book has documented was 200 years of long-wave history, demonstrating the interrelation of events that were previously viewed in isolation. These events are intimately related to demographics and to each other. Our society has been preoccupied with a growing population and the consumption of resources in previous decades. It is only now that we are beginning to reflect on the consequences of a zero or declining population growth. Just as there was no preparation to receive the millions of Baby Boomers into the consumer market and onto the job market, there has been no preparation to deal with a stable or declining population that has been the object of many noble goals in the modern era. The concept that "fewer people means more resources for more people," in the natural order of things, is a concept misapplied. The result of the miscalculation of the 1960's and 1970's was an era of misapplied economics by using tight fiscal policies to combat inflation but aggravating it even further. To achieve a stable or declining population in the long run without due consideration and preparation for the consequences will mean a decline in prosperity and intellectual progress. Existing technology and production may become more refined in the short term, but in the long term, that too will decline. With prolonged population declines, supply chains will shut down and complex manufacturing processes will be forgotten. All the knowledge and experience developed by expanding industries will disappear.

The cultural and political leadership of any country is dependent on economic leadership. Economic leadership is dependent on scientific and technological advances. Without idealism, why would anyone want to study science and spend many isolated hours developing unproven ideas that few can understand? It may be far more satisfying to become involved in areas where there is fame, fortune and popularity. A well-recognized name, by appearances, opens the doors to political arenas better than experience or knowledge. It gives a more direct line to the corporate boardroom than a good education. Political and cultural leaderships are highly subjective. Without the requisites, they are subject more to scrutiny than to imitation in the international arena. The receptiveness to any country's cultural and ideological exports is tied to the country's economic strength.

Social Orientation of Long-wave Phases		
Activity	Upswing	Downswing
Politics	Progressive	Conservative
	Activist	Legislative
Economy	Regulated	Deregulated
	Expanding	Shrinking
	Centralize	Decentralize
	Commodity Inflation	Equity Inflation
Morals	Deregulated	Regulated
World Affairs	Internationalist	Isolationist
Rights	Civil Rights	Corporate Rights
Social Orientation	Career Goals	Retirement Goals
	Idealistic	Wealth Oriented
	Women/Men Hood	Mother/Father Hood
	Young	Old
	Masculine	Feminine
Education	Progressive	Traditional
	Decentralized	Centralized
Religious/Philosophical Outlook	Secular	Traditional

Table 8.00 - Social Orientation of Long-wave Phases

Children by nature are idealistic. They aspire to be more than they are. Science is the product of idealistic youth. Engineering and technology are the application of science to solve practical problems. The wealth of nations is in the resources of the land and in the skills of the people. Without the constant regeneration of youth, without an expanding market base to pay for new products, the nation's innovative capacity and the development of science and technology will be greatly diminished. Our economies will flounder and all that we call progress will be undone.

History is full of idealistic youths. In the 1500's when the astronomer Johannes Kepler proclaimed that science is "thinking the thoughts of God after Him," he reflected the spirit of science and the thoughts of scientists at the time. Not only did people idealize the Christian God, they idealized pagan Rome. With the coming of these generations the world of modern science, art and innovation opened up and they eventually created the political structure of democracy of today. When we lose sight of ideals, we lose sight of equality and justice and corruption takes a step through the door.

With the long-wave, we have precedent for understanding historic relationships and for understanding the future. We get an expansive view of demographic change. There is historical precedent for analysis and validation. Only with the long-wave can we observe and correlate the multivariate structural changes within society and the changing social and economic dynamics over decades. Without a valid demographic model, the study of demographics is no more than a loose collection of associations lacking the ability to validate relationships. Without the ability to validate, demographics cannot move beyond the recognition of being a "soft science." The long-wave is a powerful tool for understanding social change and the hundreds of seemingly disparate events in dozens of countries over thousands of years. In the absence of controlled scientific tests in the social sciences, the long-wave ranks among the best of the social science methodologies. As we have seen throughout this book, looking back into history for less than 60 years is insufficient to account for all the relational variances of human activity. When studies fail to make correlations or make conflicting correlations, it may be that some of these studies are of insufficient time span involving correlations that change over a span of decades. The long-wave provides repetitive sets of similar historical conditions against which we can test our thesis.

What is important in understanding the long-wave is not the timing of cycles, but the interaction of demographics, for not all societies will follow the same cycle, but all societies will have a dynamic within their demographic composition. The cycles themselves will ebb and flow, appear and disappear, as societies move from new to old.

We are a generation that has lived in unprecedented prosperity. Our lifespan is longer than ever. Our standard of living is higher than at any other time in history. We enjoy more leisure time than any society before us. By 2007 there will be an escalation of people entering retirement. It is because of this great wave of savings leading up to retirement that the stock market has moved up; the future great wave of divestment to pay for retirement may have the opposite effect. Whether the working population will have sufficient resources to acquire these divested assets to prevent the lost of value or whether the global economy can uphold these asset values remains to be seen. If these asset values can be maintained as the Boomers enter retirement, the prosperity of this retiring generation would be unprecedented indeed. If these equity values cannot be maintained, monetary policy by itself will have limited effect as the ageing Boomers move beyond monetary policy's reach. Between 1920 and 1930 those over 65 years of age increased by a third. Between 2006 and 2016 those over 65 years of age will increase at the same rate. Given the historic precedents, only those without a demographic model that can validate against history can say with supreme confidence that we will all retire prosperous in our newfound wealth in the absence of political and economic initiatives.

As a result of the increase in the number of elderly population in the 1940's, the rise in concerns about ageing prompted the establishment of the fields of gerontology and geriatrics as disciplines of their own. These were followed by the publication of a large number of gerontological journals. When an increasing number of people begin to retire, as from the 1930's to the 1950's, there is a possibility that the marriage rate will go up again, to be followed by a growing birth rate.

From the 1960's to the end of the 1970's, the world was caught in the throes of inflation. Prices on goods and services rose, wages went up and interest rates increased to above twenty percent. For the next thirty and more years, economic policy makers waged a war against inflation. With tight monetary policies, high interest rates and price controls, policy makers hoped to keep inflation in check, but by the end of the twentieth century, the spectre of deflation, not seen since the 1930's, reared its head. If anyone had mentioned the possibility of deflation a few years earlier, they would have been laughed out of economic circles. That neither the inflationary pressures that appeared after the 1950's, nor the deflationary pressures that appeared at the end of the century had been anticipated as a possibility by the economic theories of the day meant that there were factors that these theories did not account for.

Social, political and economic activities follow the rhythms of demographic change. What we have delineated are a complex series of social activities, that when viewed individually and without the context of the expansive time and demographics, would lead to very different conclusions. Without demographics to tie social-economic theories together, the modern schools of thought have been examining the elephant and each identifying it as a different creature. Simply stated, as population expands, supply side economic planning is required to ensure adequate supply to meet the growing demand. As population stabilizes or declines in an ageing society, demand side economic planning is one of the possible solutions that must be examined as a way to mitigating the effects of declining demand.

The long-wave cycle in North America is well supported by social, economic and political history. The primary driver of the long-wave is demographics, as demographics is the driver for social, economic and political change. Increasing population growth supports a technologically and politically progressive society. Declines in population growth are followed by conservatism and economic decline.

Baby Boomers grew up in a world of rapidly expanding population. Population expansion created new markets and increased demand for products and services, thereby creating an environment of prosperity. Yet we emphasized population control for fear of running out of resources. Now we must consider the other side of the equation. What happens when the rate of growth of population stabilizes or declines? The consequences of an ageing and declining population are under-utilization of the capacity that was built up to meet the demands of the population boom. Over-capacity means there is no need for economic expansion and hence there will be declining prosperity. We therefore have a new challenge before us: how to maintain a high standard of living when there is no economic expansion. The challenge before us is the consequence of demographic change. On the one hand, an expanding population will give us economic expansion, but it will mean tapping further into the resources of our environment. In the deepest seas and on the highest mountains we can find traces of man-made toxins. All that we have created, all that we have consumed, it is passed back into the environment and then back to us again. As the scale of our consumption and manufacturing increases, so does the scale of our waste production. What we throw out at the other end of the earth comes back to us on our dinner plates. We have been poor stewards of the resources that we once thought were limitless and we must think in that way no more.

On the other hand, a stable or declining population will mean less demand for products and services and consequently no need to build new factories, downward pressure on prices and wages and a lower standard of living. It will mean unemployment, stagnation and a slowdown in technological progress. When we fail to be stewards of the environment that supports our health and our life, a growing population can be a destructive process. Between the two, we must find a medium where progress continues to be cultivated and in which we can maintain a reasonable standard of living.

It was said that Keynesian economics meant that paying workers to dig ditches and then paying them to fill in the ditches again, would be sufficient to keep the economy going. The other part of the equation is that the workers take their earnings to buy things to fill their garages, empty the garages into the ditches, and buy more things to fill the garages. It does wonders for the economy, but it is also an expedient way to create ecological disaster. In a free society, the economy expands with population growth.

Where there are people, there will always be needs. Where there are needs, businesses and institutions will develop to fulfill those needs. Where there is overwhelming demand, innovations and technologies will develop. This is the basis of a modern society. Social science must begin with the most basic components of society, the people and the demographics, to understand the functioning society.

The long-wave reflects the development and changing needs of individuals. Economics is about meeting the needs of the population, and determining how to produce and deliver the goods and services. As the population shifts from being proportionately young to being proportionately old, the population demands different products and services from the economy, and in different proportions, causing structural changes to the economy. These structural changes cause the dislocation of established businesses and provide opportunities for new businesses. When structural changes are unanticipated, unplanned and unmanaged, dislocation and hardship caused by the disruption of employment can be a result of the adjustment taking place. Our understanding of the long-wave should help us to create policies to alleviate the hardships induced by these changes, instead of mistakenly implementing policies that may aggravate already difficult social conditions.

The downturn of the stock market in 2000 created many pension shortfalls. In 2007 the number of people in the population reaching sixty-five will grow significantly. By 2011 the numbers will be in continuous escalation. It would be well if the political and economic systems are prepared to handle these very significant social changes. In a young society where there is growing economic demand, recovering from economic shock is relatively quick. With declining demand in an older society, recoveries take much longer. As the Chairman of the Federal Reserve Board Ben S. Bernanke summarized the demographic situation before the U.S. Budget Committee on January 18, 2007:

... because of demographic changes and rising medical costs, federal expenditures for entitlement programs are projected to rise sharply over the next few decades. Dealing with the resulting fiscal strains will pose difficult choices for the Congress, the Administration and the American people. However, if early and meaningful action is not taken, the U.S. economy could be seriously weakened, with future generations bearing much of the cost.[1]

In the past, when governments altered social policies in hopes of changing social conditions, the consequences have not always been predictable. The long-wave will open new doors of understanding in these areas. As we become more aware of our actions and the possible consequences, we may opt to alter the long-wave, but in altering the long-wave patterns, there is always the possibility that we will alter the predictability of the long-wave itself. In order to ensure the progress of society, however, government involvement in creating the correct policies is necessary. Our future depends on the wisdom and capabilities of those whom we elect to government.

APPENDIX A

U.S. POPULATION, COALE/ZELNIK, SIMON KUZNETS

Population increase comes from two sources, birth and immigration. Immigrants and those born in the country have different effects on the social system. The native-born usually spend their complete life cycle, from birth to death, in their native country. Immigrants may arrive as infants, but many arrive as adults, somewhere in their mid life cycle. Immigrants need time to settle and to assimilate into the indigenous population. Often they must take on new values in order to integrate into the social institutions. How long it takes them to assimilate depends on where they are from, what language they speak and how old they are. The very young usually assimilate much faster than the very old, the English-speaking faster than the non English-speaking, those from Western cultures faster than those from non Western cultures and the adventurous usually faster than the homesick. Their activities may not reflect that of the local population.

To evaluate the growth rate of the indigenous population, the immigrant population and the indigenous population must be separated. Since it is not practical to separate the immigrant population totally, because historically, immigrants and their offspring adopt the ways of the indigenous population, even to having the same birth rates, we have undertaken a method to delay the effect of immigration. Figure A.00 graphs the decennial change in population with the current year's immigration removed. Removing the current year's immigration number does not eliminate immigration from our statistical series because that number will be embedded in the next year's population number. In effect, we have delayed immigration by one year.

$$Y(t) = \text{Population}(t) - \text{Immigration}(t)$$

Percent Change per Decade in Population:

$$\text{Population}_{pcpd}(t) = (Y(t) - Y(t\text{-}10))*100/Y(t\text{-}10)$$

Equation A.00 - Population with Immigration Delayed by 1 Year

Figure A.01 plots population with immigration delayed by 1 year with demographers Ansley J. Coale and Melvin Zelnik's estimates of total fertility. Total fertility is the estimate of the total number of children a woman would have in her lifetime. Both the fertility estimates and birth rate estimates of Coale / Zelnik have similar patterns. Only total fertility is plotted here. The graph shows that these statistics correlate very well. There is an offset of approximately six years between the fertility estimates and population growth graph.

Figure A.02 delays immigration by five years by subtracting from the current year's population number, the current year and the previous four years immigration numbers. When immigration is delayed, the fluctuations in natural population increase become more pronounced.

$$Y(t) = \text{Population}(t) - (\text{Immigration}(t) + ...$$
$$+\text{Immigration}(t\text{-}4))$$

Percent Change per Decade in Population:

$$\text{Population}_{pcpd}(t) = (Y(t) - Y(t\text{-}10))*100/Y(t\text{-}10)$$

Equation A.01 - Population with Immigration Delayed by 5 Years

Putting statistics through mathematical processes sometimes produces side effects. One side effect of this process is that it produces shifts. Note that at usG, when there was very little immigration, the trough and peak remain unchanged at 1941 and 1961. But at usE and usF when immigration was large, the peaks and troughs shifted depending on how long immigration was delayed.

Let us compare figure A.02 with figures 4.01 and 4.02. Note that at usG, all three figures show an increasing population. If we draw a line through the three peaks toward the upswing of the third long-wave, or if we take a sample every decade, such as a census every decade, we would end up with the declining slope usF as shown in figures 4.01 and 4.02. Finally, the population increase into 1862 is shown on all three diagrams. Emigration statistics do not exist for this length of time so the role of emigration, which is very small, could not be accounted for in these charts.

Figure A.03 juxtaposes the percent change per decade in church membership with the percent change per decade in population with immigration delayed for 5 years. Although the magnitudes of the changes are different, the fluctuations of both these population statistics are well synchronized.

Figure A.04 graphs the percent change per decade in church membership with the percent change per decade in work force from figures 4.09 and 5.03, revealing direct correlations. Church membership leads work force because people enter the work force at a later age but are eligible to be church members at a younger age.

Simon Kuznets did pioneering research in what he termed "long cycles" or "long swings" in population growth, through which he relates economic changes to demographics. These swings are now known as Kuznets cycles. Kuznets does not relate long swings to long-waves. In fact, Kuznets was critical of long-waves as it was understood at the time, without the demographic component. With demographics however, the relationship between Kuznets cycles and long-waves become quite clear. Figure A.05 plots Simon Kuznets' additions to total population. These additions are calculated on a 5 year moving average, 10 years apart, centered in the middle of each decade interval. Compare this graph with figure 4.14, the percent change per decade in population 65 years of age and over. Strong correlations can be observed. There is an offset between the three peaks of the two graphs of approximately 50 years. From all these independent population estimates, we can observe well synchronized fluctuations in the wave-like nature of population growth.

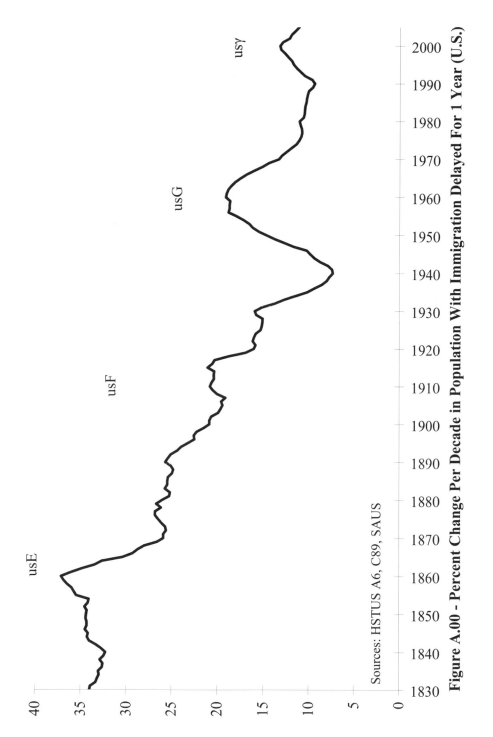

Figure A.00 - Percent Change Per Decade in Population With Immigration Delayed For 1 Year (U.S.)

Sources: HSTUS A6, C89, SAUS

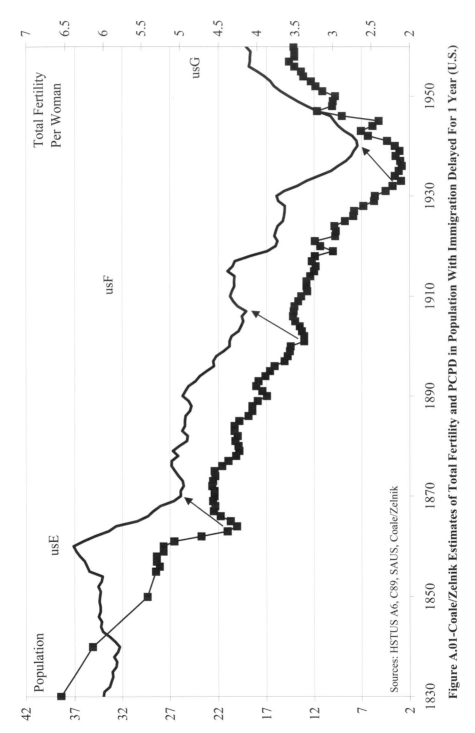

Figure A.01–Coale/Zelnik Estimates of Total Fertility and PCPD in Population With Immigration Delayed For 1 Year (U.S.)

Sources: HSTUS A6, C89, SAUS, Coale/Zelnik

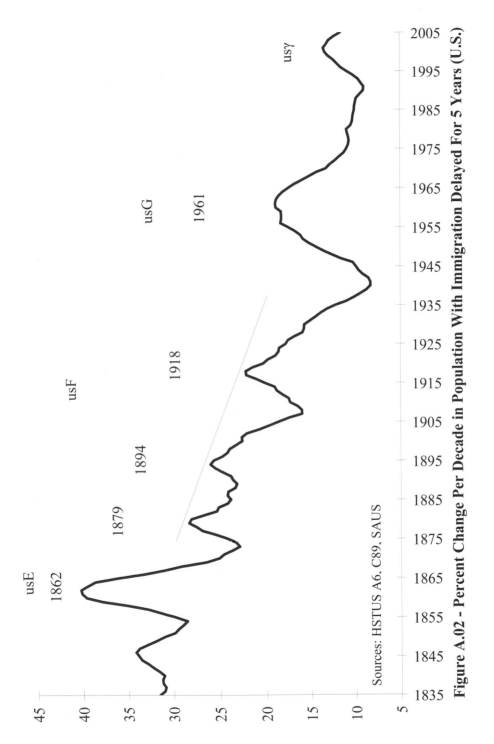

Figure A.02 - Percent Change Per Decade in Population With Immigration Delayed For 5 Years (U.S.)

Sources: HSTUS A6, C89, SAUS

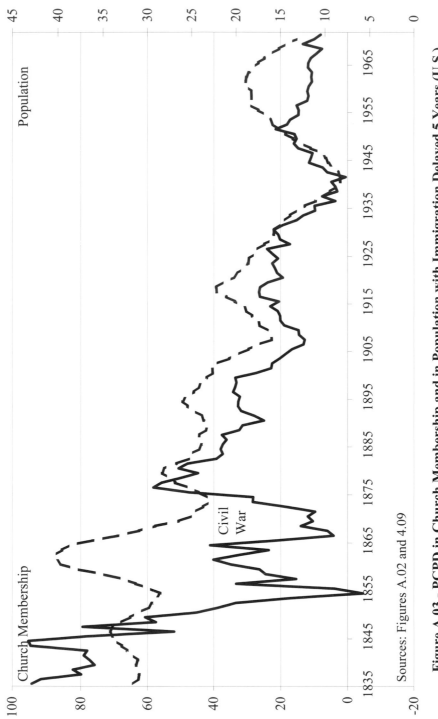

Figure A.03 - PCPD in Church Membership and in Population with Immigration Delayed 5 Years (U.S.)

Sources: Figures A.02 and 4.09

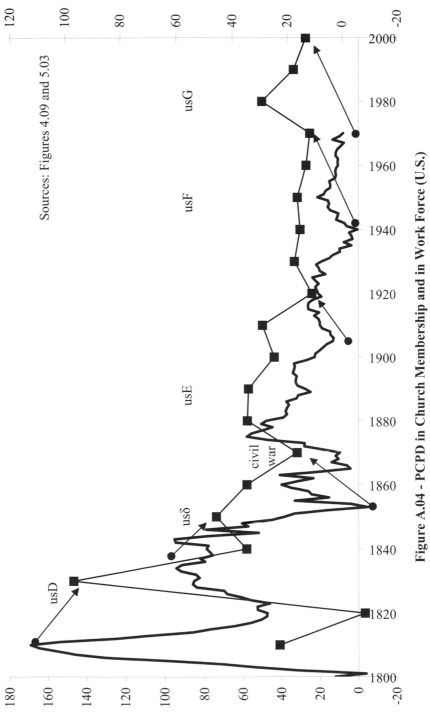

Sources: Figures 4.09 and 5.03

Figure A.04 - PCPD in Church Membership and in Work Force (U.S.)

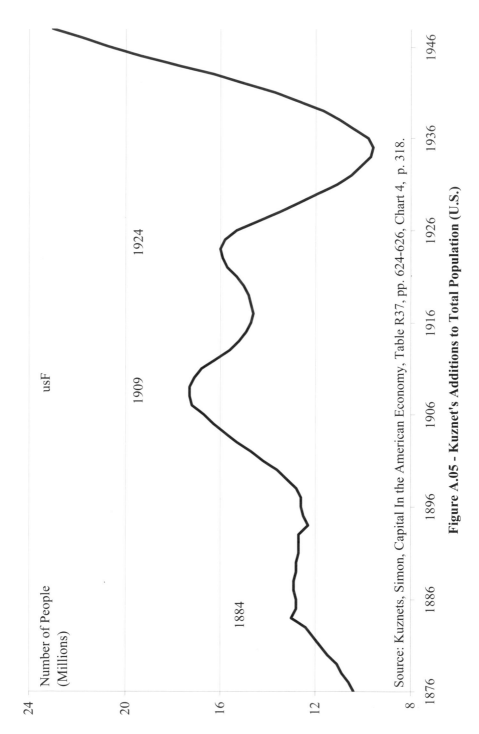

Source: Kuznets, Simon, Capital In the American Economy, Table R37, pp. 624-626, Chart 4, p. 318.

Figure A.05 - Kuznet's Additions to Total Population (U.S.)

APPENDIX B

U.S. POPULATION, MONEY SUPPLY, PATENTS
AND OTHER STATISTICS

In the main sections of this book we have shown that the major economic variables (production, wages, prices, interest rates, the stock index, mergers and acquisitions, government spending, work force, housing ownership and savings) have fluctuated with the long-wave. We will now compare money supply growth, along with some of these economic variables, with population growth.

Figure B.00 plots three money supply data series: the percent change per decade for Total Currency in Circulation in the U.S, M2 Money Supply and recent Federal Reserve estimates of M2 Money Supply. Over the last 200 years the United States has gone through many changes in the banking system, in monetary policy, in economic theory and in political philosophy. Through various periods money has been created based on the gold standard, based on treasury reserves and by fiat. Currency has been issued by independent banks, state banks, and central banks. The banks have been regulated by the U.S. Treasury, by central banks, and through central banks. There have been times when there was a central bank and times when there was no central bank. There have been times when the President, the Treasury and the central bank disagreed on how to manage the banking system. If there is anything consistent about money and banking, it is that there has been change.

There are at least two other consistencies involving money and banking in the last two hundred years. The first is that government and military spending influence money supply. Traditionally government expenditures were a fraction of the total money in circulation, except for war-time spending, as shown in figure B.01. Both government spending and military spending contribute to increasing the money supply, but how much money supply increases varies at different times. During and after WWII, government spending remained at very high levels, several times that of money in circulation.

The other consistency is that population growth influences money supply. If money supply did not grow with population, there would not be enough money to circulate and the economy would stagnate. Figure B.02 juxtaposes population data from figure A.02 with total currency in circulation. Throughout the period in comparison, for which we have data, population growth peaks lead money growth peaks on average by about ten years, except when there is a war. War spending ushers in an earlier and more intense peak. These fluctuations are also directly related to fluctuations in the percent change per decade in wholesale price index, figures 5.06 and B.03, in composite wages, figures 5.10 and B.04, in housing demand, figure B.05, and in stock index, figures 5.20 and B.06. The current pace of new housing activity has not matched the rates of the previous long-waves, possibly due to the existence of older housing stock and affordability factors. All these economic variables are related to the age and composition of the population, fluctuating according to the age related shifts in disaggregate demand from commodities, as represented by the increase in the wholesale price index, to housing, to investments, as shown in figure B.07, most notably at usF and at WWII. In a free society, wealth grows with population growth. Wealth is solely a human concept. The growth of human population is a source of growing wealth.

Figure B.08 graphs the percent change per decade in Methodist Church membership with the percent change per decade in post office revenue from figure 5.00. Since Methodist Church membership does not begin until age 13 and after, the graph for Church membership must be shifted back several years to be a better reflection of population growth. When that is done, the peaks and troughs of Church Membership precede the economic peaks and troughs of post office revenue, as opposed to what is shown on the graph. That Post office revenue follows demographic changes well is another confirmation that post office revenue, as a reflection of the economy, is also a reflection of population growth.

The relationship between innovations and demographics is a bit more complex than the other statistics that we have investigated so far. Figure B.09 graphs the percent change per decade in patents issued. There is an acknowledgement that wartime demand is an inducement for innovation. Products such as detergents and encryption methodologies can be pointed to as being invented and produced during a war. Many such products continue to be produced in modified forms for a consumer society. However does wartime urgency stimulate the growth of innovations more than a peacetime economy? If wartime demand did produce more innovations, one may expect a flood of patents issued during a war, or perhaps after a war when time is not occupied by the war effort. What the graph shows, however, is that patents issued have the greatest growth before wars. During and after WWII for example, the patents-issued growth rate was negative until after 1950. Figure B.09 can be compared to figure A.04, the percent change per decade in church membership and in work force. Innovations correlate with population growth, the composition of the population and economic progress, and is adversely affected by economic downturns and wars. The rate of innovations growth has not matched the magnitude of the antebellum years.

Capital investment is another statistical series related to demographics and to all other economic data. Figure B.10 graphs the percent change per decade in capital spending in manufacturing industries with the percent change per decade in patents issued. The growth in capital

266 BABY BOOMERS, GENERATION X AND SOCIAL CYCLES

spending during WWII did not induce growth in patents issued. Capital spending in itself is not an assurance that there would be innovative products. The relationship in the data is not immediate.

Simon Kuznets relates his additions to population in figure A.05 to what he calls additions to population-sensitive capital formation, the spending in housing construction and railroads, which resulted in the Kuznets' long cycle being referred to as the "building and construction" cycle. Kuznets also relates demographics to the per capita additions to the flow of goods to consumers. Figure B.11 can be compared to the many population graphs presented in this book.

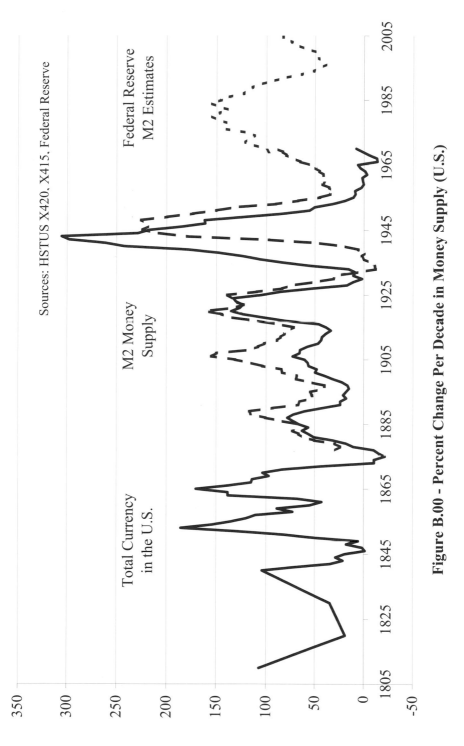

Figure B.00 - Percent Change Per Decade in Money Supply (U.S.)

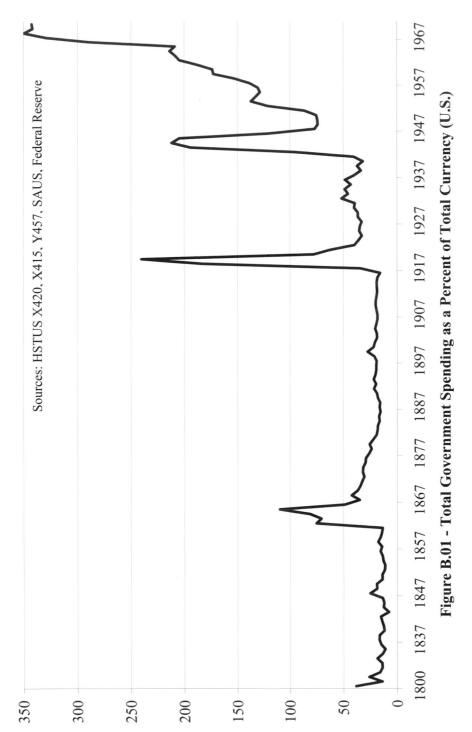

Sources: HSTUS X420, X415, Y457, SAUS, Federal Reserve

Figure B.01 - Total Government Spending as a Percent of Total Currency (U.S.)

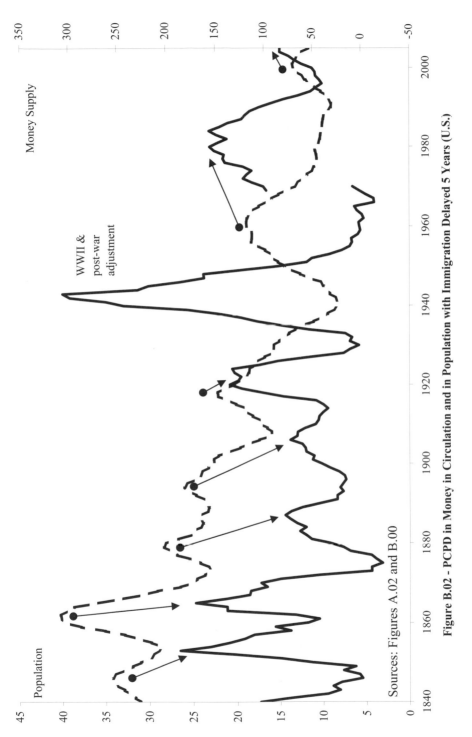

Figure B.02 - PCPD in Money in Circulation and in Population with Immigration Delayed 5 Years (U.S.)

Sources: Figures A.02 and B.00

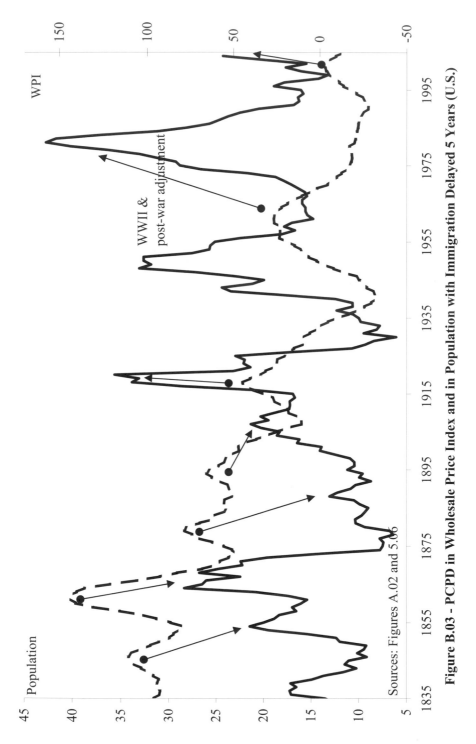

Figure B.03 - PCPD in Wholesale Price Index and in Population with Immigration Delayed 5 Years (U.S.)

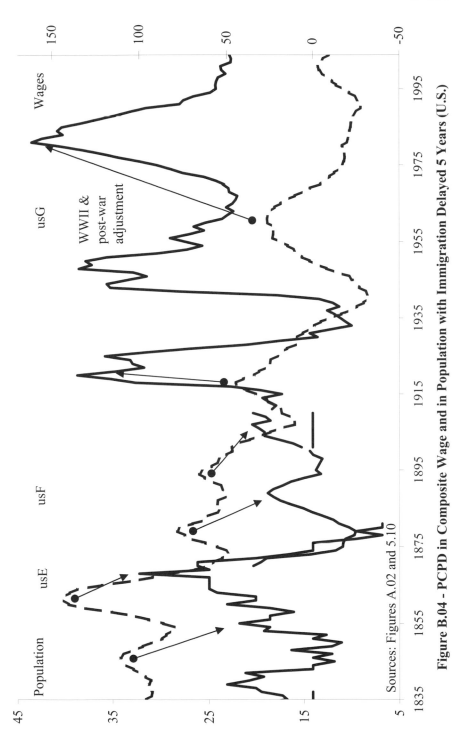

Sources: Figures A.02 and 5.10

Figure B.04 - PCPD in Composite Wage and in Population with Immigration Delayed 5 Years (U.S.)

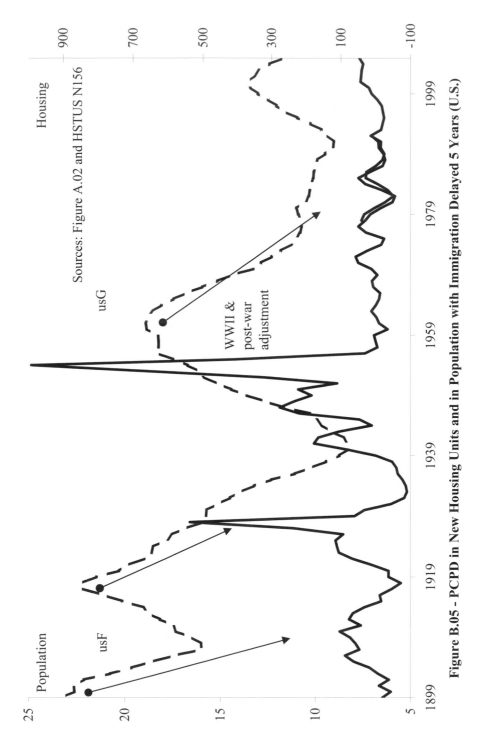

Figure B.05 - PCPD in New Housing Units and in Population with Immigration Delayed 5 Years (U.S.)

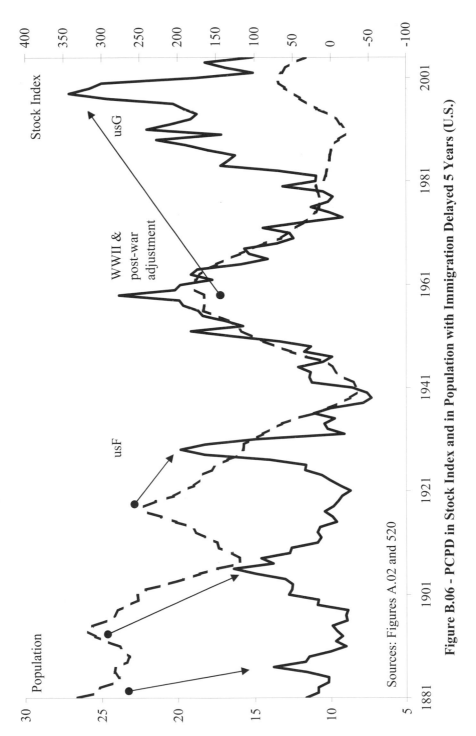

Figure B.06 - PCPD in Stock Index and in Population with Immigration Delayed 5 Years (U.S.)

Sources: Figures A.02 and 520

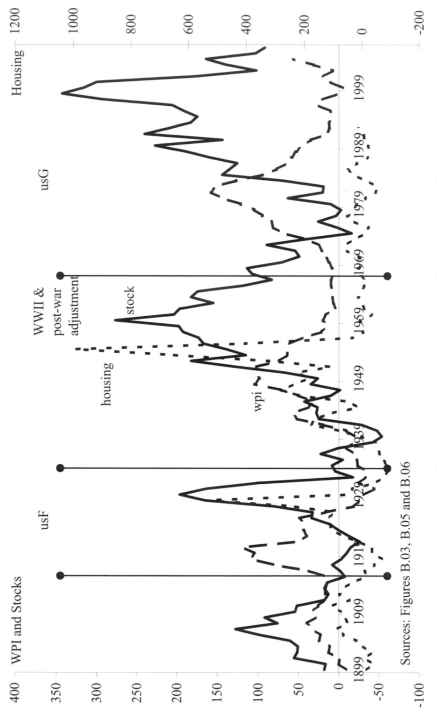

Figure B.07 - Shifts in Disaggregate Demand: WPI, Housing, Stocks (U.S.)

Sources: Figures B.03, B.05 and B.06

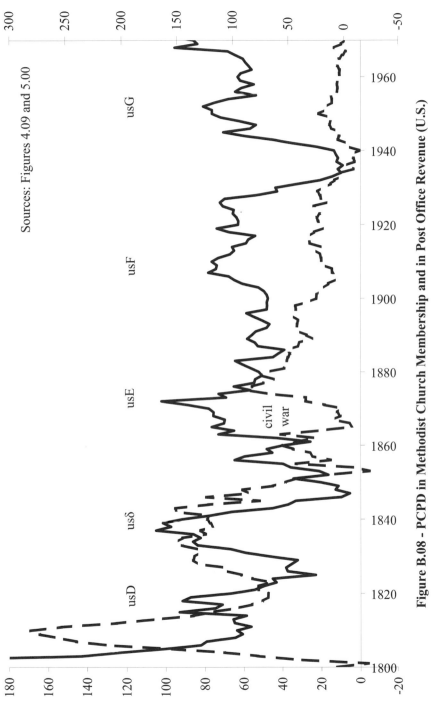

Sources: Figures 4.09 and 5.00

Figure B.08 - PCPD in Methodist Church Membership and in Post Office Revenue (U.S.)

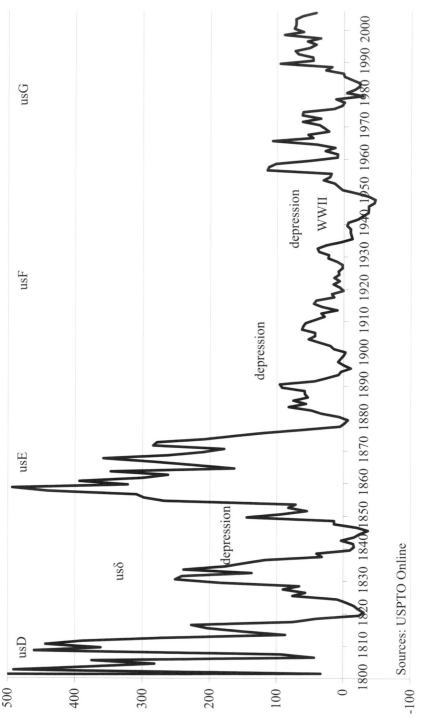

Figure B.09 - Percent Change Per Decade in Patents Issued (U.S.)

Sources: USPTO Online

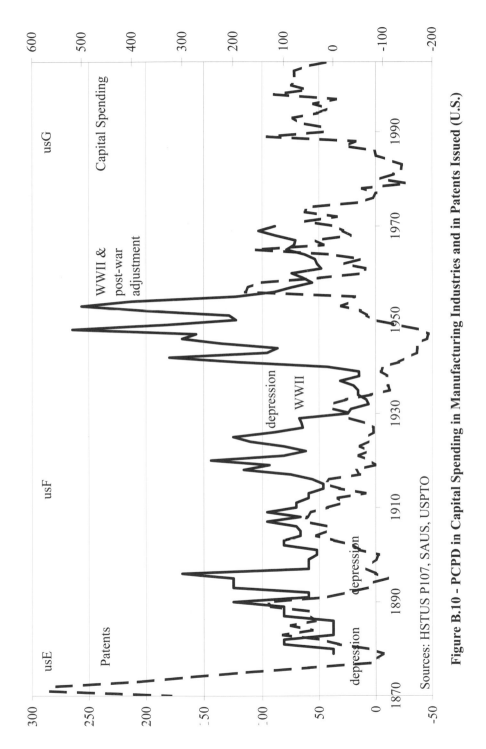

Figure B.10 - PCPD in Capital Spending in Manufacturing Industries and in Patents Issued (U.S.)

Sources: HSTUS P107, SAUS, USPTO

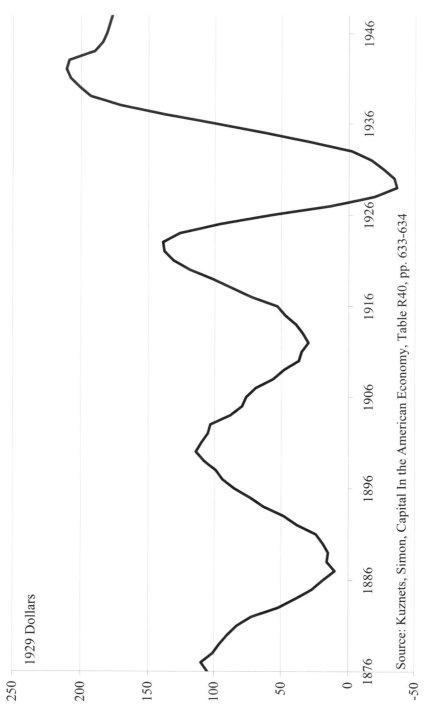

Figure B.11 - Kuznets' Per Capita Additions to Flow of Goods to Consumers (U.S.)

Source: Kuznets, Simon, Capital In the American Economy, Table R40, pp. 633-634

N_{otes}

1. THE LONG-WAVES OF SOCIAL CHANGE

1. Douglas Coupland, *Generation X*, Little Brown & Co., 1992.
2. Garnett, p. 20, Statistics Canada.
3. Morissette, Statistics Canada.
4. Beaupré, Statistics Canada.

2. SOCIAL MOVEMENTS: UNITED STATES

PROHIBITION
1. Asbury, The Great Illusion, p. 6.
2. ibid.
3. ibid., pp. 29-31.
4. ibid., p. 32.
5. Beman, Selected Articles on Prohibition, pp. 1-3.
6. Asbury, The Great Illusion, p. 67.
7. Asbury, p. 116.
8. Blocker, American Temperance Movements, p. xvi.
9. ibid., pp. 29, 65-66, 119.

WOMEN'S MOVEMENT
10. Woman's Rights Convention, p. 6.
11. Flexner, Century of Struggle, p. 80.
12. ibid., p. 148.
13. Flexner p. 223. Flexner credits this conservatism in the women's movement to the bomb explosion in Haymarket Square of Chicago in 1886 and not because "a few conservative women who took it over, through their own superior ability and the passivity of the former militants." Historians have used the Haymarket explosion as an explanation for many things during this period. It comes in almost as handy as the Industrial Revolution.
14. ibid., p. 182.
15. ibid., p. 256.
16. O'Neill, William, Feminism in America, pp. 262-263. [and thereafter] was added to this quote.
17. ibid., p.33 footnote 4.

URBAN REFORM
18. Ahlstrom p. 742.
19. Pence p. 2.
20. Davis pp. 75, 80.
21. Davis p. 275.

MUSIC
22. Toll, Blacking Up, p. v.
23. Nathan, Dan Emmett p. 171.
24. ibid., p. 55.
25. ibid., p. 118.
26. Toll, Blacking Up, p. 36.
27. ibid., p. 139.
28. ibid., pp. 154-155.
29. ibid., p. 149.
30. Berlin, Ragtime, p. 45.
31. ibid., p. 35.
32. ibid., p. 42.
33. ibid., p. 16.
34. Osgood, So this is Jazz, p. 36.
35. Brunn, Original Dixieland Jazz Band, p. xv.
36. ibid., p. 171.
37. New York Times: Feb. 12, 1922 Sect.3 p. 1.
38. New York Times: Jan. 11, 1926 p. 15.
39. New York Times: July 12, 1925 Sect.2 p. 2.
40. Brunn, Original Dixieland Jazz Band, p. 175.
41. New York Times: Aug. 11, 1924 p. 12.
42. Leonard, Jazz and the White American, pp. 112 and 118.
43. ibid., p. 110.
44. Martin, Anti-Rock.
45. New York Times Nov. 1, 1958 p. 3.
46. Ward, Rock of Ages p. 612.
47. Rolling Stone Magazine, p. 176, December 13, 1990.
48. Loesser, Men, Women and Pianos, pp. 456-457.

REVIVALS OF RELIGION
49. Edwards p. 349. Edwards notes that a Rev. Marsh had similar revivals at about the same time Edwards was having his and neither knew of each other's experience.
50. McLoughlin, Revivals, Awakening and Reform, p.45.
51. Edwards pp. 344-345.
52. Ahlstrom, A Religious History of the American People, p. 415.
53. Ahlstrom p. 415 op. cit. Bennet Tyler p.v.
54. ibid., p. 433.
55. Finney, Lectures on Revivals, pp. 286-287.
56. ibid., p. 287.
57. ibid., p. ix.
58. Smith, Revivalism and Social Reform, p. 104.
59. ibid., p. 62.
60. Carwardine, TransAtlantic Revivalism, p. 162.
61. ibid., p. 167.
62. ibid., p. 173.
63. Smith, Revivalism and Social Reform, p. 67.

64. McLoughlin, Revivals, Awakening and Reform, p.144 - 145.
65. Ahlstrom p. 745.
66. Ahlstrom, A Religious History of the American People, p. 748.
67. McLoughlin, Modern Revivalism, p. 433.
68. Ahlstrom, A Religious History of the American People, p. 747.
69. McLoughlin, Modern Revivalism, p. 453.
70. Ahlstrom, A Religious History of the American People, p.952.

3. SOCIAL MOVEMENTS: CANADA

1. Noel, pp. 15, 19.
2. Heron, p. 27.
3. Noel, p. 125.
4. Hallowell, p. 71.
5. Hallowell, p. 142.
6. Bacchi, p.30, Cleverdon, p. 26.

5. ECONOMICS

1. Samuelson, Macroeconomics, p. 795.
2. ibid., p. 58.
3. ibid., p. 133.
4. Hendrickson, p. 14.
5. Hendrickson, pp. 30, 33.
6. Hendrickson, p. 229.
7. U.S. Census Bureau.
8. Piketty; Weinberg; Wolff.
9. Samuelson, p. 196, Okun's law is used to show that shifts in aggregate demand produces economic cycles.
10. ibid., p. 204.
11. ibid., p. 160.
12. Russel, History of the American Economic System p. 277.
13. ibid., p. 261.
14. ibid., p. 261.
15. Seager, Trust and Corporation Problems p. 49.
16. L'Amoreaux, The Great Merger Movement, p. 2.
17. Russel, History of the American Economic System, p. 366.
18. Seager, Trust and Corporation Problems p. 103.
19. Russel, History of the American Economic System, p. 318.
20. Russel, History of the American Economic System, pp. 368-369.
21. Laidler, Concentration of Control in American Industry pp. 6-7.
22. Galbraith, The Great Crash 1929, p. 155.
23. ibid., p. 150.
24. Davidson, Megamergers, p. 117.
25. ibid., chapter 5 gives several accounts of this shift in opinion.
26. ibid., p. 234.
27. Fortune, Aug. 26, 1991 p. 58.
28. Scientific American, June 27, 1857 Volume XII Number 42 p. 329.
29. New York Times Feb. 20, 1917 p. 11:4.
30. Trager, James, The People's Chronology, p. 786.

6. MORE WAVES OF SOCIAL CHANGE

1. Church, p. 227.
2. Church, p. 294.
3. Church, p. 288.
4. Spring, p. 235.
5. Pulliam, p. 178.
6. Wilson, p. 206.
7. Wilson, pp. 227, 228.
8. Wilson, p. 218.
9. Stamp, p. 40.
10. Stamp, p. 45.
11. Stamp, p. 47, 48.
12. Stamp, p. 80.
13. Stamp pp. 117, 118.
14. Stamp p. 192.
15. Stamp p. 223.
16. Stamp pp. 226, 227.
17. Stamp p. 247.
18. Gidney p. 208.
19. Associated Press, "House OKs New FCC Indecency Fines," June 7, 2006.
20. Cassedy pp. 23, 27.
21. Cassedy p. 73.
22. Starr pp. 311, 313.
23. Madore.
24. Rorabaugh p.248, Blocker.
25. Weitz pp.14, 15.
26. Weitz, pp. 16, 17.
27. Weitz p. 31.
28. Weitz p. 44.
29. Weitz p. 35.
30. Weitz p. 298.
31. Sass p. 89.
32. Toronto Star, "Teachers' Pensions in Red Despite Strong Profit," March 21, 2006. Toronto Star, "Teachers' Pension Chiefs Earn Millions," May 5, 2006.

7. MALTHUS AND LONG-WAVES

1. Everett p. xviii.
2. Everett pp. 21, 26. Emphasis added.
3. Commission of the European Communities p. 5.

8. THE LONG-WAVE LIFE CYCLE

1. Testimony of Federal Reserve Chairman Ben. S. Bernanke, "Long-term fiscal challenges facing the United States," Before the Committee on the Budget, U.S. Senate, January 18, 2007.

*B*ibliography

The books contained in this short bibliographical note are not necessarily the best books in the field, but for those who are interested in a more detail history of what was covered here, the following are what the author has found to be most compatible with long-wave chronology. I have depended enormously on many of the books mentioned in the following paragraphs.

Many books on music concentrate on the history of the singers or writers without going into detail about the environment in which the music was performed. *Blacking Up* by Robert Toll, *Ragtime* by Edward Berlin, *Jazz and the White Americans* by Neil Leonard and a pro-rock book entitled *Anti-Rock* by Linda Martin and Kerry Segrave work well together in following the long-wave changes.

On social movements, Herbert Asbury's *The Great Illusion* and Jack Blocker's *American Temperance Movements* describe the rise, fall and changing character of the prohibition movement. Their descriptions synchronize well with the long-wave. Eleanor Flexnor's *Century of Struggle* and William O'Neill's *Feminism in America: A History* are standard works in the field and together show the rise and trailing off of the women's movement.

The most concise book that I have encountered on the complete history of awakenings is William McLoughlin's *Revivals, Awakenings and Reform*, but one must be careful with his dating scheme since it includes both philosophical and theological changes that may or may not be relevant to the long-wave.

The textbook by Robert Russel entitled, *A History of the American Economic System*, is a good starting point when looking into economics.

Kenneth Davidson's *Megamergers* is a good history of regulation and anti-trust. Robert Hendrickson's *The Grand Emporiums* delineates the different phases of development in the history of retail establishments. Each phase begins on the downswing of a long-wave.

Traditional/Progressive swings in education in both the U.S. and Ontario are well documented by education historians. Robert Stamp's *The Schools of Ontario*, sponsored by the Government of Ontario, is a standard work in this area. John D. Pulliam notes these swings in U.S. education and as such his *History of Education in America* reflects long-wave swings better than most books.

The historical observations of James Cassedy's *Medicine in America* and Paul Starr's *The Social Transformation of American Medicine* work well for the early part of the long-wave. The historical documentation on alternative medicine is clear for our purposes and Norman Gevitz's *Other Healers* and James Whorton's *Nature Cures* provide a good history.

The works of Waldemar Nielsen on philanthropy match the long-wave changes well. *Inside American Philanthropy* presents the three successive generations of philanthropists. Harry Weitz's *The Pension Promise* takes the history of pensions back to the first long-wave. Robert Habenstein's search for the history of early funeral services in *The History of American Funeral Directing* is documented with dates that cluster around the first and second long-wave downswings.

For the Canadian social movements, Carol Lee Bacchi's *Liberation Deferred?* and Catherine Cleverdon's *The Woman Suffrage Movement in Canada* are essential. Jan Noel's *Canada Dry: Temperance Crusades before Confederation* provides a traditional view of the history of prohibition while Heron Craig's *Booze: A Distilled History* provides an alternative perspective.

Prior to the publication of *The Longwave of Social Mood and the Dynamics of Social Change* ©1992, *Population, Politics, Social Movements and the Economy* ©1994, and *Baby-Boomers Generation-X and Social Cycles* ©1995, Kondratieff long-waves had little to do with demographics. Starting with Nikolai Kondratieff, the major schools of thought were capital investment, capitalist crisis, innovations and war. The impact of innovations on economics is widely talked about today, although little reference is made as to the origin of these ideas.

There are many people who have written about the long-wave over the last eighty years and it would be difficult to compile any complete list of names. Some may have written important papers but have not written books on the subject, others may have been relatively obscure and yet others may have supported one school or another or variations of schools. Still others may be relatively new converts. With that in mind, this list of writers of different schools of thought is meant to be only a starting point in the history of long-wave development.

Michael Barkun, Robert C. Beckman, Brian J. L. Berry, Fernand Braudel, Sherry Cooper, James T. Corredine, Guy Daniels, Carl H. A. Dassbach, Euel Elliot, Jay W. Forrester, André Gunder Frank, Christopher Freeman, Joshua S. Goldstein, David M. Gordon, Allen Greenspan, Edward J. Harpham, Heja Kim, Alfred Kleinknecht, Frank L. Klingberg, Ehud Levy-Pascal, Nathan H. Mager, Ernest Mandel, Cesare Marchetti, Terrence McDonough, Gerhard Mensch, George Modelski, David Rosenau, W. W. Rostow, Joseph A. Schumpeter, James B. Shuman, Solomos Solomou, John D. Sterman, Sidney Tarrow, William R. Thompson, Tibor Vasko, Jan Tinbergen, Andrew Tylecote, J. J. Van Duijn, Immanuel Wallerstein.

Ahlstrom, Sydney, *A Religious History of the American People*, New Haven: Yale University Press, 1972.

Asbury, Herbert, *The Great Illusion*, New York: Doubleday and Company, Inc., 1950.

Austin, William W., *"Susanna," "Jeanie," and "The Old Folks At Home": The Songs of Stephen C. Foster From His Time to Ours*, Urbana: University of Illinois Press, 1987.

Bacchi, Carol Lee, *Liberation Deferred? The Ideas of the English-Canadian Suffragists, 1877-1918*, Toronto: University of Toronto Press, 1983.

Beaupré, Pascale, Pierre Turcotte and Anne Milan, "When is junior moving out? Transitions from the parental home to independence," Statistics Canada No. 11-008, Ottawa, 2006.

Beckman, Theodore, *The Chain Store Problem*, New York: McGraw-Hill, 1938.

Beman, Lamar Taney, *Selected Articles On Prohibition of the Liquor Traffic*, New York: H.W. Wilson Company, 1915.

Berlin, Edward A., *Ragtime, A Musical and Cultural History*, Berkeley: University of California Press, 1980.

Blocker Jr., Jack S., *American Temperance Movements: Cycles of Reform*, Boston: Twayne Publishers, 1989.

Bolt, Christine, *The Women's Movements in the United States and Britain from the 1790s to the 1920s*, Amherst: The University of Massachusetts Press, 1993.

Brunn, H.O., *Original Dixieland Jazz Band*, Louisiana: Louisiana State University Press, 1960.

Cassedy, James H., *Medicine in America: A short History*, Baltimore: The Johns Hopkins University Press, 1991.

Cleverdon, Catherine L., *The Woman Suffrage Movement in Canada*, Toronto: University of Toronto Press, 1974.

Coale, Ansley J. and Melvin Zelnik, *New Estimates of Fertility and Population in the United States*, New Jersey: Princeton University Press, 1963.

Commission of the European Communities, Green Paper "Confronting demographic change: a new solidarity between the generations," Brussels: March 16, 2005.

Cremin, Lawrence A., *American Education: The Metropolitan Experience 1876 – 1980*, New York: Harper & Row, 1990.

Davidson, Kenneth M., *Megamergers*, Cambridge: Ballinger Publishing Company, 1985.

Dawson, Philip, *Cruise Ships,* London: Conway Maritime Press, 2000.

DeLand, Antoinette and Anne Campbell, *Fielding's Worldwide Cruises 1994*, Redondo Beach: Fielding Worldwide Inc., 1994.

Eberstadt, Nicholas, "What if it's a Population Implosion? Speculations about Global De-population," American Enterprise Institute, Harvard Center for Population and Development Studies, Working Paper Series Number 98.04, March 1998.

Everett, Alexander Hill, *New Ideas on Population, with remarks on the theories of Malthus and Godwin, 1826*, New York: Augustus M. Kelley, Publishers, 1970.

Flexner, Eleanor, *Century of Struggle*, Massachusetts: Harvard University Press, 1975.

Galbraith, John Kenneth, *The Great Crash 1929*, Boston: Houghton Mifflin Company, 1988.

—, *Economics in Perspective*, Boston: Houghton Mifflin Company, 1987.

Gevitz, Norman, *Other Healers: Unorthodox Medicine in America*, Baltimore: The John Hopkins University Press, 1988.

Gidney, R. D., *From Hope to Harris: The Reshaping of Ontario's Schools*, Toronto: University of Toronto Press, 1999.

Graebner, William, *A History of Retirement*, New Haven: Yale University Press, 1980.

Grimke, Sarah, *Letters on the Equality of the Sexes and the Condition of Woman*, New York: Leno Hill Pub., 1838.

Grimm, Robert T., *Notable American Philanthropists*, Westport: Greenwood Press, 2002.

Habenstein, Robert, William M. Lamers, *The History of American Funeral Directing*, Milwaukee: National Funeral Directors Association of the United States, 1955.

Hallowell, Gerard A., *Prohibition in Ontario 1919 - 1923*, Ottawa: Ontario Historical Society, 1972.

Hendrickson, Robert, *The Grand Emporiums*, New York: Stein and Day, 1980.

Heron, Craig, *Booze: A Distilled History*, Toronto: Between The Lines, 2003.

Hitchcock, Wiley H., *Music in the United States*, New York: Prentice-Hall Inc, 1969.

Hoffman, Charles, *The Depression Of The Nineties*, Connecticut: Greewood Publishing Corp., 1970.

Holmes, Jack E., *The Mood/Interest Theory of American Foreign Policy*, Kentucky: The University of Kentucky Press, 1985.

Kamin, Jonathan, "Parallels in the Social Reactions to Jazz and Rock," Journal of Jazz Studies Vol. 2, December 1974, pp. 95 - 125.

Kelley, Allen C., "The Population Debate in Historical Perspective: Revisionism Revisited," Online, Draft: April 1999.

Kobler, John, *Ardent Spirits*, New York: G. P. Putnam's Sons, 1973.

Kuznets, Simon, *Economic Growth and Structure*, New York: W. W. Norton, 1965.

—, *Capital in the American Economy: its formation and financing*, Princeton: Princeton University Press, 1961.

Laidler, Harry W., *Concentration of Control in American Industry*, New York: Thomas Y. Crowell Company, 1931.

Lamoreaux, Naomi R., *The Great Merger Movement in American Business, 1885 - 1904*, Cambridge: Cambridge University Press, 1985.

Lebhar, Godfrey Montague, *Chain Stores in America 1859–1962*, New York: Chain Store Publishing, 1963.

Leonard, Neil, *Jazz and the White Americans*, The University of Chicago Press, Chicago: 1962.

Loesser, Arthur, *Men, Women and Pianos*, New York: Simon and Schuster, 1954.

Madore, Odette, "The Canadian and American Health Care Systems," Government of Canada, Depository Services Program, Economics Division, June 1992.

Martin, Linda and Kerry Segrave, *Anti-Rock: Opposition To Rock 'n' Roll*, Connecticut: Archon Books, 1988.

Morissette, René, "Permanent Layoff Rates," Statistics Canada No. 75-001-XIE, Ottawa, 2004.

Namenwirth, J . Zvi, and Robert P. Weber, *Dynamics of Culture*, Boston: Allen and Unwin, 1970

Nathan, Hans, *Dan Emmett and the Rise of Early Negro Minstrelsy*, Oklahoma: University of Oklahoma Press, 1962.

Neil, McCart, *Atlantic Liners of the Cunard Line*, Wellingborough: Patrick Stephens Limited, 1990.

Nielsen, Waldemar, *Inside American Philanthropy*, Norman: University of Oklahoma Press, 1996.

—, *Golden Donors: A New Anatomy of the Great Foundations*, Piscataway: Transaction Publishers, 2001.

Noel, Jan, *Canada Dry: Temperance Crusades before Confederation*, Toronto: University of Toronto Press, 1995.

O'Neill, William L., *Feminism In America: A History*, New Jersey: Transaction Publishers, 1989.

Osgood, Henry O., *So This Is Jazz*, New York: Da Capo Press, 1978.

Pence, Owen Earle, *The Y.M.C.A. and Social Need*, New York: Association Press, 1939.

Pfister, Ulrich and Christian Suter, "International Financial Relations," International Studies Quarterly, September 1987. pp 239 - 272

Piketty, Thomas, Emmanuel Saez, "The Evolution of Top Incomes: A Historical and International Perspective," Working Paper 11955, Cambridge, National Bureau of Economic Research, January 2006.

Picot, Garnett, "What is Happening to Earnings Inequality and Youth Wages in the 1990's?" Statistics Canada No. 11F0019MPE No. 116, Ottawa, 1998.

Pulliam, John D., *History of Education in America*, New York: Macmillan Publishing Company, 1991.

Rorabaugh, W. J., *The Alcoholic Republic*, New York: Oxford University Press, 1979.

Rusk, Robert R., *The Doctrines of the Great Educators*, New York: Macmillan, 1969.

Russel, Robert R., *A History of the American Economic System*, New York: Appleton-Century-Crofts, 1964.

Samuelson, Paul, William D. Nordhaus, John McCallum, *Macroeconomics*, Sixth Canadian Edition, Toronto, McGraw-Hill Ryerson Limited, 1988.

Sass, Steven A., *The Promise of Private Pensions*, Cambridge: Harvard University Press, 1997.

Schumpeter, Joseph, *History of Economic Analysis*, New York: Oxford University Press, 1954.

Seager, Henry R. and Charles A. Gulick, Jr., *Trust and Corporation Problems*, New York: Harper and Brothers Publishers, 1929.

Simon, Julian L., *Economic Thought about Population Consequences: Some Reflections1*, Online, 1993.

Stamp, Robert M., *The Schools of Ontario 1876 - 1976*, Toronto: University of Toronto Press, 1982.

Starr, Paul, *The Social Transformation of American Medicine*: New York: Basic Books Inc., 1982.

Stroup, Herbert, *Social Welfare Pioneers*, Chicago: Nelson-Hall Publishers, 1986.

Toll, Robert C., *Blacking Up, The Minstrel Show In Nineteenth-Century America*, New York: Oxford University Press, 1974.

Trager, James, *The People's Chronology*, New York: Holt, Rinehart and Winston, 1979.

Ward, Ed and Geoffrey Stokes, Ken Tucker, *Rock Of Ages - The Rolling Stone History Of Rock and Roll*, New York: Summit Books, 1986.

Ward, Lester F., *Applied Sociology*, Boston: Ginn & Company, 1906.

——   , *Pure Sociology*, Boston: Ginn & Company, 1903.

Weinberg, Daniel H., Arthur F. Jones Jr., "The Changing Shape of the Nation's Income Distribution 1947 - 1988," Current Population Reports, U.S. Census Bureau, June 2000.

Weitz, Harry, *The Pension Promise: The Past and Future of Canada's Private Pension System*, Scarborough: Thomson Canada Ltd.,1992.

Whiteman, Paul and Mary Margaret McBride, *Popular Culture In America 1800 - 1925*, New York: Arno Press, 1974.

Whorton, James C., *Nature Cures: The History of Alternative Medicine in America*, New York: Oxford University Press, 2002.

Wilson, J. Donald, Robert M. Stamp, Louise-Philippe Audet, *Canadian Education: A History*, Scarborough: Prentice-Hall, 1970.

Wolff, Edward N., *Top Heavy: The Increasing Inequality of Wealth in America*, New York: The New Press, 1995.

Woman's Rights Conventions - *Seneca Falls and Rochester 1848*, New York: Arno and the New York Times, 1969.

Internet:

The Prime Ministers of Canada, The Parliament of Canada Website: www.parl.gc.ca

First Among Equals: The Prime Minister in Canadian Life and Politics. Library and Archives Canada: www.collectionscanada.ca

United Nations Population Information Network: www.un.org/popin

Film:

Gibney, Alex, Dir. *Enron: The Smartest Guys in the Room*, New York: HDNET Films, 2005.

I_{ndex}